LOST AND FOUND
Discovering Ireland's past

Edited by
JOE FENWICK

Wordwell

First published in 2003
Wordwell Ltd
PO Box 69, Bray, Co. Wicklow
Copyright © the authors

ISBN 1 869857 58 5

British Library Cataloguing-in-Publication Data.
A catalogue record for this book is available from the British Library.

Cover design: Rachel Dunne, Wordwell Ltd

Typeset in Ireland by Wordwell Ltd

Copy editor: Emer Condit

Printed by E.G. Zure, Bilbao

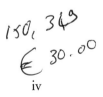

150, 349
€ 30.00

iv

Contents

Acknowledgements

I would like to express my gratitude to all the authors, who so generously contributed their time, enthusiasm and imagination to this book. I am particularly indebted to Lisa Bartlam and Elizabeth FitzPatrick for their encouragement and advice throughout the course of its compilation and editing — all errors and omissions in this regard, however, are entirely my own.

Though individual authors and private collections provided the majority of the illustrations, a number were also generously provided by the Derry County Council, the Discovery Programme, Dúchas the Heritage Service (Department of the Environment and Local Government), the Freemason's Hall Archive, the Irish Archaeological Wetland Unit, Limerick Corporation, the National Museum of Ireland, the Royal Irish Academy, the Sheffield Archive (England), the Trustees of the Museums and Galleries of Northern Ireland and the Ulster Museum. These institutions are gratefully acknowledged in the accompanying captions.

In addition, thanks are due for permission to quote a number of primary sources, letters and manuscripts housed in the archives of the National Archives of Ireland, the National Museum of Ireland and the Royal Society of Antiquaries of Ireland. My heartfelt thanks, too, to all at Wordwell, Nick Maxwell, Maura Laverty, Emer Condit and Rachel Dunne, for their patience and forbearance.

Finally, I am most grateful to the Heritage Council for providing a generous grant towards this publication.

Note

Since this book was compiled, Dúchas The Heritage Service, Department of the Environment and Local Government (formerly the Department of Arts, Heritage, Gaeltacht and the Islands), has been disbanded. Sadly, its functions and responsibilities, since June 2003, have been dispersed among various government departments. Responsibilities for the built heritage are now under the auspices of the Office of Public Works and the Department of Environment, Heritage and Local Government.

List of figures

List of plates

centre right (1). The tree-clad banks at the bottom of the field south of the church delimit the hollow way or road (2). Note the linear soil-mark of the northern bank of the road running in the field to the east (3), and the interesting alignment of field banks further west (4), to the left of the picture (photo: Con Brogan, Dúchas The Heritage Service, 1996).

Chapter 19

Chapter 21

Chapter 22

Chapter 23

bottom half of the picture, and remains of the seventeenth-century bastion towards the top (photo: C. O Rahilly/Limerick Corporation).

Pl. 71—View of Countermine 3, extending beneath the foundations of the eastern curtain wall, facing north-east. This was built by Robert Pope between 13 and 20 June 1642. The visible timber props were inserted during the excavation for safety reasons. The original timberwork was removed by Pope himself before he commenced work on Countermine 4 at some point late on 20 June 1642 (photo: K. Wiggins/Limerick Corporation).

Pl. 72—View of the western limit of Mine 3, along the base of the eastern curtain wall, seen from the north. This would have reached the base of the wall (to the right) by around 17 June 1642, but was not deep enough to continue beneath the masonry. The Irish miners opened a branch to the south, Mine 4, which eventually undermined the angle between the eastern curtain wall and the bastion on 21 June 1642. The charring of several of the props resulted from the firing of Mines 3 and 4 on the afternoon of 21 June 1642 (photo: R. Ó Baoill/Limerick Corporation).

Chapter 24
Pl. 73—Glasshouse furnace.

Chapter 25
Pl. 74—Aerial view of Dunasead Castle, which consists of a main hall with attached bawn. Extended bawn walls are evident behind the houses situated to the right of the castle.

Pl. 75—Aerial view of Ilen estuary. In the top left-hand corner is the site of Dunagall Castle, on Ringaroige Island, at the water's edge, with the remains of the castle pier lying below. Inisbeg Castle may have stood on the raised, subrectangular platform on the opposite shore. Also visible are the possible double fish-traps joining Ringaroige Island and Oilean Saor (the island to the left of the shot), and the single fish-trap on its southern side extending into the channel.

Pl. 76—Inane tower-house in foreground, with attached later corn store.

Pl. 77—Aerial view of Inane corn store following the destruction of the tower-house, the quay structure (which ran in front of the tower-house and into the water) and the substantial sea wall that encircled the site.

Pl. 78—Aerial view of Dunalong tower-house on Sherkin Island.

Pl. 79—Aerial view of Sherkin fish palace (lower left), which was attached to the east range of the friary (out of shot). The walls that retained the press beams are seen running parallel to the friary, attached to the enclosure wall.

Foreword

The romance of archaeology is undiminished and there is no doubt that the distant past continues to perplex and fascinate. This romantic attachment takes many forms: for some it is simply the excitement of discovery or the opportunity to unravel an ancient mystery, while for others it is the engagement with the lives and deaths of people who lived in a very different world but one which shaped the present in many ways. Even though digging and archaeology are inextricably linked in everyone's mind, discovery is not just the fruit of excavation; it comes about in many other ways as well, be it the painstaking study of artefact or landscape, or the application of a new scientific technique or theoretical model, any or all of which may illuminate that different world in a quite unexpected and exciting fashion.

In the nineteenth century the celebrated surgeon and antiquary William Wilde believed that groups of cairns and other monuments might mark ancient battlefields. Born in Castlerea, Co. Roscommon, he was familiar with the extraordinary concentration of ancient remains in the vicinity of Cong, Co. Mayo, and was convinced that these marked the spot of the first epic Battle of Moytura between the Fir Bolg and the Tuatha de Danann recounted in medieval manuscripts. He walked the locality with a translation of this tale in hand, happily identifying individual monuments with particular people and events. One young Fir Bolg warrior slain in combat was said to have been buried in 'The Carn of the One Man', and the enthusiastic Wilde, on digging into a likely burial mound and discovering one small cist grave holding a vase containing some cremated bone, was fully persuaded that he had found this warrior's grave. He exclaimed that 'perhaps a more convincing proof of the authenticity of ancient Irish or any other history has never been afforded'. Today we know that the Fir Bolg and the Tuatha de Danann are the stuff of origin legends and that the many burials of this sort can be accurately if prosaically dated to about 2000 BC so it is not easy to recapture the romantic colour that an epic tale could once apply to a nondescript prehistoric pot and to a simple burial cairn. Yet I can still remember a peculiar sense of intimacy and wonderment when I first saw the 4000-year-old fingerprints of a girl on one of these pottery vessels in the National Museum.

Samuel Ferguson was another nineteenth-century figure captivated by the past. Dubbed 'the inventor of the Celtic Twilight', he is renowned for his literary achievements but was a significant student of Irish archaeology as well. In poems such as *The Tain Quest* and *Congal* he depicted a heroic and essentially pre-Christian world peopled with knights, kings, warriors and maidens, and this image of a land 'glory-crowned in war' is still a part of our perception of the Iron Age. In archaeological circles he is best remembered for his pioneering work on ogham inscriptions, and I suspect that part of the motivation for his work was the hope of identifying the name of an ancient hero from some epic tale.

The subject of Ferguson's *The Tain Quest* is the medieval legend of the rediscovery of the lost story of the *Táin Bó Cuailnge*. In this tale Muirghein succeeds in identifying the grave of Fearghus mac Róich, who is then resurrected to recount the narrative of the great cattle raid. The grave is marked by a pillar stone, and in Ferguson's words:

> Shone the sunset red and solemn: Murgen, where he leant, observed
> Down the corners of the column letter-strokes of Ogham carved.
> ''Tis belike a burial pillar,' said he, 'and these shallow lines
> Hold some warrior's name of valour, could I rightly spell the signs.'

'Letter then by letter tracing', Murgen or Muirghein eventually reads the dramatic legend: 'Fergus, son of Roy, is here'. Here we glimpse the romantic excitement that the decipherment of an ogham inscription had for Ferguson; for him it held the very real promise of encountering a figure from a living past. Even in this twenty-first-century digital world—in excavation, ogham stone, pottery vessel or computer programme—it is this possibility of encountering that strange but living past that continues to furnish the romance of archaeology.

John Waddell

Introduction

The inspiration for this book came to me in a lucid moment while attending a conference hosted by the Institute of Archaeologists of Ireland (IAI). Those biannual meetings are very much a business and social event in the Irish archaeological calendar. They provide an opportunity for professional archaeologists from all parts of the country to get together to discuss the latest issues and developments in the profession, and also a platform for presenting interesting results or ideas explored between meetings. Perhaps more importantly, they are a time to catch up with old friends, conduct business and talk informally about archaeology. The mid-morning coffee break between papers is alive with conversation and good-humoured banter about such matters as the context of a find, the significance of a feature or, more often than not, first-hand accounts of discovery or amusing tales of the personalities working at the 'coal-face' of archaeological research.

There is little doubt that many archaeologists, and those in related fields, are often absorbed to the point of obsession in their chosen profession and exude an overwhelming enthusiasm for their work. The subject-matter is, after all, inherently fascinating — an attempt to piece together the past lives and beliefs of human society through the study of discarded artefacts and ruinous monuments. Even with the benefit of historical documentation and the support of scientific evidence it is often a challenging exercise, open to a myriad of interpretations. For this reason, many of us are guilty of erring on the side of caution when it comes to committing our thoughts to paper for fear of presenting a naïve or biased interpretation of the facts or, worse still, inviting the open ridicule of our peers. The tendency is to distance oneself from the reader and present a minimalist or qualified interpretation of the results and, in so doing, often overlook the key issue of archaeological research — the human dimension. In addition, the sense of excitement and enthusiasm, which is so much an integral part of archaeological work and indeed the principal topic of casual conversation at conferences, tends to evaporate in the dry formality of lecture presentations and the obscure jargon of academic publication. Although it cannot be denied that scientific rigour is entirely necessary in the pursuit of academic excellence and reliable factual information, it remains largely unintelligible to the man in the street. Perhaps it is this progressive trend towards 'serious' professionalism that is responsible for the perceived alienation of genuine archaeological research from the general public and has led, in recent years, to the unprecedented rise in the popularity of pseudo-scientific literature, based more on fantasy than fact. As explorers of the past, however, we do have a duty to redress this imbalance, communicate the relevance and importance of our work to a wider audience, and breathe life into the dust and bones of the past.

Contributions to this book were sought from archaeologists, historians and scientists working in the academic, research and commercial sectors in order to encapsulate something of the full spectrum of archaeological endeavour and elaborate on the broader archaeological picture. Authors were encouraged to adopt an informal style and share with the reader their personal insight into the world of Irish archaeology, or to share some of the thrill and excitement of a 'discovery', however big or small, which has shed some light on our understanding of the past. The only concession to academic convention is the inclusion of a short bibliography of further reading for those readers who might wish to explore the subject-matter in more depth.

The theme of this book is largely archaeological but a number of notable historians were more than willing to rise to the challenge. The result is a diverse collection of 31 essays, short stories and personal insights into the realm of research and rediscovery. In many instances they not only illuminate some darkened detail of the distant past but, additionally, something of the personality of the author.

The aim of this book is primarily to enlighten the general reader, and perhaps to remind ourselves of the diverse nature and role of the archaeologist. Hopefully, too, it will go some way towards explaining the reasons why we are often so totally absorbed in our chosen profession. This book is the product of the combined effort of all those who contributed to it — I hope you find it enjoyable reading.

1

Exploration and serendipity — approaches to discovery

Patrick F. Wallace

My favourite discovery occurred just before Christmas 2000, in the same week that one of the most exciting discoveries made by a colleague was shared with me. My discovery relates to a most unexpected personal encounter with my great-grandparents during a search through recently salvaged historical documents which I couldn't have dreamed had survived, let alone been fortuitously saved for my perusal by a childhood friend. The other experience happened while I was on the same historical quest in Limerick, when a colleague showed me archaeological finds from his excavations which brought me so close to the (1690) Siege of Limerick that I was able to smell the sulphur of the Williamite explosives as if they had been lobbed into the Abbey River a couple of hours before!

To both discoveries I shall return, but first allow me to summon a random personal selection of discoveries made both by colleagues and by me over the last thirty years. These discoveries impressed me, although they may not be those that will stand the test of time or even impress other commentators. Everyone's list of what mattered to them or impressed them will be different. I should say that the discoveries I am about to parade here are those which come to mind rather than being the considered digest of evaluations made from systematic perusals of *Archaeology Ireland,* the *Journal of Irish Archaeology, Excavations, Medieval Archaeology* and the *Journal of the Royal Society of Antiquaries of Ireland,* or of notes of lectures, conferences, seminars or any of the other ways in which news on discoveries has been gleaned over the years. They are merely a sample of what contributes to my sense of the discoveries that have impinged upon my imagination over the past three decades.

Discovery can sometimes be as much about a hunch, blessed with a bit of luck, as the result of controlled research. How often have we seen the newest recruit on an excavation site make a find of a quality the site director has never emulated? In this regard, I recollect then-student Anne O'Sullivan's find of an Anglo-Saxon penny in a Fishamble Street house on her first day at work. Serendipity does come into it, as it did when, while alone one evening at home after work, I noticed what I thought was an unusual beetle-like insect on our dining room table. I carefully 'captured' it (in the language of entomologists) by placing my wallet on top of it to sadly crush it to death without destroying any of its diagnostic details. I put it in a matchbox and brought it to my colleague at the Natural History Museum, Dr Jim O'Connor, to whom I had brought a procession of specimens over the years but never hit the jackpot. He would invariably write back a courteous and encouraging note informing me that my latest offering was of such and such a well-known type. This time it was different. My hunch paid off for — surprise, surprise — I had made a significant discovery; it was the first sighting in Dublin of this insect (*Palloptera muliebris*) in almost two centuries! My joy on receiving Dr O'Connor's note was only surpassed by the pleasure a little later at seeing my name in print as a co-author in an entomological journal. Sometimes hunches do pay off even for enthusiastic amateurs — or, in this case, rank charlatans — but you must be prepared for many disappointments and always be guided by the specialist professional, especially in archaeology.

George Eogan's discovery of the second passage at Knowth in 1968 (see Chapter 6) has to loom large among the great Irish archaeological discoveries. This was the result of an informed hunch and a bit of luck. M.J. O'Kelly's identification of the roof-box at Newgrange was more personal — the inspired discovery of an inquisitive genius. Michael Connelly's identification of a unique miniature passage tomb and later of a remarkable pagan Viking Age cave in the vale of Tralee are the discoveries of an inspired prospector who has the Midas touch. Talking of prospectors past and present, may I also salute the discoveries of William O'Brien at Ross Island (see Chapter 16) which have taken us back to the beginning of our first metal age, a few centuries before 2000 BC. Discoveries by metal-detectorists like those who stumbled on the Derrynaflan hoard and other Early Christian treasures have no place in this roll-call because greed and ignorant haste should never attend upon discovery lest the objective of the search be destroyed or the scientific circumstance be compromised. Anyway, discoveries should not be made either for profit or fame.

Discoveries in archaeology are not always made by men with torches squeezing their way through tight underground passages with leaking roofs — that is, apart from Tom Fanning and George Eogan! They can result from hunches like Eogan's or strokes of luck like the two Anglo-Saxon coin hoards which turned up on the excavations at Castle Street, Dublin, or Jim Lang's identification of the hogback at Castledermot.

Jim Lang also once described how he made a significant discovery in Anglo-Saxon sculpture. He and a colleague, Richard Bailey, made the discovery quite by accident. They were laying out a number of tracings of panels of crosses on the floor of Lang's living room when, accidentally, one drawing fell the wrong way up on top of another in such a way that what had been the body of a bird fitted exactly over something like a helmet. They were astonished because it immediately occurred to them that the sculptors of a thousand years ago must have produced patterns by using (wooden) templates which were used over and over in different positions. They were soon to demonstrate the validity of their hunch well beyond the north of England. It was more than just another case of 'eureka', or even of wondering why this had not occurred to anyone before; it had also to do with connecting with the mind-set of a sculptor whom they had encountered as a man trying to work things out for himself. 'Meeting' the sculptor in this way humanised him and brought his work, his art and his era closer to modern-day students. This sense of encountering a person's way of doing something is what makes discoveries really exciting and more pleasant (for me at any rate) than even scientifically or historically significant discoveries made in libraries or laboratories from methodical observation and statistical process. I recall in this context laughing when, at Wood Quay, I found a small lead lump thrown away with its clay mould which had broken before it could be finished as a weight because I thought I could imagine the lead-worker as he tossed away the offending mould and its contents in anger, probably accompanied by a stream of unprintable Old Norse (or Middle Irish) expletives!

Discoveries also result from flashes of inspiration in which an experienced eye, thorough background knowledge, and a desire to put a number of jigsaw pieces together combine to answer a conundrum so that both the solver and his envious colleagues will ask why they hadn't thought of it before, the answer being so obvious now that it is solved. Con Manning's explanation for the apparent eccentricity of the doorway in the west wall of the cathedral at Clonmacnoise must rank as the best example of this in Irish archaeological annals. Just as it was the evening light at Clonmacnoise that provided Manning with his flash of inspiration, so it was at Ballyportry Castle where Siobhan Cuffe discovered a late medieval wall-painting featuring St Sebastian.

Michael Dolley's conclusion that a mint existed in late Viking Age Isle of Man from his work on the Kirkpatrick coin hoard was a discovery which only somebody steeped in the subject of the Irish Sea and Hiberno-Norse coins could have made. Mary Cahill's inspired interpretation of the use of late Bronze Age gold boxes and the contemporary gold spools, both of which she believes on ethnographic grounds to have been worn in slits in the ear lobes of the wearers, is the result of a similar set of circumstances — unrivalled knowledge of a subject and the ongoing quest for an answer (and an approach instilled by M.J. O'Kelly!) which took her outside conventional archaeology to the parallel literature of ethnography and the flash which brought the answer. In Ms Cahill's case the flash of inspiration was supplied by a severely pierced person whom she saw on the *Late Late Show*.

Ethnology or folklife studies can be as useful as ethnography when seeking explanations for the uses of archaeological objects. Such quests can result in discoveries and suggestions about the continuity over the centuries of certain practices or implement types. The National Museum's folklife collection was originally mainly accumulated to explain objects in the archaeological collection and the practices connected with their use, and, in a complementary way, to demonstrate the continuity of objects and practices then still current in parts of Ireland about a century ago. I was pleased to accidentally make a minor discovery in this vein one day while in the folklife stores, where I noticed lead fishing weights shaped like boats. It immediately occurred to me why lead weights of this type from Viking Dublin did not fit into our weight scheme. They were for fishing lines and used with line frames. In a related way, familiarity with the artefacts of tenth- and eleventh-century Dublin has led to my noting several instances of presumed continuity in both artefact types and construction methods over the centuries. For instance, there was a day on an island off Bergen in Norway when I noticed a farmer using a wooden shovel with an iron shoe on its edge like those found at Fishamble Street. There was the load-bearing roof post in the old house at Loughindrain Folk Museum in Argyll and the sloped roof support in the folk farm at Rydale, Yorkshire, which recalled the foundations of a related house (of undoubted English rather than Scandinavian or Irish origin) of the eleventh century at Fishamble Street. And at the Weald and Downland Folk Museum near Singleton, Suffolk, an explanation of how fence-makers used perforated frames or templates to make their products revealed how the *klinhus* technique came about and was used especially in the bench sides, mobile beds and doors of Dublin.

Other discoveries are the consequences of work experienced elsewhere! Michael Moore's and Ben Murtagh's remarkable deduction that there were Dublin type one buildings in Waterford (this was way before the well-preserved Arundel Square campaign) arose from their both having recently worked on preserved samples of such buildings at Fishamble Street, Dublin. My own reassessment of the size of some of our earliest Early Christian oratories came from familiarity with the same buildings, most particularly the positions of the roof supports in relation to the walls.

While all excavations add in varying degrees to the sum of knowledge, there are some in which very exciting artefacts are discovered, apart altogether from the structural, chronological and environmental evidence which 'finds' people often lose sight of! Yet who could fail to be impressed by Valerie Keely's discovery of the copper-alloy 'biscuit tin'-shaped urn of British Celtic origin which turned up in Laois, or the pair of seventh-century glass cruets of Merovingian origin which were discovered on John Bradley's site at Moynagh Lough? Linzi Simpson's exposure of ploughing beneath Viking Dublin as well as of round (animal?) pens in some of the earliest plots, not to mention her sunken-floored structures and the large rectangular building (of Germanic type, possibly Danish rather than Saxon, if she'll permit me!) and her early radiocarbon dates which necessitate a rethink of many previously received views, all rate as significant discoveries.

Among the scientific techniques which facilitate discoveries in archaeology are dendrochronology, ground-penetrating radar, X-ray photography and metallographic analysis of the trace origins of impurities in metal.

Dendrochronology, which was pioneered in Ireland by Michael Baillie, has given a remarkable second-century BC date for one of the main features at Navan Fort/Emhain Macha as well as for the bog road near the Shannon at Corlea. It has pushed back the dates of crannog use for Christina Fredengren at Lough Gara and has permitted us to consider that the stone castle at Trim was, after all, built during the time of Hugh de Lacy himself.

Baillie's master chronology was also to enable his Danish counterpart, Nils Bonde, to demonstrate from its tree-ring growth pattern that the great warship raised from Roskilde Fjord at Skuldelev had a keel that was laid down in Dublin in the 1060s. This breathtaking discovery established what we had always suspected but couldn't prove from our excavations, that there was a shipyard at the later Viking Age port of Dublin capable of turning out the largest warships of the age.

X-ray photography by Anthony (Roly) Read revealed to Raghnall Ó Floinn that the faint rattle in the 'Mias Tighernán' was made by a folded piece of metal entrapped in the dish, possibly the original reliquary, and that the present dish also conceals a smaller and later flattened-out precursor. Aerial photography, mainly exploited by the late Leo Swan, has resulted in the discovery of countless new sites and of types new to the record. Advanced photography also exposed the phases of Raffin to Conor Newman who, along with Joe Fenwick, used a range of geophysical techniques to expose a wealth of new sites at Tara (see Chapter 8). Carbon 14 and the painstaking work it involves have allowed Anna Brindley and Jan Lanting to change the whole chronology of the Neolithic and the early Bronze Age and the cultures which have had to be rearranged within them. From being previously ascribed to the end of the era, the single-burial group (including, I am pleased to say, my own site at Ardcrony with its fine pot which I salvaged over a weekend back in 1977) now belongs nearer to the beginning of the Neolithic, about 6000 years ago. The same dating method has established Lough Boora as one of the earliest known settlement sites in Ireland to date (about 8000 BC).

My own main archaeological discoveries are deductions based on observations of coincidences and patterns, such as the floor-plans of Dublin's tenth- and eleventh-century buildings which yielded a number of building types, how they were built and how they relate to the broader Irish, Scandinavian and European world. Neither they nor identification of Dublin's weight unit of 26.6g, observations on the carpentry of the waterfronts, work on the general characteristics of the Hiberno-Norse town, or trying to understand the plots and layout of towns and how they came about come near encounters with details which either betray the mind-set of a craftsman or the accidental preservation of something which ought not to have survived. The discovery not only of the planks used for slipping ships from the front face of one of the mud banks in their final position as a horizontal reinforcement raft for a later bank, to which they were turned over like the page of a book, but of the actual impressions they made in the mud as they lay in their original position is hard to beat. So was the finding of grass used as bedding material in Fishamble Street which was still green, so quickly had it been covered after it was placed in fresh condition on the wall benches. The discovery of insect pupae (probably an indication of a filthy, smelly environment in which they originally lay) in places such as the defensive mud-banks and revetments, where they were covered over by shovelfuls of estuarine mud; the discovery of mosses used as 'toilet paper' in Dublin's cesspits; the very smell of newly excavated layers of animal and human manure containing cherry stones and other inclusions; the charred remains of what had been a roof purlin that had collapsed (presumably burning) on the corner of a post-and-wattle house wall which it had caused to catch fire; the several coins which were deposited or lost in bedding materials and other places only to be found a thousand years later; the kite brooch whose mould was also turned up but in a different part of town; the skulls of cats with knife-nicks on either side of their eye sockets which indicated that they were skinned for their pelts; the Ardenberg jug trapped under a collapsed wooden revetment wall; the human skeletal remains, including those of a young adult female buried in the inward slope of an early waterfront embankment, and another split with a sword which was then used to slash across the mouth of the (presumably!) screaming victim; these were the kinds of discoveries that were almost taken for granted on a daily basis at Wood Quay from 1974 to 1981.

Levels of excitement generated by discoveries are relative to what the discoverer has already experienced. The more exposed to the excitement of discovery the discoverer has been, the more it takes to impress him. Every archaeological debutant believes his first site is on a par with Ur of the Chaldees or Çatal Huyuk. I recall asking the then Keeper of Irish Antiquities, who had just treated me to lunch after inspecting my excavation at Oyster Lane, Wexford, whether he would like a final look at the site before taking the afternoon train back to Dublin. His reply disappointed me then, but I can better empathise with his position now: 'Pat, a hole is a hole and I've seen your hole!' His former assistant Etienne Rynne never grew cynical and has remained an enthusiast all his life. His joy at the discovery of a ritual deposit of hazelnuts under the base slab of the main burial cist of my first excavation at the ring-cairn at Sroove, Co. Sligo, was as uncontained as mine.

Sroove is also an example of being in the right place at the right time as regards making another discovery which outranked anything found at the early Bronze Age site. My being at Sroove in 1973 led to my meeting the then locally based teacher (now artist) Joe Sweeney, who brought me one evening to see Carntemple and what turned out to be its incomparable set of *c.* ninth-century decorated graveslabs. These were lying about on the graveyard surface as if they had been relatively recently deposited around part of the Early Christian enclosure. I couldn't believe my eyes as I confirmed Sweeney's hunch about the antiquity and artistic importance of the slabs. The slabs were later stolen from the graveyard, and, after a tip-off from Paul McMahon, Martin Timoney and I were to 'discover' them a second time after a car chase across the Sligo countryside.

While at home in Limerick before Christmas 2000 on another mission — about which more presently — I accepted Ed O'Donovan's invitation to see the bed of the Abbey River; this had been drained to accommodate a new sewer pipe in advance of being reflooded after the fitting of an unused mid-nineteenth-century lock gate of gigantic proportions and the associated erection of a marina at the old Custom House side of Curragower Falls. To walk on the soupy gravel of the river bed along by Barringtons Hospital was one thing, as indeed was the privilege of seeing the new concrete revetment wall built into the Shannon to regulate the water serving the marina. But it was nothing compared to the surprise that O'Donovan had in store (literally) when he brought us to his finds depot. The finds reflect the civic history of Limerick, its trade and commerce, its everyday life and, most dramatically, its famous late seventeenth-century sieges. The fifteenth-century spur, the silver groats and the sixteenth-century port seal are very impressive. But the unexploded Williamite mortar bombs and cannon balls are something else. The shells had quenched as they landed in the river, having been slung at the walls and the bridge from well over a mile away. By drilling into the soft filling in the shell apertures under expert guidance, O'Donovan and his colleagues were able to siphon out the unexploded contents of these 300-year-old bombs. To smell their sulphuric loose earth-like filling was to smell the siege of Limerick — its menace, its fires, its terror. I will never forget how close to it all the smell of the explosive content of those unexploded bombs brought me. I had seen the Sarajevo touring car, bullet marks on Berlin buildings, mortar craters in north-west Russia and even Beal na Blath's muck on Michael Collins's great-coat, but they did not bring me as close to the historical theatre from which they survived as did the smell of these shells. Sad to say, future visitors viewing them on display will probably lose out on the drama and history conveyed by the smell, a sensation of unmatchable value in bringing you to an ancient scene but one which is difficult to preserve and impossible to communicate.

When I confess to my principal discovery from over three decades of excavation, research, museum work and historical research, the reader, if convinced of the sincerity of my case, will conclude that, in the final analysis, all anyone is trying to discover is himself or herself. It may be that as we get older we are inclined to become autobiographical; we also have less to prove to ourselves, so that the individual can to his 'own self be true' about what really matters now that ambition and insecurity have released their former prisoner.

The discovery that has meant most to me probably tells a great deal about me and my values. It is middle age and the associated contemplation of mortality that frees me in a sadly cynical world from any desire to impress but rather urges me to share the excitement of the discovery in question. Picture the scene. Alone in the kitchen of a County Limerick farmhouse a week or so before Christmas, I'm flattening out and noting the paper contents of half a dozen black tin boxes of polling-booth size. Over the course of the previous couple of days I have encountered the records of a local landlord which had been salvaged from destruction by the neighbour charged with the task. There are notes on family history, election posters, newspaper cuttings, indentures, diaries, plans of shops, estate time-books, rent-books and the bills of the local blacksmith. The records related mainly to the forty years or so after the Great Famine, with some strays from the Edwardian period and a few nuggets from before the Famine. The finder and saviour of the papers hadn't fully prepared me for the importance of the records, particularly those that pertained to my great-grandfather and his son, my grandfather, the blacksmiths who issued bills of works done for the estate (their main customer) at the forge. I was in the process of bringing together the bills for the various years from the black boxes when I made the best discovery of all — my great-grandmother's handwriting. Her husband had obviously been absent from the forge on an August day in 1877 (a century and a quarter ago) when she signed her name (Catherine Wallace) with the date over a penny stamp of Queen Victoria with the phrase 'paid in full'. She had literally signed off on the account on behalf of the family, her writing being tall, careful, slow and deliberate, in contrast to that of her husband, their daughters and son, which I know from the other bills. I couldn't believe my luck. It was as if I had met Catherine and was the first of my family to have done so in well over a century. She had died in 1895, her husband lasting into the new century to be present (just, I suspect) for the census of 1901. Her grandchildren, including my father, were born long after her death and had never been privileged to meet her as I had just done. I was stuck to the chair in grateful astonishment, conscious of the accident which had preserved these old bills for so long when at any time they might have been burned. It was almost as if I was fated to meet her and to commemorate her memory as I am now doing. Could all this have been meant to occur? I have described the bills elsewhere. Here I am merely sharing the joyful moment of a wonderful personal discovery, one I couldn't have imagined possible. For a family for whom handwriting had mattered so much, who were obsessed with the clear concise style they all shared for at least three generations (presumably because they learned it from one another as they compiled bills and ledgers) and who, up to the last generation, actually took pride in their writing, to have not only evaluated their various hands but, in contrast, to have also seen the writing of somebody who wasn't as used to writing as the smiths and their children was a rare privilege. I remember literally standing up from the table and looking across the black boxes ranged in an arc on the floor around my feet, tracing my finger across Catherine's signature and the stamp, and reflecting as I walked out into McDonogh's yard for a breath of winter air that this was the brightest of all the nuggets preserved in the cache. I was fortunate to have discovered it, and I would probably never be so lucky again. I don't think I could be!

But, of course, this was before I saw the bones and other remains of Kevin Barry and his comrades in their graves at Mountjoy jail before they were removed to Glasnevin, but that is a story for another archaeologist to retail… It just shows that discoveries will continue to be made in the funniest of ways and in the strangest of circumstances as long as people stay interested in what went before them.

2

Raising a glass to Professor M.J. O'Kelly

Margaret Gowen

The urge to discover in archaeology is grounded in an intense interest in the material remains of the past and the irresistible challenge of uncovering and piecing together the shape and character of ancient structures, places and lives, though the remains can be cruelly scant. Archaeological work can produce results that are a source of great wonder. New discoveries can be intensely rewarding and the act of discovery can excite huge public and professional interest.

As a fearful, awestruck student in the first of our first-year archaeology lectures, I watched and listened — attentively — as Professor M.J. O'Kelly lowered his glasses, peered out at a group of 50-odd of us, raised his hands (in the way that he did) and introduced us to our chosen subject by making a single important point that has remained with me through my archaeological career: 'If you can't see people in your archaeology by the end of this year, you have no business doing it'. He suggested that if we failed to connect our studies to people we would, quite simply, fail to become archaeologists.

On very many occasions it has been this close connection to the lives of people and the material remains they have left behind, both casually and carefully, that has excited my own personal interest. At another, completely different level I have found that 'peopling' our developing consultancy business in the once-demonised commercial sector of archaeology with individuals who are now some of the best in the profession has been almost as rewarding.

Over the years there have been a few singular discoveries that probably bear mentioning in the context of this publication. These were points at which there was a real thrill and an almost visceral pleasure in knowing that the choice of study and later work was absolutely right.

During my very first season of excavation as a student at Newgrange, I was invited to take and hold a gold Roman coin that had been found at the base of the mound. Its glittering weight was a shock at first and its mint condition was a stunning introduction to the beauty and wonder of special, well-preserved archaeological artefacts. What followed was realisation that the archaeologist had to understand and place artefacts in their context. In this instance, and to my student mind, the object was a potent evocation of the universal urge of people throughout time to leave votive offerings when visiting sacred places.

It also illustrated, after my first year of learning, the nature and structure of archaeological thinking and interpretation. The elegance of accurate deductive thinking charmed and excited me. Just what were the Romans doing in the Boyne Valley? What other evidence for their presence existed in the record? Newgrange clearly must have remained a sacred site up to that time. The River Boyne was clearly used as a route. Did they travel on foot or use boats? What sorts of boats did they travel in? What is the evidence for Roman boats in Ireland? Were they simply reconnoitring the territory? Perhaps they just came, saw and didn't make the effort to conquer? I was hooked! And so I sought out J. D. Bateson's 1973 article and read a bit. Later, in second year, O'Kelly placed the following question on our examination — 'The Romans came to Ireland as tourists. Discuss'!

That excavation had started with wrist-numbing (and mind-numbing!) trowelling on concrete-hard boulder clay, at the eastern side of the mound, in which, to our poor student eyes, nothing could be discerned. After two weeks, and before the discovery of the coin, I wondered about the merits of choosing English as a second-year subject. We 'greenhorns' were placed adjacent to the Beaker settlement area where O'Kelly had noted a subcircular trend in the soil the previous year. He confidently anticipated the remains of a very large Beaker house. We were encouraged to probe the boulder clay for soft 'spots' that might represent post-holes. A spread of burnt bone was revealed that O'Kelly suggested might be domestic debris on a Beaker house floor. Adjacent to this spread of material, which it became my task to uncover, one of the senior volunteers, a drop-dead gorgeous English student (there was always at least one, who inevitably ignored the juniors), demonstrated that he had discovered a promising post-hole. He was sitting in it before we all realised that this was something quite particular — and definitely not a post-hole. It was the socket of one of the stones that formed the passage of a satellite tomb — Site Z (Fig. 1). My spread of bone was found to be concentrated on, and to reflect the size and location of, the V-shaped passage floor.

This, declared O'Kelly, was the essence of archaeology. Discovery may occasion changes in interpretation. Preconceived ideas are dangerous and archaeological interpretation may have to be fundamentally reviewed at times.

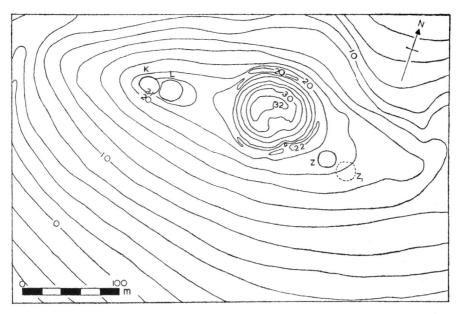

Fig. 1—Contour plan of Newgrange ridge, contour interval 2m
(after M.J. O'Kelly et al. 1978).

We had built models with beach pebbles in sand on baking trays in our university practicals — a very good way of learning the variations in megalithic tomb structure. I started to see variations in colour and texture emerge in the soil that I could translate into a plan. It was a marvellous time.

Having spent my working life in development-led archaeology, I have rarely had the opportunity to participate in the excavation of standing monuments. Unexpected and unusual archaeology has, however, punctuated my experience, and the discoveries that have excited my interest most are quite unconnected.

As a postgraduate student in the late 1970s John Barber's rescue excavation of a medieval burial site at Ballincubby, near Kinsale, found me excavating a female skeleton with a fully grown, engaged foetus. Clearly both had died in childbirth. It was as remarkable as it was chastening to a young woman of 21.

Ritual care was evident in the placing of white quartz pebbles in the sockets of the stones that form the alignment at Aughnasilly, Co. Cork, reminiscent in some ways of the use of white quartz at Newgrange. I started to make connections that were not articulated in my academic reading at that stage.

The slanted layers beneath Skiddy's Castle so marvellously identified, excavated and interpreted by Dermot Twohig illustrated the extraordinary subsidence of the heavy stone structure into soft, organic ground on its massive timber raft foundation.

Supervising the excavation of two Viking house plots on Fishamble Street for

Pat Wallace in 1979–80 was a formative and wonderful experience for a young archaeologist (Pl. 1). To work with such preservation and in such immensely rich archaeology was such a privilege — the very best opportunity that one could dream of at that time. The site, already well understood, read like a book once you developed an eye for it. Starting with four weeks of drawing sections in FS II before going on to supervise in FS III taught me a great deal about the subtlety and derivation of the soft organic layers that had accumulated one by one to a depth of over 2.5m on the original boulder clay. These peeled one off the other like butter, each one providing the most extraordinary and complex definition.

The challenge, however, was to capture it. Every day presented exciting and stunning discoveries and every day the pressure to reach the bottom grew as the patience of Dublin Corporation wore thin.

The only discovery of relative consequence made by me during my own period of site supervision was a collapsed roof of fire-blackened sods with their pared, wooden twig scollops *in situ*, some as fresh-looking as if they had been placed there the year before, though they had all snapped. This rested on a rough

Pl. 1—Building level 10, Fishamble Street (plots 10 to 12, left to right), in course of excavation (after Wallace 1992).

lattice framework of branches and twigs. The main roof supports had been extracted for reuse. Up to that time, the only other really well-preserved collapsed roof had been a burnt roof of straw, excavated by Noel Dunne on FS II. My discovery (I proudly marched Dr Wallace onto the site to show him!) revealed that at least some of the very common sod subfloors that had been previously excavated in these congested Viking houses may well have first served as the roofs of the previous buildings on the property.

My period at Fishamble Street was made all the more special by the opportunity to work with Siobhan Geraghty, who undertook a concerted and structured study of plant macrofossils in the property plots that it was my responsibility to supervise and record. She discovered some very rare items, but also illustrated the range of plants used for bedding, floor-covering, food and foraging. She captured hints of food shortages in the huge numbers of seeds of the weed 'fat hen' which suggested that a porridge was made from it. A parallel hint of privation and food shortage was revealed in the animal bone study undertaken by Finbar McCormick, suggesting times of near-famine in the city. Siobhan showed us bramble seeds, apple pips, sloe stones, mosses, ferns and rare plants. It was evident (and I suppose logical) that groups of people would have left the city to forage and gather wild fruit, or that people made their way to a gathering at a market-place to buy from or barter with people who collected enough to make the sale of their pickings and the journey into the town worthwhile.

During that time discoveries of a very special nature were being made on a daily basis: rich evidence of a merchant class; a large house filled with locks and keys; foreign objects; imported ceramics; marvellous fabric from Constantinople; beautiful clothing pins and ornaments. Shellfish were found in huge quantities (gathered from which shores nearby?). The finds that impressed most, however, were a beautiful toy boat and a toy sword, while skeletal remains sometimes showed signs of very violent death.

Vikings ate horses (the butchering marks on the bones revealed this), they skinned their cats and they beat their dogs to the point that they occasionally broke their noses. They used exquisite bone combs to comb teeming, itching lice out of their hair. They used tweezers, files, ear-picks and masses of moss as part of their toiletry. Low wattle walls around their cesspits were probably designed to stop small children and animals from falling in! All human life was there.

What a privilege, then, to return to the opposite side of the street, twenty years later with the splendid Linzi Simpson directing, to collaborate on the excavation of a very different side of Fishamble Street, with new, computer-assisted ways of managing the riches of information retrieved.

In the area of development-led archaeology, challenging discoveries are regularly made and some have occasioned change in academic thought: for example, the discovery during gaspipe-laying in 1986 of a well-preserved Neolithic house at Tankardstown, with the high-precision accelerator ^{14}C dates of 5105 ± 25 BP (uncal.) — approximately 3970 – 3880 BC — for charred emmer wheat from possibly one growing season. The site was first identified by Christine Tarbett during monitoring of topsoil-stripping when a linear gully with heavily oxidised edges appeared, filled with charcoal-rich soil and large stones. After two days a burnt, fire-damaged but still remarkably intact lozenge-shaped arrowhead was found. I needed no further evidence. The absolute certainty with which I made the decision that we had found the remains of a Neolithic structure still surprises me — we only had one corner of it. But the dimensions and the character of the remains were incredibly similar to those described and illustrated by Sean Ó Nualláin at Ballyglass. It was enough to allow me to encourage the Bord Gáis Project Manager to be far more generous than he really had to be in the circumstances. We used that generosity and engaged in a rigorous sampling of the foundation trench and two main internal post-holes, one of which possessed the cache of charred material. The identification of emmer wheat at the time was a very important discovery, as were the remains of apple pulp and hazelnut shell.

The interest generated within the profession was so great that the Royal Irish Academy generously funded a further three years of excavation, during which — it seemed extraordinary at the time — a second, larger house was found. Later, in 1990, another Neolithic house was revealed during gaspipe-laying at Newtown, Co. Meath. Since then, many more have been found and our company has been responsible for the discovery and excavation of a unique site at Corbally near Kilcullen, Co. Kildare, where were found two groups of three closely built structures (Pl. 2).

The last of the discoveries that bears recounting in the context of this publication relates to linking excavation results to interdisciplinary palaeoenvironmental work. The project involved the study of an archaeologically rich peat basin in Derryville Bog, Co. Tipperary, prior to the development of the Lisheen lead zinc mine tailings lagoon. Intensive contour survey of the peat basin floor, used to record and place the numerous archaeological sites in their microtopographical context in antiquity, proved to have a far-reaching benefit in providing the template for the particular knowledge, survey and observations of the project's peat expert, Wil Casparie. Wil used the contours to illustrate the growing size, changing character, flora and hydrology of the bog system over time (Fig. 2). He was able to link elements and events in the peat profiles and to interpret the palaeohydrology of the bog system with amazing clarity, providing the project with chronological definition regarding the times when particular conditions on the bog surface made human access possible and even attractive.

Pl. 2—House 5, Corbally, Co. Kildare: general view from the east with House 6 visible to the west, excavated 2001.

Even more exciting was Wil's ability to understand the impact of human activity on the bog and to illustrate the impact of this 'interference' in the very delicate balance of the bog's hydrology and drainage.

The bog was traversed by a 600m-long, narrow and largely stone-paved Bronze Age track which crossed the peat basin but fell short of the present bog margin. Again, the certainty with which I decided that this must represent the limit of the peat in the Bronze Age surprises me as it had a huge bearing on the focus of the project management of the work. Excavation revealed that the track had been carefully paved at its eastern 'entrance', while at its western end it had become mired in a treacherous and very wet area where the track-builders wove a tangled, incoherent web of wood and brushwood in their apparently increasingly desperate attempts to get to the other side safely. This wet stretch was found to be the bog's main outlet channel. Wil identified the evidence for the channel, helping the interpretation of the track's disintegration into

3300-2350 BC

1700-1200 BC

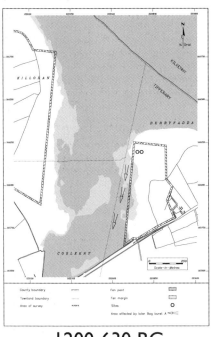
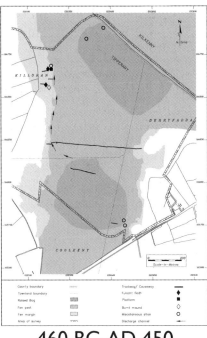

1200-630 BC

460 BC-AD 450

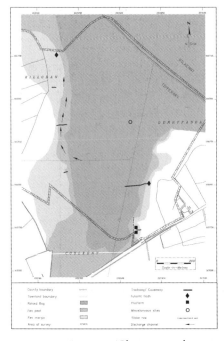
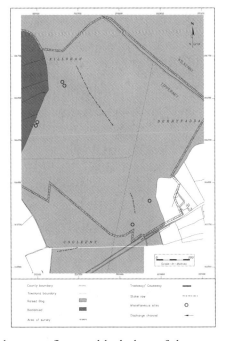

Fig. 2—Changes in the size, character, flora and hydrology of the Derryville bog system, Co. Tipperary, over time.

structural chaos, but he added much more. The track had been built across the peat basin during a short dry spell of just some 25 years in the Middle Bronze Age (the regeneration of alder and the later demise of these trees provided the detail in this context), while a dendrochronological date of 1440 ± 9 years for a repair to a part of the track that had sunk into the peat provided a singular reference point.

What had caused this short-lived dry spell that had only once encouraged the creation of a track across the entire bog, and what factors encouraged building at the margins? Why was it never crossed again? We had no mechanism for a site-focused study of climate change, but answers emerged when the contour survey was analysed. A low ridge underlay the track alignment and Wil's observations led to the discovery that the hydrology on both sides of this ridge had been independent prior to and during the Bronze Age. He also demonstrated that

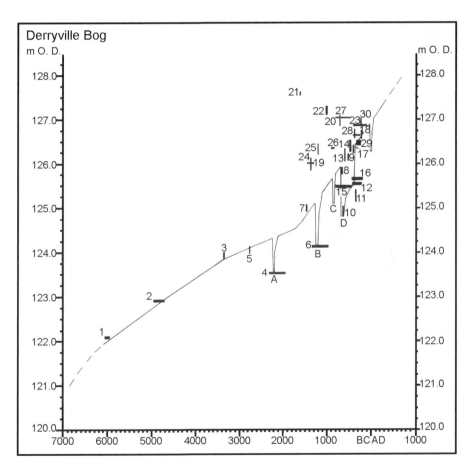

Fig. 3 –Wil Casparie's time/depth graph, indicating bog bursts in the Derryville Bog, Co. Tipperary.

there had been a number of significant bog bursts, after which rapid drainage created conditions for short-lived access through surface drying. Wil illustrated the results of his, at first, tentative interpretation using a time/depth graph (Fig. 3).

Picture the excitement, then, when the results of a completely independent study on testate amoebae (as hydrological indicators) produced almost exactly the same graph! The remarkable coincidence was revealed at one of our project round-table sessions when we first learned of the results and were able to add the archaeological site location and dating results to them. We went on, as a team, to create chronologically secure definition as to how the peat basin developed as an environment and how human activity had used it opportunistically. Wil also demonstrated how the impact of this interaction had changed the natural system, sometimes to a devastating degree. Track 18, described above, depressed the peat very marginally, but had caused the two independent hydrological systems on either side of it to coalesce, thereby creating the conditions in which raised bog peat would develop and the bog could no longer be crossed. This explained the total absence of further long tracks within the study area. Also, he illustrated how one bog burst had been caused by a large Iron Age track crossing the main drainage channel at the south-west of the peat basin and blocking its discharge function. A great part of it had been swept away.

Our company's work continues on another branch of discovery — one that has revealed the value of promoting teamwork, integration, technical innovation, accurate resourcing, good research and a real interest in communicating the subject.

So, let me now raise a glass to Professor O' Kelly, who taught me how to see with an archaeologist's eye; to understand the value of good survey, plans and cross-sections ('If you can't explain it, draw it!'); to appreciate the great richness of Frank Mitchell's work and the value of interdisciplinary collaboration; to understand the first principles in archaeological excavation and deductive thinking; and to seek people in the past.

Further reading

Bateson, J.D. 1973 Roman material from Ireland: a re-consideration. *Proceedings of the Royal Irish Academy* **73**C, 21–97.

Casparie, W. and Gowen, M. 2001 Die zahlreichen Moorwege von Derryville bog, Co. Tipperary, Irland: Über den Zusammenhang von Bautechnik und Moorhydrologie. *Proceedings of the Oldenburg Moor Symposium 1999*, 91–106.

Corlett, C. 2001 Neolithic housing development at Corbally, Co. Kildare. *Archaeology Ireland* **15** (3), 4.

Geraghty, S. 1996 *Viking Dublin: botanical evidence from Fishamble Street*. Dublin.

Gowen, M. and Tarbett, C. (forthcoming) *Excavations at Tankardstown, Kilmallock, County Limerick*.

Mitchell, G.F. and Ryan, M. 1997 *Reading the Irish landscape*. Dublin.

O'Kelly, M.J. 1982 *Newgrange: archaeology, art and legend*. London.

O'Kelly, M.J., Lynch, F. M. and O'Kelly, C. 1978 Three passage graves at Newgrange, Co. Meath. *Proc. Roy. Irish Acad* **78**C, 249–352

Ó Nualláin, S. 1998 Excavation of the smaller court tomb and associated hut sites at Ballyglass, County Mayo. *Proceedings of the Royal Irish Academy* **98**C, 125–75.

Purcell, A. 1999 Neolithic houses at Corbally, Kilcullen, Co. Kildare. *Archaeology Ireland* **13** (1), 15.

Twohig, D.C. 1997 *Skiddy's Castle and Christ Church, Cork: excavations 1974–77*. Cork.

Wallace, P.F. 1992 *The Viking Age buildings of Dublin* (2 vols). Dublin.

3

An axe in three plays...

Gabriel Cooney

Prologue

Lambay Island, Co. Dublin

OS 6-inch sheet 9.   NGR O 317508

Circumstance of discovery: found in 1997 during the archaeological excavation of a Neolithic quarry site (93E144).

Context: topsoil (Context 1001), Cutting 10.

Collection: none.

Petrology: porphyritic andesite (Macro ID).

Axe. Pecked, ground and polished. FS 02. Lower left side nearly straight, upper left side curves towards butt. Right side curved along its length. Both sides rounded in section in the lower part of the axe. In the upper part sides flatter, with pockmarks remaining from primary manufacture. Junctions of the sides with the edge are clear. Edge is sharp with two very small chips removed from centre and right. Edge is curved, symmetrical in plan. Blade profile is symmetrical, blade area is defined by a higher level of polish than the faces. Face 1 is well ground and polished in the lowest two thirds; in the upper third there is a small area on the left where grinding has not fully obliterated primary treatment. Lower two thirds of Face 2 are well ground and polished but to a lesser degree than Face 1. The upper third of Face 2 is more irregular, with remnant areas of primary working. Junction of sides and butt clear. Butt is flat in plan, also flat in profile but slightly oblique (sloping towards Face 1). The butt is ground but not polished. Profile is asymmetrical; thin; cross-section oval.

L. 16.1cm, W. 6.2cm, T. 2.6cm, Wt. 397g.   ISAP: 20649.

University College Dublin, Archaeology Department (93E144:7000).

Cooney 1998a.

Going to the island

It was a warm, sunny day. The sky seemed to join with the sea a great distance away, unlike some of the days in the dark part of the year. Then the world seemed very small and waves crashed against the land. They had come to the island earlier in the day when the currents made it easier to row the skin boat. His father was related to people on this island, which they called the Rugged Island. His grandmother had told him that the people called it this when they first came to the land because of the high cliffs with many bays that formed the edge of most of the island where it entered the sea. This morning they had steered for the cairn of the ancestors on top of the island that was visible from their home. This was the landmark by which you could find the safe, sandy landing place on the side of the island facing the land. It had been a relief to feel the wet sand under his feet. Now they were walking up to the high part of the island. The boy could feel the warmth of the earth through his feet and the wind, which had appeared as they climbed, was lifting his hair as he listened to the talk of the group. They chatted about how good the crops might be this year and the great feast that could be held after they were harvested.

They were going up a well-worn path but it was quite steep. Seagulls flashed and dipped above them. One of his older relatives stopped and turned to stand facing the sea and the mainland. Pointing with his right arm outstretched he talked about the distant mountains from where the sea currents came. He swung his arm around and named the hills and places on the coast. The one the boy always remembered was the mountain that looked like the tip of an arrowhead.

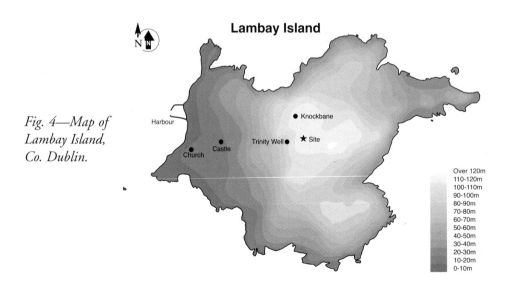

Fig. 4—Map of Lambay Island, Co. Dublin.

This lay below where the sun sat in the sky in the middle of the day. It was known as the Shining Peak. There the sacred white stone that had the power to cure and kill could be found. The boy remembered his grandmother telling him the story of the man with evil in his heart, who when he went to get stone at the peak had been turned into a rock. This rock could still be seen on the path that led up into the mountains. The Shining Peak reminded them of why they had come to the island and they hurried on.

Soon they came to the valley known as Where the Water Springs from the Ground. This was the most important place for water on the island. The people said that the ancestors must have known that it would also be needed to shape the green and white rock that lay beyond and above the spring. They climbed up out of the wet valley and into a narrower one that rose in front of them. Now they could hear voices and the sun was glistening off the face of the rock. Someone said it was as smooth to touch as those stones that the sea threw up on the land. There were heaps of broken rock at the place where people always came to make axes during the lighted part of the year. Even now they could see two men smashing a large block to pieces and looking to see how many possible axes it had provided. It was from here that the axe which was his father's most treasured belonging had come. When the boy had asked when this was his father had said: 'As many cycles of the moon ago as there are branches on the largest oak tree in the woodland'. There were many stories told about their axe and the effect of the white sparkles in it. These were said to be drops of milk that had dropped from a woman's breast as she had fed her twin sons. When the axe was being re-ground to lengthen its life in his home the grains were kept and given with a little water to people who were sick or could not have children.

Now his father had decided to bring back the axe to its birthplace. They had come as part of the celebration that the elders of all the communities who had ties to the island had agreed on. This would be a good way to show respect to the ancestors after the recent unsettled times. Ahead of them they could see the new cairn taking shape. It had been placed where for as long as could be remembered people had put offerings in the ground to ensure that they could work the stone in the right way. Now objects were being placed above the ground. Someone whispered that it was beginning to look a little like the monument for the ancestors on the highest point of the island that they could see over their left shoulders. His father took the axe carefully out of its basket and slowly, regretfully, placed his right hand on its smooth surface for the last time. He called the boy and told him to place it on the surface of the growing cairn. The boy did as he was told, noticing at the same time that many of the other objects that were placed there had been broken. He turned and saw that his father was already making his way down the valley. He ran to him and pulled at his arm. His father turned, looked back and said, 'I have given part of myself to this place'. As they made their way back down to the sea they saw the ravens circling overhead. They all agreed that this was an auspicious sign, both for what had been done and for the journey home.

Clearing the ground

It was a Monday morning in March and the woman was busy planting the seed potatoes. It had been a wet spring until a week or so ago. Then her husband had dug the ground. Now there was a good chance that the potatoes would be all in the ground by St Patrick's Day, so they should have a good crop. They had put manure on the small field over the winter and he had cut a line along the centre of each furrow and then thrown up earth on either side onto a ridge. The ridges were about three stalks wide. She was crouched over the ground with her ciséan or basket over her right shoulder and a stick in her right hand. With this she poked a hole into the ridge, a mixture of sods and manure, and then threw in half a seed potato with part of the eye so that it would grow.

This was the best and the highest of the three small fields that had been made in the valley, which now looked like three wide steps on a stair. The cabins of the families who had made this land were on the rough, rocky ground overlooking the fields. When the wind was blowing they would have liked more shelter, but it was more important that they had a good crop of potatoes. As she worked rhythmically her thoughts wandered. She wished it were later in the day when the children would be home from school and they could help her. Sometimes they wanted to stay at home when the potatoes were being planted, but she had no intention of crossing the master. She had seen him the day before when the priest had come over from Rush to the small chapel above the shore to say Mass. It was a good chance to see all the people on the island and to get news from the mainland. As it had been a stormy Sunday people had been remembering the day when the church was dedicated and a boat sank on the way back to Rush. But that wind had dried the ground and now all the men were busy working down on the castle farm to get the ploughing done. She knew that her husband, who was a good ploughman, would turn his horse with the sun, from left to right, so that God would bless the work.

She felt the ash in the bottom of the basket, which had come from the bonfire lit on St John's Eve the previous year. This had been mixed with the seed potatoes to ensure a good crop. She could tell from the pains in her feet that she was coming to the stoniest bit of the field where they had already removed lots of stones and thrown them to the side. Here her husband always cursed when he

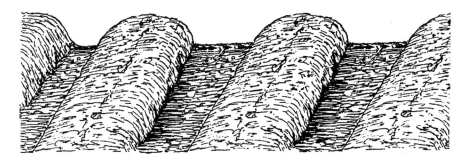

Fig. 5—'Lazybed' cultivation ridges.

was digging. Because of the stones they had left the ridges in the same position for several years (Fig. 5). Their friends and neighbours wondered whether this would bring them bad luck, but they had had good crops from the field. She stood up to stretch and ease the pain in her back and she could feel the sun warm her bones. Looking onto the higher ground she could see the ravens circling above Cnoc Bán. This was where the good people or the little people lived.

There were lots of stories about this hollow hill and other places on the island where the little people lived. They caused no trouble as long as you remembered to take precautions, like placing an iron thong over a baby's cradle if you had to leave it alone in a cabin and sprinkling the crops and animals with holy water from Trinity Well on May Eve. It was then that the little people liked to be around and up to no good. Of course there were stories about children who had been taken away and changed into seals and who were thought of when the seals cried out on quiet nights. The maid in charge of the dairy down at the castle, who had lived on the island a very long time, long before the pier was built, had whispered to her a while ago that their little field was a fairy place as well. The maid claimed she had a thunderbolt, or what one of the gentry in the castle had called a stone celt, from that field. She said she sometimes had placed it in the milking pail to increase the flow of the cows' milk. But nobody else seemed to have heard this story.

Bending down again she decided that she would pitch some more stones to the side of the field before carrying on with the sowing. She picked up a smooth, green stone with white speckles. That's strange, she thought, it is almost as if it has been shaped by a human hand. The stone was longer than the length of her hand, and as she felt its polished surface she thought that it was just like a stone that you would see down on the seashore. It was like a chisel, but much too broad. While it had an edge like an axe, she could not see how it would be attached to a handle. As she remembered the small, bright pieces of sharp stone that often came up when the sod was turned over she thought of the dairymaid's story about the field. Could this really be something belonging to the little people? She also thought of her father's story about a man who had found a thunderbolt and put it in the roof of his cabin to bring protection against lightning.

What should she do? If she brought it into the house there was sure to be much talk and speculation. People would remind her and her husband that there was something strange about their lovely small field, which was so important in making sure the family had enough food through the year. No, she quickly decided, better to leave well enough alone. She threw the stone to her right, out of the field, and covered it with a few other stones. As she began to plant the potatoes again she heard with relief and happiness the sound of children's voices coming up the valley.

The discovery

Monday, 28 July 1997. The weather was sunny if a bit windy, but not as cold as it had been earlier in the month. Looking out to the west the sea was calm and I could see the Dublin coastline from Skerries to the mountains, with the red and white of the Pigeon House towers clearly visible. Ireland's Eye looked sombre in the shadow of Howth. Overhead a low-flying jet on one of the flight paths to Dublin Airport seemed to be taking in a Lambay tour. Thankfully the seagulls were quieter now that the young gulls were confidently flying around the place and deserting the nesting spots. The ravens had come from the eastern side of the island as they always did at this time in the morning. They were soaring on the currents to the south, with Raven's Rock beyond them. I was thinking that things seemed to be going well on the site as I did a few quick record photographs while the team headed for a sheltered spot at the Eagle's Nest for our morning coffee break.

In Cutting 1 West Diarmaid was excavating what we were interpreting as the original soil surface. This is what Neolithic people would have stood on as they started to work the west-facing rock outcrop nearby. Then the angular pieces of quarried and broken-up porphyry would have covered this surface. The problem of interpreting what happened before the surface was covered with stone was exacerbated by the rabbit burrows that had appeared at this level. This reminded me to take a shot of Cutting 8 to the north, where Emmet was working. Cuttings 8 and 7 nearby had occupied Emmet and Beatrice for much of the season. We had opened these areas to get a better understanding of the activities that had taken place in the valley while the rock outcrop which formed the sides of the valley were being quarried. We took off the cultivation soil with its many episodes of spade cultivation and pieces of nineteenth-century pottery along with the small bits of coal and beach pebbles. This raised lots of questions about this relatively modern activity. Had the field been manured with seaweed? Did the pottery come from the cabins nearby or had it been brought up from the castle? But there was also lots of flint and some pottery dating from the Neolithic in the cultivation soil, suggesting that the spade cultivation had disturbed much earlier features. At first the context (807) under the cultivation soil had looked promising, with a number of stone concentrations like those we had come across just to the west. Now it seemed that the whole area was a mass of rabbit burrowing with remnants of features surviving, such as the short length of trench that Emmet was currently excavating.

Turning to the west I took a shot of the section (Drawing No. 94) that Conor was recording. It showed up the ridge and furrow episodes in the cultivation soil very clearly. On the current surface below the cultivation soil just in front of the section face was Feature 11. This was a low mound of stones that had been placed on the surface during the Neolithic, or the stones might also be the top layers in the fill of a pit. This was one of the most exciting features on the site at the moment as it was close to the large pit (Feature 1) containing deliberately placed stones — hammerstones, rubbers and pieces of porphyry — as well as carefully placed deposits of flint artefacts and pottery. We had discovered Feature 1 in one of the test pits that we had dug in a line along the length of the valley to see what was the extent of Neolithic activity. It was to look at the connection between the quarrying of the porphyry to make axes and these features on the valley floor that we had decided to continue Cutting 1 to the west right across the valley. These new excavation areas were called Cuttings 9 and 10. There had been a laugh about what would happen when it came to Cutting 12 as everyone knew that to stave off bad luck I avoided using the number after that wherever possible, so the notebooks, film numbers, contexts and everything else went from 12 to 14! The only lucky thirteen that I knew of was the birthday of my daughter Emma.

In Cutting 9 Sarah was taking off the topsoil. Large stones had already started to appear. This was very promising as it suggested that the cultivation soil was thin and that there might be good preservation of the Neolithic levels. We had started work on Cutting 10 this morning and had just taken off the sod. Photos taken, I was walking along the edge of this cutting to join the others for coffee when I noticed a curving, polished piece of porphyry in the newly exposed surface. I was tempted to clean off the earth around the stone with one of our small paint-brushes. This judicious brushing revealed one face of a complete, large porphyry axe — what we would call in 'stone axe speak' an FS (Face Shape)

02 type axe, with an asymmetrical shape. It was lying with the blade pointing to the west close to the edge of Cutting 10. I thought how lucky we had been not to hit it with a spade earlier in the day when we had been de-sodding! Since it was on top of the cultivation surface it had clearly been moved in the nineteenth century.

I was struck by the notion that this axe encapsulated the striking history of the site that we were bringing to the surface again. There had been two major episodes of activity. The first occurred in the fourth millennium BC, when people had quarried the rock and at the same time carried on a number of activities in the valley. These seemed to focus on placing objects in or on the ground. The second phase was in the nineteenth century, when people had made a field out of this rocky ground. This both disturbed and removed some of the prehistoric evidence, but also covered it up in the area of the field because people had added to and deepened the soil. This beautifully finished stone axe confirmed that all stages of axe production took place on the site well over five thousand years ago. Not only that, but in some cases axes along with other objects came to rest there. Fantastic, a cause for celebration! It would be fun telling Emmet, Conor, Diarmaid and Sarah about the find and ringing Beatrice with the news. Now of course I also had a good story to tell the next time someone asked me what was the most interesting thing I had ever found! Definitely time for a cup of coffee.

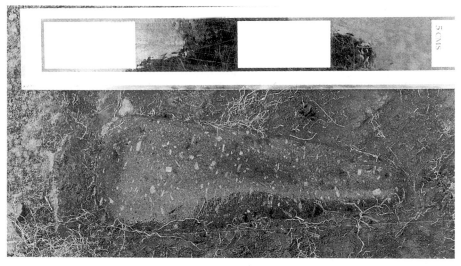

Pl. 3—The stone axe photographed in situ.

*Pl. 4—Gabriel Cooney
examining the new find.*

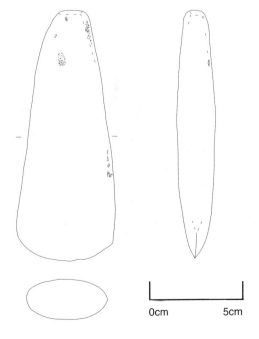

*Fig. 6—Line drawing of the
stone axe.*

0cm   5cm

Acknowledgements

My thanks to Dúchas The Heritage Service, on the recommendation of the National Committee for Archaeology of the Royal Irish Academy, for grant aid for the excavation, and to the Lambay Island Trust, in particular Dr Patrick and Mrs Margaret Kelly, for their enthusiastic support and continued hospitality. Thanks are due also to Barbara Leon for the description of the axe in the prologue and the illustrations that accompany the text. The photographs were taken by David Jennings. I am very grateful to Emmet Byrnes, Eoin Cooney, Mary de Courcy, Melanie Giles, Barbara Leon, Stephen Mandal and Aidan O'Sullivan for their comments which have improved the telling. I would also like to thank Conor Brady, Beatrice Kelly, Linda Fibiger, Sarah Halpin, Finola O'Carroll and Diarmaid O'Keeffe for their work and thoughts on the site. I take full responsibility for the script!

Further reading

Cooney, G. 1993 Lambay: an island on the horizon. *Archaeology Ireland* **26**, 24–8.

Cooney, G. 1998a Neolithic site on Lambay Island, Co. Dublin. In I. Bennett (ed.), *Excavations 1997*, 57–9. Bray.

Cooney, G. 1998b Breaking stones, making places: the social landscape of axe production sites. In A. Gibson and D.D.A. Simpson (eds), *Prehistoric ritual and religion*, 108–18. Stroud.

Cooney, G. 2000 *Landscapes of Neolithic Ireland*. London.

Cooney, G. 2002 So many shades of rock: colour symbolism and Irish stone axeheads. In A. Jones and G. MacGregor (eds), *Colouring the past: the significance of colour in archaeological research*, 93–107. Oxford.

4

Beyond the Gap:
Knockroe passage tomb and the people of the Slate Quarries

Muiris O'Sullivan

'They're a rare breed, that crowd beyond the Gap' was the enigmatic response when I explained to an acquaintance that I planned to conduct an archaeological excavation at a megalithic tomb south of Windgap in County Kilkenny. It was 1989 and I knew little about the neighbourhood, while my informant had taught in nearby Callan. His endorsement seemed ambiguous at the time but, in hindsight, it is strangely appropriate in a good sense.

Windgap is situated to the south of Callan, where the old road to Carrick-on-Suir (Carrick to local people) crosses a saddle in the low foothills stretching east from Slievenamon mountain. A few miles beyond Windgap is Lamou Cross. Beyond that again is Delaney's Pub, an old-world local renowned for its musical sessions, traditional and otherwise. The road continues through Skeough and on to Carrick-on-Suir, about five miles to the south. Delaney's is located across the road from the site of a former rural RIC station, a focus of strife in the nineteenth century before being destroyed during the War of Independence and now marked only by a handball alley. This complex occurs at the lower end of the Slate Quarries, while the townland of Castlejohn marks the upper end. The Lingaun River forms the spinal cord, flanked by the sheer quarry faces, abandoned spoil-heaps and ruined dwellings of a once-thriving slate enterprise, now reclaimed by nature. Winter rain, brought down from the hills in cascading torrents, swells the volume of the river, but in the summer it is reduced to a rippling stream punctuated by deep pools rich in freshwater fish.

Lying above the quarries, in the townland of Knockroe, is the passage tomb known to the wider archaeological community by its townland name but to the local people as 'the Coshel' (caiseal). This side of the Lingaun is in County Kilkenny but the other side is in County Tipperary. Local identities are formed around this frontier, adding spice to the varying highs and lows of the respective county hurling teams. Long ago Kilkenny, represented by the Slate Quarries, reached a Leinster Gaelic football final only to be disqualified when it was found that some team members were from the Tipperary side of the valley. On a more recent occasion, while addressing the Kilkenny Archaeological Society at Knockroe, the writer of this piece was pointing out the proximity of the passage tomb to the county boundary when an insistent voice in the attendance exclaimed: 'But it's in Kilkenny!' It was the legendary Margaret Phelan, the indefatigable champion of Kilkenny's heritage. These incidents underline the abiding significance of a short frontier that links not just the two counties but the provinces of Leinster and Munster and also the dioceses of Ossory and Cashel. In early medieval times this stretch of borderland was disputed by the armies of Ossory and Munster, and it has played a role in forging the distinctive Slate Quarries character. A reference to 'the crowd on the other side of the river', relatively innocuous elsewhere, could be laden with powerful meaning to someone standing at the Coshel or Clashnasmut, facing each other from the two sloping sides of the Lingaun.

A thin slab of the local slate was inserted, in prehistoric times, in the south recess of the east tomb at Knockroe. According to the Ormonde Deeds for 1348, slate from the Ormonde Quarries was used to roof and floor Kells priory. In the 1560s it was used to roof the Tudor mansion in Carrick, and in the following century it roofed other buildings in the town. By the nineteenth century the various privately run quarries had been amalgamated into a single enterprise. Water-powered and steam-powered machinery was installed, a canal and a private road were constructed, and more than a hundred men were employed.

During the armed rebellions of the mid-nineteenth century the Slate Quarries were within the area in which the uprisings occurred and the police station came under attack. In December 1858, a Chief Inspector Curtis from Piltown visited the neighbourhood to investigate reports that a secret society was meeting locally. His report specifies that he had visited the Slate Quarries police station and questioned both the constable and sub-constable, examined the station diary and patrol books, and advised the resident policemen to 'send a man in plain clothes through the neighbourhood' to gather intelligence. He concluded, however, that no secret society existed specifically in the Slate Quarries, although he was convinced that some of the locals were probably low-ranking sworn members of 'the Society'. Whatever threat existed in the 1850s, the life story of the Slate Quarries police station took a fatal turn in 1921 when it was burned down during the War of Independence. By then, however, the heyday of the Quarries was over and the slate enterprise was beginning to face technical and marketing difficulties. Although small-scale extraction continued into the 1940s the commercial value of the Slate Quarries had been undermined by a variety of circumstances and the mile-long complex is now reduced to water-filled quarries, abandoned mounds of waste slate, terraces of roofless cottages, a collapsed concrete bridge — testimony to a botched public works initiative — and a dwindling store of memories.

Discovery and excavation of the megalithic tomb

The earliest account of Knockroe passage tomb is to be found in Canon Carrigan's *History and antiquities of the diocese of Ossory*, published in the early years of the twentieth century. The monument came to archaeological prominence in the 1980s and the occurrence of megalithic art on several of the stones attracted immediate interest. At this stage the site was heavily overgrown, its northern half buried beneath a field margin, and the presence of a second chamber on the eastern side no more than a possibility. By contrast, carvings were visible on the orthostats of the western chamber, which stood out of the cairn, and decorated kerbstones were visible on the southern side. Archaeological excavations began in 1990 when a cutting was inserted into the southern half of the cairn. The north-west quadrant and the edge of the cairn were explored in 1991, the eastern tomb in 1994 and the western tomb in 1995. Excavation grants were provided each year through the Royal Irish Academy.

Over the four seasons a large number of students, from the Department of Archaeology in UCD and several overseas institutes, worked alongside experienced excavators and some local collaborators, notably Ed Shea and Ned (Butcher) Fitzpatrick, both of whom maintained a helpful interest over several years. Many of those who collaborated at the site have established considerable reputations as archaeologists in the meantime, notably Dr Carlton Jones, who subsequently brought important material in the Burren to light, Deirdre Murphy, who with her brother Donal has established a respected contract archaeology company, and my colleague Dr Tadhg O'Keeffe, now an even more renowned medievalist than he was then.

One of the more exciting seasons at Knockroe occurred in 1991 when Trojan work on the part of several people was rewarded with the revelation that the kerb was still intact on the northern side, followed by some disappointment when it transpired that, in contrast to the southern side, only one of the kerbstones was decorated, and that with two barely visible arcs. The examination of the cairn in 1991 and 1992 led to the suspicion that only the lower course of stones, and possibly not even that horizon, could be regarded as an original filling. This was confirmed by the discovery of a footpath near the base of the cairn. Subsequently, for some reason, the cairn was restored. The upper layer is made up of dumped fieldstones, but the lower layers are made up of larger stones and organised into distinctive horizons. The complex history of the cairn brings to mind Joseph Raftery's discovery of La Tène material beneath Cairn H at Loughcrew, and serves as a reminder that many passage tombs do not have a complete cairn. It would seem that cairns associated with some megalithic tombs may have an interesting story to tell, which involves several phases of activity.

The Knockroe excavations revealed numerous parallels with the Boyne Valley, particularly Knowth. This is manifest in the siting of the complex in relation to the nearby river, in the incorporation of a straightforward western chamber and a cruciform eastern chamber, in the use of special stones in significant parts of the structure, in the alignment of the western tomb with the setting sun of 21 December, and above all the intriguing artwork. In due course both chambers at Knockroe were found to contain cremated bone representing large numbers of individuals, accompanied by classic passage tomb grave-goods as well as late Neolithic pottery, with the inevitable addition of Bronze Age Food Vessel ware. In the north recess of the eastern tomb, sherds constituting the lower half of a Carrowkeel pot were encountered, representing a classic passage tomb inclusion of pre-3000 (cal.) BC. Fragments of what appears to be a large decorated pin were also recovered, a further example of a type identified previously at Fourknocks and Knowth. So strong is the Boyne Valley comparison that a programme of geophysical survey in the ground around the Knockroe site is an imperative, to check whether other features occur beneath the sod nearby, as at Knowth and Newgrange. A major survey of Neolithic and early Bronze Age settlement in the region is also required.

Local support

The excavations could never have occurred without the blessing of Tom Morrissey, owner of the land on which the site occurs, and his father Willie. They facilitated the work in every way imaginable, never placing obstacles in our way, even when they might have felt entitled to say that enough was enough. Willie, an octogenarian at the time of his death a few years ago, had been brought up on the Morrissey farm in Knockroe. In his youth, during the 1930s, he had bought a lorry and earned a living as a haulier in the Slate Quarries. When the lorry was bought by the state on the outbreak of the Second World War his enterprising nature led him to establish a farm-machinery sales business in Carrick. This concern thrived for half a century. Meanwhile his brother ran the family holding on which the archaeological site occurs. In 1995, when innumerable pieces of cut leather were recovered from relatively modern layers in the east chamber of the megalithic structure, Willie remembered that his grandfather had made shoes for local people. In conversation he made an impromptu identification of the various cuts of leather, incredibly all in Irish. Irish as a spoken language was clearly alive in this region until a few generations ago. *Bóisín* is the local pronunciation of the boreen that leads down to the site, a pronunciation that mystified the writer until he learned that this was a distinctive rendering in the once-thriving Gaelic dialect of the area. On another occasion a mysterious slab of slate was found, too large by far to be a roof slate and yet perforated near one end, which was correctly identified locally as a horse-drawn platform on which a farmer would kneel between the drills while thinning or weeding mangolds or turnips.

Around 1987, on an early visit to Knockroe, I met Seán Power, who brought me on a guided tour of the antiquities in the neighbourhood. Seán is a local landowner who takes a special interest in the passage tomb site and appears to have the remains of a destroyed *fulacht fiadh* on his land. He is one of several people and organisations without whose assistance the excavation programme would have been diminished. The vital excavation grants from the Royal Irish Academy were supplemented by the donation of site offices and implements from the South of Ireland Asphalt Company (SIAC) and further assistance was provided by Mr Paddy Hickey, an engineer who supplied a level and produced a contour survey of the site (sadly Paddy, the father of David Hickey of 1970s Dublin Gaelic football fame, died in the summer of 2001). One day, in May of 1990, an SIAC lorry brought a sizeable Portakabin from Dublin on the first day of the excavation. Manoeuvring his cargo slowly along the narrow, twisting laneway leading down to the site, the driver struggled to avoid the stone walls and other obstacles on either side. At Tom Morrissey's gate, about halfway along the laneway, he admitted defeat and confirmed that he could go no further. The cabin was unloaded in the gateway, the lorry withdrew and we were left stranded. Along came Seán Power who announced that one Liam Meagher would be our saviour. Half an hour later a large tractor came down the laneway and by various skilful means the driver worked it to nudge the cabin into the yard. Liam Meagher, the good-humoured driver whose casual manner conceals a sharp mind and a farmer's natural physical strength, then insisted that the entire excavation group should come to his house for lunch. Our protests were brushed aside and we soon found ourselves around a table in a big farmhouse in Kiltrassy as Liam's wife, Catherine, produced a meal seemingly from nowhere. Liam and Catherine then surprised us further by showing us an unoccupied three-bedroom prefabricated bungalow at the other end of the garden, recently vacated by their own family, and told us that we were welcome to use it as a base. Thus began an enduring friendship with the Meagher family.

By an incredible coincidence, a retired uncle, Johnny Maher (brother of Liam's mother), lives in the Meagher household. Johnny is an antiquary with a deep and extensive knowledge of the local area, informed by superb judgement. His advice has been crucial on matters ranging from archaeology to geology and from history to folklore and placenames, regarding all of which he has a collection of literature and a knowledge of critical sources. His collection would be much larger but for his inherent generosity, which prompts him constantly to hand over his own material to anyone who shows an interest. In his young days Johnny, who is now into his eighties, heard locally that there was writing on the stones at the Coshel. One day, while passing along the trackway overlying the cairn, he noticed petroglyphs highlighted by the sunlight raking across one of the stones, and he came to understand the true significance of the writing and the nearby Devil's Altar. His enthusiasm for archaeology and his willingness to provide information to professional archaeologists working locally was eventually rewarded when specialist attention turned to the Coshel. Although the archaeological excavations have given Johnny Maher tremendous satisfaction and he has been a supportive friend to the field programme, he could not be prevailed upon to speak publicly to any visiting group, preferring to remain in the background while the present writer took the spotlight, often presenting information supplied by Johnny.

Our involvement with the Meaghers has been an uneven relationship in that we could never hope to repay their generosity. Another household we came to know well was that of Pat and Eileen Power in Knockroe townland. Their friendship found expression in a myriad acts of kindness, and Pat's trailer features in many site photographs because he made a practice of leaving it on site to be filled with spoil from the excavations, which he would then empty at a designated spoil-heap before returning the trailer to be filled again while he got on with tending to his busy farm. This voluntary assistance was in addition to cordoning off a corner of his farm as a location for the site office and equipment container. Eileen Power, who held down a nursing post as well as rearing two sons and helping Pat with the farm, provided accommodation for selected members of the excavation team over the years. It is a feature of the Knockroe project that, when needed, help seemed to materialise from all over the countryside. The backfilling of the site at the end of each excavation season always attracted a *meitheal* and over the years a core group emerged. This group once found itself in a Chinese take-away in a neighbouring town, where good-humoured banter about references to Drunken Chicken and Bird's Nest Soup in the menu brought the house down and almost led to a rift with the management. Elsewhere a pub manageress once found herself temporarily locked outside the door as she tried to encourage her patrons to leave 'shortly' after closing time. It goes without saying that the archaeologists were blameless on all these occasions. A more businesslike occasion was the removal of a stubborn ash root from the western chamber in 1995. This root, around which the archaeological excavation had delicately proceeded, was eventually lifted out by means of a rope attached to an ingenious extension to the front loader of Liam Meagher's tractor. A sculptor who visited the site removed the stump with the intention of carving it, which appears fittingly appropriate.

The Slate Quarries have provided a rural setting of incredible tranquillity for the excavations. It is an area of outstanding natural beauty, especially in summer. Over the years the excavation team became familiar with the sight of hawks, foxes, badgers, rabbits, pheasants and herons. During the early part of the 1994 season we shared the archaeological site with a family of stoats. Ravens nested in the quarries further down the valley. The grassy laneway linking the megalithic tomb with the site offices was enlivened by the presence of living balls of fur, which we took to be rodents of some type. A few times each week, at the end of the day, we would receive a visit from Michael Egan, a local farmer from the other side of the valley, who more than once commented that the voices from the excavation broke the loneliness of the countryside and lifted his spirits. John Joe Dunphy, another local farmer, also visited occasionally. Eddie Grinsell (RIP) was a local man who went quietly about his daily work with a horse and cart. Eoin McCarthy was a craftsman who made clocks and other souvenirs from the local slate. John Denby, a photographer from Carrick, supplied a few spectacular photographs. Paddy Walsh, former Kilkenny hurler, made drawing frames. John Delaney, who runs Delaney's pub, has continued to visit the site at key sunrises and sunsets and has produced an important photographic record of these events. On and on it went, there being too many people and favours to mention.

The archaeology at Knockroe is spectacular, but the social side is no less memorable. In the early 1990s a sculpture festival was held in the Slate Quarries. Some of the exhibits, which have become a permanent feature of the Lingaun valley, were inspired by the megalithic tomb. The event spawned an annual Slate Quarries festival, animated by Jim Power (RIP), during which a variety of cultural experiences are introduced. Local people speak of a memorable day when, during Mass, lighted candles were floated out on the surface of the water resting in one of the quarries. The Slate Quarries festival often revolves around Delaney's pub, surely one of the more remarkable places in the area. Thursday night in Delaney's brings together a gathering of local musicians, including the redoubtable John Delaney himself. One afternoon during a Slate Quarries festival patrons witnessed the spectacle of John's piano being passed over the head of the crowd to the open area outside the pub so that he could play for the large gathering assembled there. The assembly at these events would often include

Pl. 5—In the evenings, after work, some members of the excavation team would go swimming in this quarry.

Pl. 6—View of the north-western end of the quarries, showing the Lingaun River and the megalithic tomb, visible as a light patch below the horizon at the right edge of the photograph.

Pl. 7—One day during the 1991 season the excavation team decided to visit Cody's coffee shop further downtown (or downstream?).

Pl. 8—Suzi Klemm from Austria, a key member of the 1990 and 1991 excavation teams, has attracted unexpected attention.

local celebrities such as Paddy Clancy (who died a few years ago) and his brother Bobby, members of the famous singing Clancy clan, and the writer Michael Cody. A favoured experience amongst the visiting archaeology students in the mid-1990s was to witness a weekly rendition of the ballad 'The Carrick-on-Suir Brass Band' in Delaney's, always preceded by an explanation of the band's origins as a travelling musical accompaniment to Duffy's Circus. Other local hostelries, such as Guinan's of Windgap, were also patronised.

In the early days of the excavations I came to hear about Ned Fitzpatrick, an all-round local handyman. Ned was 69 at the time, but retirement had never crossed his mind, and he remained active as a casual worker until about a year before his death, which occurred at the age of 79 in the latter part of 2000. He worked daily at tasks such as fencing, painting, cutting timber and milking cows on behalf of farmers in the locality. Even in his mid-seventies, he would show strength and resourcefulness as he took centre stage whenever large boulders, such as displaced capstones, were to be moved around the excavation site. Ned's involvement in the excavations was wholehearted, although subject to ground rules which he laid down from the beginning: (1) he would do only his type of work, i.e. fencing, mixing concrete, barrowing waste and other physical activity, and (2) he would come into work only when there was a specific job to be done (no delicate work and no waiting around for barrows to be filled!). After his first day on the excavation, I learned subsequently, Ned regaled the patrons of his local, Guinan's of Windgap, with mythical stories of the archaeologist's activities, to the extent of claiming that he had been handed a spoon with which to load a barrow of soil. Ned had a gift for telling apocryphal stories as if he were describing events that he had witnessed, invariably peopling the tale with neighbours whose personalities fitted the characters in question.

Ned was regularly to be seen on his large black 1930s bicycle, travelling the roads around Lamou Cross and the Slate Quarries, with his scythe, crowbar, sledgehammer or shovel strapped neatly in place. He explained that his father had been a very heavy man and that he himself cycled to avoid getting into a similar condition. Wasted muscles in one leg, which he attributed to the effect of poisonous chemicals encountered while working with cereal crops, did not inhibit his activities. He had a wrought-iron constitution, and he needed it! His day began early, with a glass of poitín and a wholesome breakfast, and he would arrive early at his place of work. He worked until early afternoon, at which stage he returned home to eat, after which he cycled the few miles to Windgap where he was a regular fixture until closing time in Guinan's, seated with one elbow on the bar and a pint of Guinness nearby. He demanded respect for anyone who was singing and would occasionally be prevailed upon to sing one of his own favourites:

If I had to do it again,
I doubt if I'd do it the same ...

Oh before I had reached twenty years
I was an expert on whiskey and beers ...

And if I had to do it again
I'd certainly do it the same.
For the sake of being good
I certainly would,
If I had to do it again.

Having enjoyed the Guinness and the company he would cycle home, catch some sleep and rise at the crack of dawn to face another day. To swop rounds with Ned was to invite disaster, because he was both a sprinter and a stayer when it came to drinking. Only once in my experience did he show any sign of being affected by the drink. During the 1995 season he arrived at work one morning after a particularly heavy session at a race meeting in Gowran Park, warning that he might not be able to last the day. Nothing would dissuade him from starting work, but he eventually had to admit defeat around 10.00 a.m. He was back after lunch, explaining that he had boiled and eaten a head of green cabbage and was now feeling in the best of health.

Ned was an institution in the Slate Quarries. He was a big man, a larger-than-life character who was friendly, gregarious, reliable, sensible, physically strong and singularly talented. In his youth, until he was well into middle age, he had played handball and hurling, and he was a renowned set dancer. Spectators had to beware when Ned and his troupe danced the vibrant Lancers, as the ladies in the set were flung from man to man with ever-increasing gusto and impeccable timing. Because of his proficiency as a dancer and his role in keeping the Lancers set alive in south Kilkenny, people came from many countries to meet Ned, and he was even brought to Moscow on one occasion in the early 1990s. The first attempt to visit Russia had to be aborted when the occasion happened to coincide with an attempted coup against Mikhail Gorbachev. Ned was sitting in his place in the aeroplane when the journey was cancelled, but the visit went ahead some time later. His father and at least one uncle had worked in the Slate Quarries, before the enterprise closed down (his uncle died with a work colleague when something went wrong as they primed explosives on the rock face prior to a blasting operation). Until his death, Ned maintained a set of traditional slate-working tools and was much in demand amongst visiting groups who marvelled at his demonstrations of the once-thriving craft. Ned's huge hands made the task

Pl. 9 (right)—The late Ned Butcher demonstrates the slate-cutter's craft, using traditional tools.

Pl. 10—(below left) Johnny Maher contemplates the megalithic art of a kerbstone at Knockroe. For him the excavations fulfilled a lifelong ambition.

Pl. 11—(below right) Susan Hogan-Conrad from the United States gets a bear hug from Ned Butcher.

Pl. 12—From left, Robbie and Liam Meagher, Pat Power and Ed O'Shea, on one of the many occasions when local help was indispensable.

Pl. 13—My wife Debbie during the 1991 season, a year in which three couples who would later marry met for the first time at Knockroe.

of marking and cutting the slate look easy. He was as tough as he was skilled: when tightening barbed wire, he would frequently grasp the barbs in his unprotected closed fist. He fished in the Lingaun River and fashioned blackthorn sticks from suitable stems located along the boundaries. He took a keen interest in the local area and kept a fatherly eye on the ducks, which he had introduced to the landscaped lake in Windgap. He never married ('Why tie yourself to a tree when you have the run of the orchard?') and he was very close to his family and an extensive range of friends. This was clear from the crowds at his funeral, not to mention the guard of honour and the draping of his coffin with the colours of the local hurling club. Like *An tOileánach*, Ned represented a lifestyle that may never again exist.

Conclusion

As research continued at Knockroe, the local community's involvement deepened. Even those who might not have an interest in archaeology were drawn to the site. On one occasion a trainer of horses was persuaded by a friend to visit the excavations. He showed little interest in the guided tour until it was mentioned that the upright structural stones were known as orthostats. 'Orthostat', he exclaimed, 'now there's a good name for a horse!'

Further reading

Ó Nualláin, S. and Cody, E. 1987 Passage tombs in the Suir valley region. *Journal of the Royal Society of Antiquaries of Ireland* **117**, 69–83.

O'Sullivan, M. 1987 The art of the passage tomb at Knockroe, County Kilkenny. *Journal of the Royal Society of Antiquaries of Ireland* **117**, 84–95.

O'Sullivan, M. 1993a Recent investigations at Knockroe passage tomb. *Journal of the Royal Society of Antiquaries of Ireland* **123**, 5–18.

O'Sullivan, M. 1993b *Megalithic art in Ireland*. Dublin.

O'Sullivan, M. 1995 The eastern tomb at Knockroe. *Old Kilkenny Review* **47**, 11–30.

O'Sullivan, M. 1996 A platform to the past: Knockroe passage tomb. *Archaeology Ireland* **10** (2), 11–13.

O'Sullivan, M. 1996 Knockroe and the Neolithic settlement of Munster. *Irish Historic Settlement Newsletter* **6**, 1–5.

O'Sullivan, M. 1996 Five thousand years of unwritten history. In M. O'Dwyer (ed.), *Coolagh — history and heritage*, 80–4. Kilkenny.

O'Sullivan, M. 1997 On the meaning of megalithic art. *Brigantium* **10**, 23–35.

O'Sullivan, M. 1998 Retrieval and revision in the interpretation of megalithic art. In C. Jones and C. Hayden (eds), *The archaeology of perception and the senses,* 37–48. Cambridge.

5

Two stones make a line

Stefan Bergh

There may be hundreds of reasons why people study archaeology, and likewise why people become archaeologists. One aspect of archaeology as a subject of study, which at the same time constitutes a major part of its fascination for us, is the ever-present element of unpredictability. This unpredictability is, of course, most evident in the fieldwork aspects of archaeology, such as excavation or survey. Our archaeological interpretations are based mostly on methodical and often time-consuming research, and are arrived at in part by the study of what others have done before but also through our own 'primary' analysis of different or unexplored aspects of past society. Sometimes during the course of our investigations we encounter a sudden 'eye-opener' or make an unexpected discovery.

Even though we may have a relatively good idea of the kind of finds we expect to make during an excavation at a particular site, we can never tell beforehand exactly what those finds might be and what they can tell us. The 'thrill of the trowelling' is an exciting and ever-present element of any archaeological excavation. Of course, we rarely make ground-breaking discoveries of the calibre that will make headlines in the press. Occasionally, however, we do stumble upon something that, to the general public, might seem relatively insignificant but to us is of great importance as it may illuminate a certain aspect of a past society. The chance discovery of a fragment of a certain type of pottery made during the excavation of a Neolithic house, for instance, may be of major importance in the interpretation of the contacts its occupants may have had with other communities. This, in turn, may lead to certain conclusions concerning trade and exchange, and could also help us to understand the nature of ritual patterns expressed in, for example, the megalithic tombs contemporary with the house.

During some types of archaeological investigation, particularly reconnaissance field-walking undertaken primarily to explore, find and record hitherto 'unknown' sites, the element of unpredictability and surprise makes our work all the more compelling. The satisfaction and excitement of finding an unrecorded prehistoric site, if only indicated by a scatter of flint flakes, or something as spectacular as a previously unrecorded megalithic tomb are admittedly a fundamental part of the fascination of archaeology. All of these findings, big and small, add up to a greater understanding of the prehistoric society we are studying. Sometimes they only reinforce what we already know, but occasionally they force us to rethink, change or fundamentally alter our interpretation of certain aspects of the prehistoric past.

The subject-matter of this essay does not concern the unexpected discovery or 'rediscovery' of a spectacular object or site, but rather concerns my sudden awareness of the importance of a particular construction feature of a megalithic tomb. It might not sound particularly exiting, but the significance of two large stones, passed and noted by thousands of people over countless years, turned out to be of fundamental importance in the interpretation of a whole ritual landscape from the Neolithic.

Background

To put the discovery in context it is necessary to outline the general background to the story.

I have, over the last 20 years or so, had the privilege of studying the archaeology as well as the landscape of County Sligo. The county of Sligo can be divided into two distinct regions, with the igneous Ox Mountains creating a dramatic border zone between the inland, southern part of Sligo and the land along the Atlantic to the north. Even though I have spent considerable time getting to know the landscape south of the Ox Mountains, my main focus has been the dramatic and varied coastal landscape to the north. This part of the landscape has a long coastline created by the three bays of Ballysadare, Sligo and Drumcliffe. The most characteristic and remarkable feature of this landscape is, however, the dramatic contrast between the rugged heights of the Ox Mountains to the south and the clear-cut 'table-top' limestone mountains to the north. These mountains enclose the region to the north, east and south, while the sea forms the natural border to the west. The centre of this topographically well-defined region is the Cúil Irra peninsula, just west of Sligo town. At the western end of this peninsula is the singularly impressive mountain of Knocknarea, the visual focus for the whole region. I call this area the Cúil Irra region (Fig. 7).

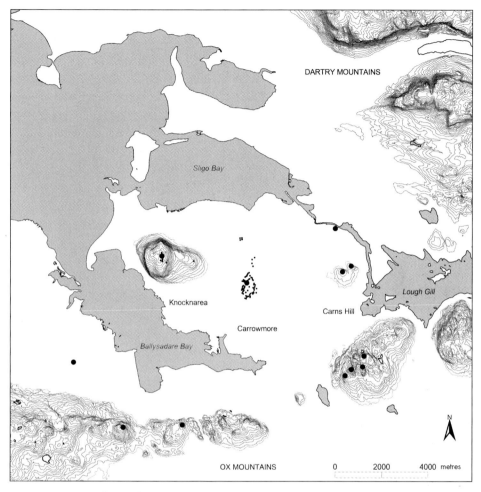

Fig. 7—The Cúil Irra region, Co. Sligo, with the passage tombs indicated.

In the Neolithic, some 5000 years ago, this coastal region was one of the key social and ritual centres of Ireland, indicated by the very large number of passage tombs. Some 80 of the roughly 250 recorded passage tombs in Ireland are found in the Cúil Irra region. The passage tomb cemetery of Carrowmore, one of the largest clusters of megalithic monuments in western Europe, is located at the foot of Knocknarea on its eastern side. The large cairn of Miosgán Meadhbha is conspicuously situated on its flat summit (Pl. 14).

During my first summers in Ireland, when working as a student on the excavations at Carrowmore, the mountain of Knocknarea was a distant place where we went once or twice a summer with a few beers to enjoy the magnificent sunset. Its relationship to the great megalithic cemetery at Carrowmore was little explored by me at that stage!

Pl. 14—A view of Knocknarea mountain from the east, with Carrowmore 27 in the foreground (photo: Stefan Bergh).

During the course of research for my PhD thesis in the mid-1980s, which primarily involved a study of the passage tombs in the Cúil Irra region, I undertook an extensive programme of survey. This consisted of a landscape analysis as well as detailed surveys of all the known passage tombs of Cúil Irra. The best-known passage tomb in Sligo, and probably the most spectacularly located prehistoric monument in Ireland, is the huge cairn of Miosgán Meadhbha on the summit of Knocknarea. This large cairn is an ever-present and dominant feature of the region, and a distinctive landmark for any passer-by.

One of the general features recognised within the other passage tomb clusters in Ireland is the existence of large focal tombs, such as Newgrange, Knowth and Dowth at Brú na Bóinne, Co. Meath, or Cairns D and T at Sliabh na Caillighe, Co. Meath, around which smaller tombs had been arranged. The centrally placed tomb C51 has been interpreted as the focal monument within Carrowmore. It was also in general terms accepted, but not explicitly discussed, that the large cairn of Miosgán Meadhbha was a focal point for Carrowmore as a whole. The interpretation and context of this large cairn had, however, never been discussed in any detail, nor had the monument on Knocknarea been surveyed in modern times.

As my fieldwork progressed, and more and more passage tombs were surveyed, I came to realise that I could never attempt an understanding of the Neolithic ritual landscape of Cúil Irra without a greater understanding of

Knocknarea, and especially Miosgán Meadhbha. This large cairn had in the Neolithic (as it has today) a role and meaning in this region far beyond the sheer mass of stones from which it is constructed. My aim was to attempt to explore and understand some of that meaning.

On the summit of Knocknarea

The cairn of Miosgán Meadhbha, with a diameter of some 60m and a height of around 10m, has never been opened. By analogy with other similar cairns, however, it is likely to contain a passage tomb, and probably a rather elaborate one. Thanks to its remote location it has not met the same fate as many other large cairns that became a source of stone for local building needs. The only building requirement on the top of Knocknarea has been the building of field walls, and thankfully this has been fairly limited.

So the next, and final, part of my plan to survey all the passage tombs in Cúil Irra was to survey all eight sites on the summit of Knocknarea. The last time these sites had been surveyed was almost exactly 100 years previously, when Wood-Martin studied them in the mid-1880s for his *Rude stone monuments of Ireland*. Before him, the large cairn was surveyed by Gabriel Beranger in 1779. It seemed like Miosgán Meadhbha was scheduled for survey once every hundred years!

Beranger's plan and section of the cairn show no details but feature a slightly oval cairn with a (marginally exaggerated) diameter of *c*. 210ft (70m) and a flat summit measuring *c*. 100ft (30m). The cairn is described as 'an enormous heap of small stones', which admittedly is a rather accurate description of its general appearance! Wood-Martin's plan is slightly more elaborate (Fig. 8). One detail noted on this plan is the 'Site of probable Cist' marked just outside the cairn on the north side. And just outside the cairn on the south side there is a large stone marked on the same plan, but without any comment. None of these features are described or mentioned by Wood-Martin in the text.

Without having analysed Wood-Martin's plan in any great detail I set out to survey the sites on Knocknarea in early June 1984 (Fig. 9). The survey, which was carried out with a theodolite, was a rather arduous task as every working day started with a 40-minute uphill climb, with all the surveying equipment and provisions on my back (in hindsight this was not so bad, compared to the high-tech total station equipment weighing some 17kg which I used to resurvey the same sites eighteen years later!). The 1984 survey was carried out with the assistance of Agneta Shierbeck, then a student of archaeology at the University of Stockholm.

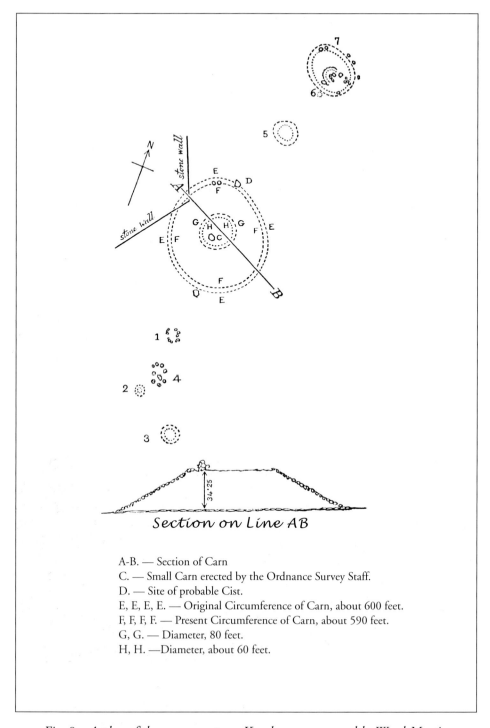

Fig. 8—A plan of the monuments on Knocknarea, surveyed by Wood-Martin in the 1880s.

Section on Line AB

A-B. — Section of Carn
C. — Small Carn erected by the Ordnance Survey Staff.
D. — Site of probable Cist.
E, E, E, E. — Original Circumference of Carn, about 600 feet.
F, F, F, F. — Present Circumference of Carn, about 590 feet.
G, G. — Diameter, 80 feet.
H, H. —Diameter, about 60 feet.

A limestone slab and a gneiss boulder

In addition to making a ground-plan, my intention was also to survey a number of profiles across the cairn, in order to estimate as accurately as possible its total volume. When setting out the very first north–south profile with a 50m measuring tape I started at the large gneiss boulder to the south of the cairn, climbed due north up the steep side of the cairn, walked due north over the flat top, and aimed again due north with the compass to descend the steep northern side of the cairn. To my amazement the compass was pointing directly towards the large flat limestone slab just outside the cairn. I walked back to the southern edge of the summit of the cairn, just to check that my measuring tape was actually aligned north–south from the gneiss boulder where I had started. And it was! I then realised that these two large stones were not randomly placed but in all probability marked a line that must have been of significance to the layout of the monument.

The existence of two boulders aligned approximately north–south might not be considered particularly remarkable in any way were it not for the fact that they are the only stones of this size present in the vicinity of the large cairn. The

Pl. 15—The gneiss boulder just south of Miosgán Meadhbha. Note sites 5 and 7 in the background, and the pointed profile of Croaghaun mountain on the skyline (left of centre). The view is taken from the north, looking south
(photo: Stefan Bergh).

Pl. 16—View (looking south) of the limestone slab just north of Miosgán Meadbha (photo: Stefan Bergh).

dimensions of the gneiss boulder (Pl. 15) to the south are approximately 2m x 2m x 1m, while those of the limestone slab (Pl. 16) to the north are roughly 2m x 2m x 0.3m. Besides the gneiss boulder, the only other boulder on the summit is a massive glacial erratic, nearly three times as large, located slightly downslope and approximately 70m to the north-west of the cairn. Other than this huge erratic, all the other large stones evident on the summit are used in the construction of the smaller burial monuments. So the large recumbent limestone slab lying just outside the perimeter of the cairn on its north side and the large boulder situated just outside the perimeter of the cairn on the south side must be considered as constituent elements linked to the layout and construction of the large cairn of Miosgán Meadhbha. These large stones have of course been noticed and photographed by thousands of tourists (and archaeologists) visiting the site over the years, but because of the cairn they could never have been viewed at the same time (unless from an aeroplane!) and their significance was therefore never fully appreciated.

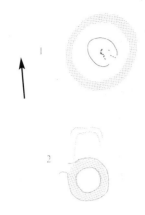

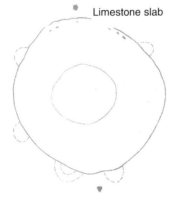

Limestone slab

Gneiss boulder

Fig. 9—A plan of the monuments on the summit of Knocknarea, surveyed by Stefan Bergh in 1984.

0   20 M

So, what is the significance?

How does the rather trivial fact that two stones apparently define a line that bisects the cairn north/south have any impact on our understanding of a prehistoric society?

We must start by looking at the immediate surroundings on the summit of Knocknarea. The north/south axis of the line seems to have been of significance not only to the large cairn, which it neatly transects, but arguably also to the general layout of the monuments on the mountain itself (Fig. 9). If this alignment is extended southwards it is immediately evident that two of the three smaller megalithic tombs (nos 5 and 7) also share this alignment.

In general, the smaller 'satellite' passage tombs appear to pre-date the very large tombs, which has also been demonstrated to be the case with some examples at Newgrange and Knowth in Brú na Bóinne. Applied to Knocknarea, it seems likely that at least two earlier monuments were placed along a significant north–south alignment initially marked by the large limestone slab and gneiss boulder to their north. Perhaps at a later stage, the large cairn was deliberately built in between the two large stones and centred on the alignment. This suggested sequence offers the possibility that an earlier monument occupied the central space between the two stones but was later covered by the construction of the large cairn.

Why, then, a north–south alignment, as it hardly points towards any of the well-recorded celestial phenomena? This line certainly appears to provide an axis or 'baseline' for the layout and construction of the monuments on the mountain and it could hardly have been picked at random. There is, however, one very tangible explanation for the axis they chose. If one extends the line south beyond the summit of Knocknarea it aligns directly with the very characteristic peak of Croaghaun in the Ox Mountains, some 7km away. Significantly, on the summit of this distinctive mountain is a small passage tomb (Pl. 15). Even more significant is the fact that this part of the Ox Mountains, around Croaghaun, is rich in quartz, a type of stone recognised as very important to the passage tomb ritual, and undoubtedly of special significance to the tomb-builders. So, one possible interpretation of the north–south alignment is that it was based on the distant source of quartz. The two stones may have acted as markers aligned on this source, which in turn served as the basis of the layout of monuments on the most important focal site in the Cúil Irra region.

The identification of this north–south alignment on the summit of Knocknarea provides an interesting parallel with Newgrange. The large mound at Newgrange and the two smaller sites to the west (K and L) lie in a straight line, while the two sites on the eastern side of the great passage tomb (Z and Z$_1$), though on the same general axis, are misaligned a little to the south (see Fig. 1, Chapter 2). This general pattern is repeated at Knocknarea. Here, however, the two monuments to the south (nos 5 and 7) are aligned on the great cairn, while those to the north (nos 1 and 2) are offset a little to the east of this alignment. In both cases, therefore, if one views the monuments from the direction intended by their builders (from the east at Knocknarea and from the south at Newgrange), the two monuments on the left of the principal mound are aligned with it while those to the right are located a little off-line.

It is interesting to note that both sites are not only similar in their linearity but are also almost identical in their formal layout. Clearly, this is a repeated formal pattern or plan whose layout concerns the use and organisation of ritual space. By the same token, each site has its own characteristic set of unique attributes. The group of monuments at Newgrange are located on a low ridge overlooking the River Boyne, while those at Knocknarea are located on the flat summit of this spectacular mountain — the visual focus for a whole region.

Another aspect of the north–south alignment recorded on Knocknarea is its role in a wider landscape perspective. The linear arrangement of monuments are all facing east, overlooking the Carrowmore passage tomb cemetery in the centre of the Cúil Irra peninsula, and by so doing turn their back on the sea. It is now obvious that the whole arrangement of monuments on Knocknarea, partly revealed by the relationship between the limestone slab and the gneiss boulder, was intended to create a real as well as a symbolic ritual façade of the flat summit, with the sky and the sea as a backdrop. The deliberate transformation of the skyline of Knocknarea with the construction of the huge cairn of Miosgán Meadhbha must have made, as it still does today, a profound impression on any traveller entering this region.

During recent fieldwork on Knocknarea a complex system of banks along the eastern side of the mountain has been identified, and excavation has demonstrated that these too date from the Neolithic. The banks seem to reinforce the symbolic screening of the landscape, expressed by the alignment on the summit, as they share the same general north–south trend. So, an impressive façade, facing east, consisting of an alignment of monuments on the summit of the mountain and an extensive series of banks of earth and stone on its eastern slopes, seems to have been of critical importance to the role of Knocknarea in the Neolithic.

The end of the beginning

This essay has attempted to illustrate how a minor discovery, or a sudden moment of awareness of the relationship between two stones and the cairn of Miosgán Meadhbha, has made possible new interpretations concerning this enigmatic site and the layout of monuments on the summit of Knocknarea. As a consequence this has implications regarding the position of monuments within the ritual landscape of the Cúil Irra region. Interestingly, there is a suggestion that this spatial patterning is echoed at the great passage tomb cemetery at Newgrange.

The Irish passage tombs were an integral part of a complex ritual, displaying different layers of spatial and morphological patterns, which we attempt to read and understand. Some of these patterns consist of both general and widespread features common to many of the passage tomb areas throughout Ireland, while others seem more regional in character. These ritual patterns and their characteristics are reflections of the society in which they were created and used, and it is in this context that they can be interpreted and given meaning. The inferences made in this essay are part of such interpretations. They should be seen, therefore, as the beginning of some new avenues of future research that will increase our understanding of Irish passage tombs and the society that built them.

Further reading

Barnatt, J. 1998 Monuments in the landscape: thoughts from the peak. In A. Gibson and D. Simpson (eds), *Prehistoric ritual and religion: essays in honour of Aubrey Burl*, 92–105. Stroud.

Bergh, S. 1995 *Landscape of the monuments. A study of the passage tombs in the Cúil Irra region, Co. Sligo, Ireland*. Stockholm. Riksantikvarieämbetet Arkeologiska Undersökningar.

Bergh, S. 2000 Transforming Knocknarea — the archaeology of a mountain. *Archaeology Ireland* 52, 14–18.

Bradley, R. 1998 *The significance of monuments*. London.

Bradley, R. 2000 *An archaeology of natural places*. London.

Cooney, G. 1983 Megalithic tombs and their environmental setting, a settlement perspective. In T. Reeves-Smyth and F. Hamond (eds), *Landscape archaeology in Ireland*, 179–94. BAR, British Series 116. Oxford.

Cooney, G. 2000 *Landscapes of Neolithic Ireland*. London.

O'Kelly, M.J., Lynch, F. and O'Kelly, C. 1978 The passage-graves at Newgrange, Co. Meath. *Proceedings of the Royal Irish Academy* 78C, 251–352.

Tilley, C. 1994 *A phenomenology of landscape*. Oxford.

Wood-Martin, W.G. 1888 *The rude stone monuments of Ireland (Co. Sligo and the island of Achill)*. Dublin.

6

The great mound at Knowth and the discovery of its passage tombs

George Eogan

The great mound at Knowth is one of a number of such monuments that exist within a relatively small area of the valley of the River Boyne, a short distance downstream from Slane in Brugh na Bóinne, Co. Meath. With Newgrange and Dowth it forms part of a group of vast passage tombs — amongst the largest of their class known in Europe. In early historic times (the latter centuries of the first millennium AD) literary sources refer to features in that area, which appear to have been passage tomb mounds. The first archaeological mention concerns the discovery of the tomb chamber at Newgrange in 1699. Dowth had been noted in accounts from 1769 and substantial digging took place there in 1847–8. Knowth was mentioned in 1848 by Wakeman but it was only in 1941 that the first archaeological investigations took place there. These were carried out by Professor R.A.S. Macalister, and during the course of that work several of the large kerbstones that surround the base of the large mound were revealed. Some large stones independent of it were also revealed, as was a souterrain.

Certain issues and problems arose out of excavations carried out during 1960–1 at the passage tomb at nearby Townleyhall. It was felt that an investigation at Knowth might assist in answering some of these questions. Accordingly, excavations were initiated in 1962, and these and other forms of research have been ongoing since then (Pl. 17). Initially these concentrated on areas outside the large mound, but before long information was coming to light that demonstrated that the great mound was not an isolated structure but part of a cemetery complex. We now know that that complex consisted of twenty passage tombs. But what was also exciting was the fact that passage tomb occupation sites were coming to light. These consisted of the remains of houses, circular in plan, averaging 8m in diameter and constructed of wood. But what a

*Pl. 17—Aerial view of the great passage tomb cemetery of Knowth with the
River Boyne in the distance (photo: Dúchas The Heritage Service).*

contrast there is between those secular structures and the tombs! The houses are
altogether simple and unimpressive wooden buildings, the design and
construction of which required no great skill or expertise. But other and
unexpected discoveries were also emerging. Amongst these was the fact that the
passage tombs were not the first monuments to be erected. On the contrary,
occupation had commenced a thousand years previously. Back about 4000 BC
early Neolithic people settled on the hilltop. They lived in rectangular houses
and, on the western side of the hilltop, a circular area up to 100m in diameter
was protected by a palisade. There was also post-passage tomb activity. The
passage tomb people were succeeded in the centuries before 2000 BC by
Grooved Ware people who had a different ritual regime, and for ritual purposes
a circular, open-air 'temple' replaced the tomb. A century or more later the
earliest metal-using people, the Beaker folk, settled there, but apart from a few
pits they left very limited structural traces. However, they left abundant evidence
of artefacts, including pottery sherds and flint tools.

After the Beaker people, and for close to two thousand years, there is no
evidence for human activity at Knowth. A revival of interest in the site took place
during the course of the Iron Age. Evidence for this is provided by a number of
inhumation burials with grave-goods and also by a limited number of isolated
finds.

Although changes were taking place in the region from the fifth century AD onwards, Knowth initially participated in these only to a limited extent. Around the seventh century, however, an important remodelling of the great mound took place with the digging of two concentric ditches around it. As a result it became a well-protected settlement that seems to have served as a royal residence for the kings of North Brega. Royal occupation expanded considerably during the tenth and eleventh centuries when a substantial, but unprotected, settlement was established. People lived in rectangular houses, various crafts were practised and a variety of goods were manufactured. But at Knowth nothing remained unchanged. In the course of the twelfth century the native Brega settlement came to an end and the lands of Knowth became part of the property of the nearby Cistercian abbey of Mellifont, which had recently been founded. This situation continued down to the sixteenth century, when Mellifont was dissolved and its lands granted to new, incoming people. Those new arrivals also farmed the land and continued to do so for centuries although successive influxes of new settlers were a feature of the times. This pattern continued up to the relatively recent past.

The excavations at Knowth revealed a succession of cultural complexes, each of which was of considerable importance and added to our knowledge of the development of the site. Knowth remained a place favoured by diverse cultural groups over a period of 6000 years. However, its passage tombs stand out as the most elaborate and impressive of all the remains. Excavations have shown that amongst them is one of particular note owing to its enormous size, covering about an acre (*c.* 0.4 hectares) and nearly 10m in height. By virtue of its location, size and the presence of megalithic art it was assumed that this too was a passage tomb. However, there were no surface indications to suggest that the mound contained chambers, so a programme of investigation was designed to address the overall structural history of the site, and a careful, systematic and ordered scheme of work was embarked upon. This started on the northern side of the mound and proceeded westwards.

The western tomb

From an early stage of our excavations it was becoming more obvious that the monument was indeed a passage tomb as one of the first features to be revealed was a series of large stones (kerbstones) placed end to end in an ordered fashion. But there was more: the outer face of practically every one was decorated with megalithic art, and the closer one approached the western side the more elaborate this art became. Another feature in this area was evidence for a settlement dating from the developed Early Christian period, with, in addition, drystone walls indicating the presence of a passage, possibly a souterrain. That was our understanding when that season terminated at the end of August 1966 — there was still no evidence for a passage tomb.

Work resumed the following year and it soon became obvious that the line of the kerb was curving inwards from both sides towards a kerbstone that had a distinctly different scheme of art to any of the others revealed up to then. In contrast to curvilinear motifs, its art comprised a series of parallel lines. The presence of a suspected souterrain, noted during the previous season, was also confirmed. This ran parallel to the kerb on its inside but there were also some flat stones resting on two parallel walls which extended inwards at right angles from the approximate northern end of this souterrain. Further excavation revealed that their inner end was spanned by a fairly substantial capstone. Despite the presence of the flat stones, which seemed to span the drystone work, the space between the walls was filled with soft dark earth. This earth extended only as far as the outer edge of the large capstone, and a cavity existed beyond that point. On the following day, 11 July 1967, careful excavation enlarged the opening and enabled an assistant, Martin Colfer, to peer in with the aid of a torch. He reported that he could see a passage extending inwards for a distance of several metres. This certainly was significant, but as this might still have been another souterrain normal excavations continued so as to elucidate the situation. After the removal of further material, additional lintels that spanned the space between the drystone walls were revealed. A definite entrance was now visible, and with the use of the flash-lamp I could see that, after a short distance, the drystone work gave way to much larger side-stones of orthostatic proportions, together with substantial capstones. Of greater significance was the fact that the surface of one of them was decorated with megalithic art. We were now confident that, at last, we had found the entrance. Thrilled at the discovery, the group — Quentin Dresser, Tom Fanning, Seán Galvin, Fiona Stephens and myself — speculated excitedly on the extent and nature of the tomb (Pl. 18). The only way to resolve our curiosity was to investigate further and so we set off up the passage.

In some places the side orthostats were leaning inwards owing to the immense pressure of the overlying mound so we had to crouch and wriggle or go on hands and knees in those parts, and in one place to contend with a pool of muddy water. As there were loose stones over the floor this was often a painful and uncomfortable operation. In places, however, one could proceed in the relative comfort of a hunched position. At one point there was a stone basin astride the passage with a sill-stone beyond. Other interesting features emerged in that area; as we flashed our lamp we saw that practically every orthostat was highly

Pl. 18—Discovery of the western passage: (left to right) Quentin Dresser, Seán Galvin, Fiona Stephens, George Eogan, Tom Fanning (photo: Seán Galvin).

Pl. 19—View of the face-like decoration with two large staring eyes carved on the surface of an orthostat, No. 50, in the western tomb passage (photo: Dúchas The Heritage Service).

decorated. Immediately on the inside of the sill, the art on one orthostat appeared to represent an anthropomorphic figure with two large, staring eyes (Pl. 19). In view of the design and its location we speculated on the possibility that this ghostly figure might have represented a guardian, a protector of the inner sanctum of the tomb.

Further inward the passage was much better preserved and the capstone roof was now higher. There were still plenty of stones over the floor, but there was no sign of an end to the passage. We could now walk almost erect and soon we reached the chamber, an undifferentiated structure containing two transverse sill-stones, one of which was decorated, as was the back stone, with parallel lines like those of the entrance stone (except, in this instance, these did not have the vertical line). By now we were a most excited bunch and had lost all sense of time and distance, so Quentin Dresser volunteered to return to the outside world to inform the rest of the team (who had been getting worried about our 'fate') of the news and collect a measuring tape. On measuring the tomb we discovered that it was slightly over 34m from end to end — an incredible monument, an incredible occasion, and certainly one that remains as vividly in my memory today as it did on that July evening 36 years ago. This was indeed a remarkable discovery, and what an extraordinary experience to have entered a tomb that has been standing for about five millennia, surely one of the greatest monuments of Neolithic Europe. We were truly privileged to have been present on such an auspicious occasion, an occasion that in our wildest dreams we could not have anticipated and which would never be repeated — or so we thought.

Close to thirty years were to elapse before excavation of this tomb commenced. This was largely due to the fact that the site proved to be an incredibly rich and complex one, with twelve successive phases of activity represented. These phases extended from the early Neolithic of 6000 or so years ago down to modern times (though a number of periods of inactivity are also witnessed in the stratigraphical record). Most of the phases of activity at Knowth occurred after the construction of the passage tombs and are represented, in places, by a deep and complicated stratigraphy of overlapping archaeological sediments. These overlying layers had first to be carefully excavated and meticulously recorded before investigations of the passage tombs, lying below, could take place. Even then, before excavation of the tombs could commence it was essential that a detailed survey was completed. This involved producing a ground-plan, a series of cross-section drawings and a number of elevation drawings, in addition to making a preliminary study of the art. Attention was also paid to the drawing up of a programme of excavation. In fact this only took place during the mid-1990s and, out of necessity, it was a broadly based enterprise in which a programme of conservation by the National Monuments Division (Dúchas The Heritage Service) went hand in hand with the excavation. In fact only the outer two-thirds of the passage has been excavated, the purpose of that work being to assist conservation as well as research. As a result the tomb is now in an excellent state and is well maintained and managed.

The eastern tomb

During the remainder of the 1967 season and the beginning of the 1968 session work continued along and outside the perimeter of the large mound largely on the southern side, but by the beginning of July 1968 cuttings were opened parallel to the east–west diagonal, and on the opposite side of the mound to the previous season's tomb discovery. This soon demonstrated that there was a considerable deposit of soft dark earth, the by-product of Early Christian occupation. Excavation revealed that this overlay a stony layer that contained cavities, hinting at the presence of another souterrain. On Tuesday 30 July, a small aperture appeared in what we believed to be a souterrain, and drystone walling was observed. This cavity existed because a lintel did not span the drystone work at that point. On the next day (31 July) we expanded the hole to enable us to partially enter the cavity. Immediately I was surprised to find that, at that very point, there was an elaborate junction where as many as four passages converged. The walls of three of these were of drystone construction, consistent with the structure of a souterrain, but the fourth, extending westward, was entirely different. Its sides were built of large orthostats, while the outermost capstone was decorated with megalithic art. These features aroused immediate suspicion as to its nature, and in view of that it was decided to explore further. Perhaps it was just a more elaborately built souterrain. Two capstones, a short distance in from the entrance, had partly fallen, and in the interests of safety it was necessary to secure these by inserting props underneath before proceeding further up the passage. A few loose stones also needed to be removed. In order to allow this work to take place further exploration was postponed until the following day, 1 August, at midday.

By coincidence Jim Banbury of the National Monuments Branch, Office of Public Works, had arrived on site to take some general photographs, and for that work he also had a small portable electrical generator. We got the generator going, and with additional lighting from a hand-lamp, accompanied by John Rock, I made a more thorough visual inspection of the immediate area. Before long we established that one of the drystone passages led towards the edge of the mound, but soon we could explore it no further owing to an accumulation of

Pl. 20—(top) Discovery of the eastern passage: (back row, left to right) Cearbhall O Meadhra, Frank Hickey, Tom Fanning, George Carson, Rolf Elm Larsen; (middle, left to right) George Eogan, Hilary Wynne, Anne Gannon, Máirín Markey, Lucy Corbett, Mia Delaney, Martin Timoney; (front) Máire de Valera.

Pl. 21—(left) View along the eastern passage looking inwards from capstone 38 (photo: Dúchas The Heritage Service).

fill. It did appear, however, that this could have been the original entrance/exit area to the souterrain complex. Another drystone passage extended northwards, approximately parallel to the edge of the mound, but owing to a collapse it was only possible to continue along it for a short distance. At a right angle to the entrance area of that passage another drystone passage extending downhill became visible. It was in good condition and we soon established that this was another souterrain leading to a beehive-shaped chamber.

Having established this much, we turned our attention to what seemed to have been the most substantial passage of all, a metre in width and slightly more than that in height at the point of entry. We moved along the passage but after a couple of metres or so we encountered a number of obstructions — a downward-sloping capstone and inward-leaning orthostats. Having overcome those obstacles, we came to a well-preserved stretch of passageway, but soon we had to return to hands and knees and grope our way along a stone-littered passage. The source of the stones was evidently the cairn overhead, from which they had slipped in the course of structural settlement and adjustment. Beyond that point conditions improved once more and one could almost stand up. In this area there was a cracked, inward-leaning capstone decorated with a chevron design, and many of the orthostats to either side were also elaborately decorated (Pl. 21). By now we were certain that we had found another tomb — how astonishing! But this was only the beginning of a series of remarkable sights that still awaited discovery.

We proceeded slowly along the passage, impatient to explore further, but before long we encountered more obstacles to our progress caused by a number of inward-leaning orthostats touching each other at the top. Above this there was a void, both sides of which were defined by almost vertical drystone walling. I now believed that the tomb consisted of a two-tier structure and so, in my excitement and probably not considering the danger, I climbed to the 'upper' passage. In reality I was now walking along the top of the orthostats and over the spread of stones that had slipped from the cairn above during the settlement and subsequent adjustment of the passage at this point. At any rate, I decided that it was easier to follow this upper passage than to crawl along and over the spread of cairn stones at ground level. The floor of this 'upper' passage sloped gradually upwards but came to a sudden and abrupt end. Staring into an apparently bottomless void, unable to see the ground below, it felt as if I was suspended in mid-air! I could never have anticipated what lay before me as my eyes adjusted to the gloom. I flashed the lamp around and an astonishing sight emerged — a massive corbelled roof built of large slabs that narrowed in beehive-shaped fashion to a point where it was closed with a single large flag. I shone my light downwards to an even more remarkable sight, a great chamber with a rounded ground-plan.

I descended into the chamber. I have no recollection of how I did it, but, without thinking, I suspect that I actually jumped down from the top of the orthostats, a height of 2m or so! The chamber provided further wonders. Two side recesses and a single end recess opened off it, while the surrounding orthostats, as well as some of the overlying corbels, were decorated, some most elaborately. One of the side recesses had a portal-like entrance consisting of two tall jambs, again bearing decoration. On entering the recess: more art but also something quite unexpected and truly astonishing. Before me was a large stone basin, over 1m in diameter, ornamented externally with parallel horizontal grooves and internally with a series of arcs and rays.

We eventually confirmed that the distance from the kerbstone before the entrance to the inner face of the back stone was some 40.4m in length. We now realised that the great mound at Knowth contained not one but two chambers placed back to back! We had never anticipated, on initiating the programme of excavations only six years previously, that such extraordinary discoveries awaited us.

Remarks

The sophistication of the art and architecture of these remarkable structures was not only unexpected but astonishing. To have entered these tombs for the first time was an indescribable experience, but the fact that it was possible to do so, considering their great antiquity and the nature of their construction, is all the more remarkable and a tribute to the extraordinary achievements and skill of those who built them five millennia ago. As Colin Renfrew put it in his foreword to my book *Knowth and the passage-tombs of Ireland* (1986),

> 'it is rarely given to any man to enter, for the first time in centuries or millennia, a well-preserved structure from the prehistoric period which is already older than the Pyramids of Egypt by several hundred years'.

To have had the privilege of doing so is, for me, one of the greatest events that one could ever experience.

Further reading

Eogan, G. 1986 *Knowth and the passage-tombs of Ireland*. London.

O'Kelly, M.J. 1982 *Newgrange, archaeology, art and legend*. London.

O'Kelly, M.J. and O'Kelly, C. 1983 The tumulus of Dowth, Co. Meath. *Proceedings of the Royal Irish Academy* **83**C, 135–90.

7

A medieval guided tour of the Hill of Tara

Edel Bhreathnach

'A thulaigh an bhláth' chrín, gé gur chinnte barrlaoch is éigse ar do bhruach,
Cá bhfuil na hardríthe a mbíodh gach sárfhile ag déanamh dóibh duan?'

'O hill of the withered flower, though there was surely the best of heroes
and poets on your slope,
Where are the high-kings for whom every excellent poet composed verse?'

(from a dialogue with the Hill of Tara by the eighteenth-century poet
Peadar Ó Doirnín).

Precious moments for a medieval historian, topographer or linguist vary from the dramatic to the minor detail. The dramatic is similar to the experience of an archaeologist unearthing a spectacular artefact or feature, and is equally rare. We dream of unearthing an unknown or lost manuscript, discovering a new version of a text or finding the papers of an earlier, great scholar. Many of us will experience such a spectacular discovery once in our career, especially in Irish studies, where there is a plentiful harvest for a small community of scholars. However, as with any profession, pleasure must be gained from a subject during the daily routine if one is to persist. How many of us have felt a surge of delight on opening for the first time the manuscript in which *our* text is preserved, on breathing the musty smell of a favourite library (in my case The Duke Humphreys in the Bodleian Library, Oxford) or disentangling the etymology of a word, understanding the origin of a place-name, unravelling the tangled web of propaganda woven into our annals and genealogies, wondering at the literary and intellectual skill of a medieval Irish author … The pleasure is endless …

Pl. 22—Aerial view of the Hill of Tara looking north. The conjoined earthworks of the Forad and Tech Cormaic lie in the foreground and, immediately north of them, Duma na nGiall enclosed within the rampart of Ráith Ríg. Further north, Ráith na Senad stands to the west of St Patrick's churchyard, and the parallel banks of Long na mBan can be seen in the far distance (photo: Dúchas The Heritage Service).

There may be a popular perception that the craft of the medieval historian, unlike that of the modern historian, whose sources are plentiful and personal, is purely 'academic', devoid of an emotional relationship between practitioner and source. Yes, there is a great chronological gap, many texts are anonymous and only the voices of the noble and literate classes are accessible. Frequently, the medieval historian has to be satisfied with a glimpse of the medieval world through the equivalent of newspaper headlines (annals), legal documents (law-tracts) or court poetry (bardic poetry). It is difficult to find the personal touch in such sources. This view denies the existence, however, of countless documents where the author's character has survived or of the marginal notes and doodles scattered throughout our manuscripts describing the most basic of human feelings: love, anguish, hunger, cold, discomfort, loneliness, jealousy ... what you yourself might express in an emotional moment ...

For the past ten years I have worked on the history and literature of the Hill of Tara, Co. Meath — not an easy task since every generation from the seventh century to the present day has felt obliged to weave their own legend around it and to claim this as *the* explanation for its importance. As a result many texts concerning Tara are deliberately mysterious or magical and lead one to the supernatural. There is one text, however, with which I can readily identify and, even though it is anonymous, I feel particularly close to the author since we are both treading the exact same path of describing and 'solving' Tara. The text is *Dindgnai Temrach*, 'The landmarks of Tara', the earliest copy of which is preserved in the twelfth-century manuscript known as the Book of Leinster. It was probably composed around the year AD 1000 by someone who had a detailed knowledge of the visible monuments on the hill. I would regard it as the first in a series of surveys of Tara, a survey to which subsequent surveyors — John O'Donovan, George Petrie, R.A.S. Macalister, Seán P. Ó Ríordáin and Conor Newman — turned for assistance and inspiration. This medieval surveyor was an archaeologist, historian and mythographer in one. So let us walk the Hill of Tara and view it through medieval eyes ...

The landmarks of Tara

Translation (from the Book of Leinster, folio 30a)

Nemnach, a spring beside the mound in the south-east of Tara. The small stream that flows from Nemnach eastwards, on it the mill was made for Ciarnait, Cormac's slave.

The site of *Tech Mairisen* is opposite the mound to the north of Nemnach with three small stones around it. Thus the house was arranged: a high interior, a very low (?roof). Mairisiu was a widow who lived at the same time as Cormac. Any house that is built in that manner will not be unlucky and will not be without wealth there.

Ráith Lóegaire son of Niall to the north of that monument. Four main doors at every cardinal point in it. Lóegaire's body was placed under his shield so that he was buried against the outer ditch in the south-east of Ráith Lóegaire in Tara with his face to the south fighting the Leinstermen.

Lecht Matta — Matta was a mercenary of the Leinstermen who served Cormac — is beside Ráith Lóegaire to the south-east. One day four youths were playing games by Ráith Lóegaire on the south-east. Matta cast a slingshot there and it hit against the wall(?) of its two courtyards and the youth died as a result.

Ráith Ríg beside Ráith Lóegaire on the north. There are three remarkable wonders in that [monument]: the site of Cormac's royal house in the south-eastern part of the enclosure on the side to the south of Ráith Lóegaire, the site of the *Forad*, *Múr Tea* between them on the south. Tea was wife of Éremón. *Liathdruim* and *Druim Caín* and *Múr Tea* and *Cathair Chaín* were the names of

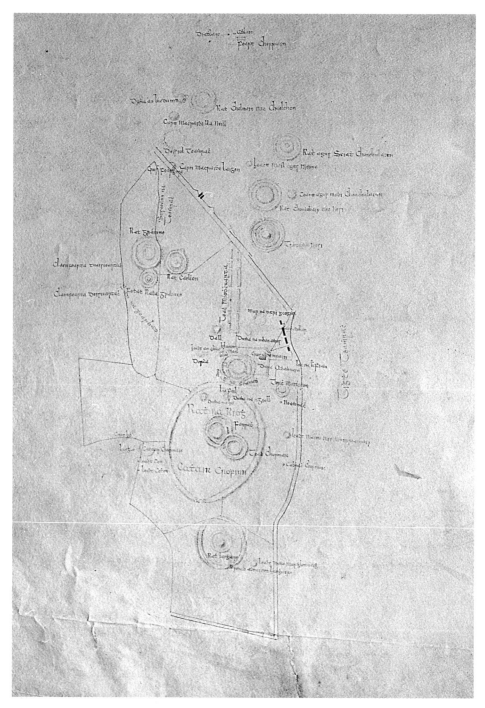

Fig. 10—George Petrie's sketch-map of the Hill of Tara, discovered in a miscellaneous folder in the Royal Irish Academy (reproduced by kind permission of the Royal Irish Academy).

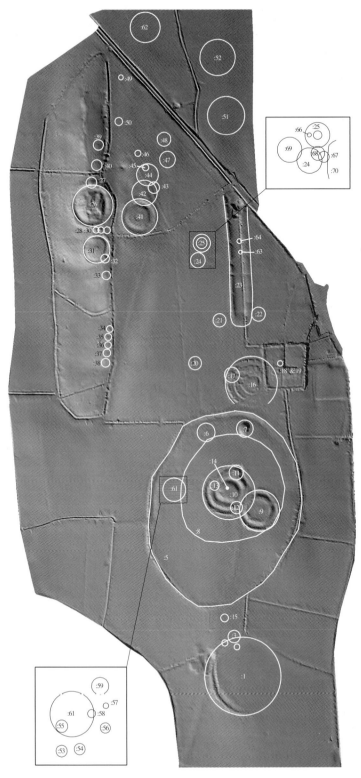

Fig. 11—A topographical map of the Hill of Tara with monuments numbered according to Newman 1997 (reproduced by kind permission of Conor Newman and the Discovery Programme).

Tara at first. Then Tea, Éremón's wife, was buried between the site of the Forad and the royal house. It is from that, Tea's wall, a small hill between the two walls on the south, that Tara is named.

There is a spring by the side of the enclosure on the east and it has three names: *Liaig, Tipra Bó Finne* and *Derc nDub*. Thus it is said: 'its "calf" does not go to its "leech"' — one comes from the east of Tara, the other from the west of Tara.

Duma na mBó west of *Duma na nGíall*, namely, *Glass Temrach*.

Duma na nGíall to the north-east of the Forad. *Fál* beside Duma na nGíall to the north. That stone would cry out under he who would take the kingship of Ireland. Fál was the name of that stone, a false rock, a rock under a king.

Lecht Con and Cethin in the slope against Ráith Ríg to the west. There are two stones there, one Lecht Con and the other Lecht Cethin. From that the misunderstanding: 'You have acted for me Cú and Cethe', namely, Cú and Cethe killed Cormac's dispenser of food in the middle of the royal house in Tara. After that he went directly to the height of Tara in the west and was overtaken. And the brother of the man whom he had slain slew him. And Cormac had said that Cú should not be killed. Intercession was of no avail so they were both killed.

There is a spring in the slope north of Lecht Chethin. *Lóeg* is its name and it flows directly west. The site of Cormac's kitchen is on its bank above the slope over Lóeg to the east.

Ráith na Senad opposite Duma na nGíall to the north.

The site of Adomnán's tent in that earthen rampart with his cross in front of the rath in the east and his seat to the south of the cross.

The site of the house that was burned over Benén, Patrick's servant, and over Lucat Máel is a short distance from Adomnán's cross to the south-east, namely, beside the pathway a little to the east.

There are three small stones beside Ráith na Senad to the north: the three stones that were placed over the druids. Their names are Máel and Bloc and Bluicne: Máel to the east, Bloc to the south and Bluicne to the north-east.

Lecht in Abaicc is east of them. The grave is [orientated] south-east, south-west. Only three feet its measure. A small depression below. Its grave is thus: a small stone underground in its eastern part and another in its western part. Three feet are found at one time and three and a half feet at another time.

There are two mounds to the north of the grave: *Dall* and *Dorcha* except that there is no wall between them and the stones and the grave. Dorcha is the name of the western mound. Dall (and Dorcha) the name of the eastern mound.

Long na mBan is north-east of the eastern mound. This is how that house was arranged: the lower part to the north and its higher part to the south and the supporting wall about it to the east and the west. It is slightly bent in its northern half. It is correctly north and south. The shape of a long house: fourteen doors in it or fifteen according to others, seven in the east and seven in the west. They say that it is there that Feis Temrach used to be celebrated. That is truly correct for the greater number of the men of Ireland used to fit in there and this it is the house with a thousand soldiers.

There is a small mound to the south-east of the site of the house at its southern end. It is called *Duma na mBan*.

The grave of Caelchú (*cubat Caelchon*) and his charioteer is opposite the north-eastern end of Long na mBan. That Caelchú was the son of Loarn son of Ruad son of Cas of Éoganacht Chaisil. Túath Cais at Tara are descended from his family and Aicme Rois of Tara come from them.

The triple rampart of Nessa, Conchobar's mother at the north-eastern end opposite the north-eastern end of Long na mBan to the north-east. *Ráith Chonchobair meic Nessa* beside the triple rampart to the north with its door in the east opposite *Méide Con Culainn*.

The site of *Scéith cona Thuil* is opposite the Méide to the north-east. Thus is this rath: level on the ground with a small hill in its middle, it hollow full of clay.

Sescend Temrach is opposite Ráith Chonchobair to the north-east at the same height as Long na mBan to the north-west, a dirty, little marsh there beside Carn na Macraide.

Ráith Gráinne is west of Sescend Temrach on the summit of the hill.

Fán na Carpat is by the foundation of Ráith Gráinne from the north opposite the northern Clóenfherta to the east.

The two *Clóenfherta* are to the west of Ráith Gráinne. In the southern Clóenfherta the maidens were killed in Tara. In the northern Clóenfherta the judgement (was given) against (....) of the judgement that Cormac gave concerning the destruction of the field of woad by sheep.

Carn na Macraide Laigen is beside Sescend Temrach to the north.

Cros Fhergossa, the holy pilgrim. It is he who is [buried] in *Carraic Clumáin*. [His cross is] beside Carn na Macraide to the south-west.

Dessel Temrach is between the two Carn na Macraide, namely, the northern carn and the southern carn.

Carn Macraide Uí Néill is beside Dessel Temrach to the north.

Ráith Cholmáin meic Caelchon is to the north-east of Carn Macraide Uí Néill, that is, from the northern carn.

Duma in Luchdoind is beside Ráith Cholmáin meic Caelchon to the west.

Adlaic and *Diadlaic* are opposite Ráith Cholmáin to the north-east by the side of the slope to the north-east of the rath. They are two wells, Adlaic one of the two, the other Diadlaic, but there is no difference between them.

Notes

The names of monuments highlighted in the text are translated and explained (with normalised spelling). Where possible, they are identified with existing monuments, as catalogued by Conor Newman in *Tara: an archaeological survey*.

Nemnach '?sacred, bright'. Ciarnait was a Pictish slave girl who became Cormac mac Airt's mistress and for whom he built the first mill in Ireland at Tara.

Tech Mairisen 'Mairisiu's house'. The complete tale of Mairisiu's conflict with Cormac mac Airt is unknown.

Ráith Lóegaire 'Lóegaire's rath'. Newman 31:33:1. Lóegaire son of Niall Noígiallach, king of Tara, was reputedly buried in the ramparts facing southwards towards his enemies, the Leinstermen. This description may have been borrowed from Anglo-Saxon sources since this burial custom was practised among the Anglo-Saxons but is not known in Ireland.

Lecht Matta 'Matta's grave'. The text tells of the death of Matta, a mercenary from Leinster in Cormac mac Airt's court at Tara. A version of the place-lore (*dinnshenchas*) of Slieve Aughty, Co. Galway, describes it as the abode of Matta mac Meirc.

Ráith Ríg 'Rath of Kings'. Newman 31:33:5. This large hilltop enclosure may have marked out the sanctuary from which the name *Temair* 'sacred space' is derived. An early Irish poem which describes Tara states: 'He saw the outer trench which closed against the height; vaster still was the encircling rampart (?)...'. This may refer to Ráith Ríg.

Tech Cormaic 'Cormac's house'. Newman 31:33:9. This was the reputed house of the heroic king of Tara, Cormac mac Airt.

Forad 'a mound or platform'. Newman 31:33:10. This is a technical term, possibly cognate with Welsh *gorsedd*, which describes either the mound on which a king was inaugurated or from which royal spectators viewed an assembly.

Múr Tea 'Tea's wall'. Newman 31:33:12. The reputed grave of Tea, wife of Éremón son of Míl. She was brought from Thebes in Egypt and died of homesickness at Tara.

Liathdruim 'green hill'.

Druim Caín 'fair hill'.

Cathair Chroinn 'Cronn's fort' or *Cathair Crófhinn* 'Crófhinn's fort'. Cronn or Crunniuc mac Agnomain was husband of Macha, goddess of Emain Macha (Navan Fort, Co. Armagh). Crófhinn daughter of Allod belonged to the mythical Túatha Dé Danann and was niece of the Dagda, 'the good god', often associated with the River Boyne.

Liaig 'leech, physician'. A spring at Tara.

Tipra Bó Finne 'the spring of the white cow'. The white cow had mythical and sacred attributes and is particularly associated with Bóann (goddess of the River Boyne), which possibly means 'she who has white cows'.

Derc nDub 'dark pool, well'.

Lóeg 'calf'. Similar to the association with white cows, rivers had 'calf' names, as in the case of the old name for the River Bandon, Co. Cork (*Lóegde*).

Duma na mBó 'the mound of the cows'. Newman 31:33:6.

Duma na nGíall 'the mound of the hostages'. Newman 31:33:7. This Neolithic tomb was probably used as the location on which hostages were occasionally handed over by kings as guarantors for a legal contract or an agreement.

Glass Temrach 'the green (*faithche*) of Tara'. This name presumably refers to the area where assemblies were held at Tara.

Fál. Fál, the oracular stone which cried out as part of the recognition of a particular king's right to rule at Tara. The sources suggest that it was a recumbent stone and therefore not the pillar stone which now stands on the top of the Forad (Newman 31:33:14). There is a suggestion in the sources that the 'real' Fál or Lia Fáil was transferred to Tailtiu (Teltown, Co. Meath) in the early medieval period.

Lecht Con 7 Cethin 'Cú and Cethe's grave'. ?Newman 31:33:61. Although Cethe is described in this text as Cormac mac Airt's *rannaire* ('dispenser of food'), Cú and Cethe appear elsewhere as the sons of Dian Cécht, the healing god or physican of the Túatha Dé Danann. They were killed, according to *Lebor Gabála Érenn* 'The book of the takings of Ireland', at *Aircheltrú* (unidentified).

Ráith na Senad 'the rath of the synods'. Newman 31:33:16. The site of four reputed ecclesiastical synods: the Synod of Patrick, the Synod of Brendan, the Synod of Rúadán and the Synod of Adomnán.

Tech Benéin. This is the location where Benén, St Patrick's disciple, miraculously escaped from a burning hut, unlike a rival druid who met his death.

Cros Adomnáin 'Adomnán's cross'; *Suide Adomnáin* 'Adomnán's seat'. Adomnán, ninth abbot of Iona (died 704), was a highly influential cleric who wrote the Life of Columba and who caused the enactment of the Law of Adomnán, which sought to protect non-combatants (women, children and clergy) during warfare.

Máel 'shorn (of hair)', *Bloc, Bluicne.* Bloc may mean 'round' or 'fragment' and Bluicne may be a diminutive of *bloc*, both possibly referring to the shape of the stones.

Lecht in Abaicc 'the dwarf's grave'. The dwarf is said to have intervened between Dall and Dorcha (see below) and was killed by them owing to their blindness.

Dall 'blind'; *Dorcha* 'dark'. According to the metrical version of this text, they killed one another over alms given to them. In the prose text this tale is associated with Cú and Cethe.

Long na mBan 'the ship of the women'. Newman 31:33:23. One of the many names given to the *Tech Midchúarta* 'Banqueting Hall'. The use of the word *long* or *bárc* in relation to a building probably describes a type of long house known from medieval Dublin. An imaginary plan of the Hall at Tara is illustrated in the Book of Leinster (folio 29a).

Duma na mBan 'the mound of the women'. Newman 31:33:22. Otherwise known as Duma na mBanamais 'the grave of the women mercenaries'.

Cubat Caelchon 'the grave of Caelchú'. Caelchú belonged to the Munster dynasty of Éoganacht Chaisil.

Tredua Nessa 'the triple rampart of Ness'. ?Newman 31:33:51. Ness daughter of Eochaid Sálbuide bore Conchobar mac Nessa for the druid Cathbad. She also became Fergus mac Róich's wife.

Ráith Conchobair meic Nessa 'the rath of Conchobar mac Nessa'. ?Newman 31:33:52. Conchobar is not usually associated with Tara, but rather with Emain Macha.

Méide Con Culainn 'the (decapitated) neck of Cú Chulainn'; *Sciath cona Thuil* 'a shield with its boss'. When Cú Chulainn was killed, one version of his death-tale relates how his head and forearm were buried by Erc mac Coirpri Nia Fir at Tara. The impression of his shield was also said to be evident in the ground at Tara.

Sescend Temra 'the marsh of Tara'. A marsh existed in the northern part of Tara until the nineteenth century when it was drained by a local landowner.

Ráith Gráinne 'Gráinne's rath'. Newman 31:33:41. Gráinne was the daughter of Cormac mac Airt and betrothed to Finn mac Cumaill. She eloped with Diarmait úa Duibne, a story which is told in the medieval romance 'The pursuit of Diarmait and Gráinne'.

Fán na Carpat 'the slope of the chariots'. This probably refers to a path that led to the centre of the complex on the hill's summit. See Deisel Temrach below.

Na Clóenfherta 'the sloping burial mounds'. Newman 31:33:26, 31. There are three explanations for the unusual form of these barrows. The southern part is said to be the spot where thirty princesses of Tara were killed by Dúnlaing, king of Leinster. Two different false judgements caused the collapse of the king's house and therefore the creation of the northern monument: one judgement (referred to in this text) was by Lugaid mac Con against a widow whose sheep were grazing in the king's field of woad. The other false judgement was made during a contest between Lóegaire mac Néill and St Patrick.

Carn na Macraide Lagen 'the grave of the Leinster youths'. With regard to the remaining monuments, see complex defined in Newman 31:33:42–50.

Cros Fhergossa 'the cross of Fergus'. Fergus, the holy pilgrim, may have belonged to the Osraige (a people whose territory was approximately coextensive with the diocese of Ossary) or to a northern alliance known as the Airgíalla. He is reputed to have had a vision that a cross would be erected in his honour at Fán na Carpat.

Carrac Clúmain 'Clúmáin's rock'. This does not refer to a monument at Tara but to Fergus's home, possibly the townlands of Carrickcloney, barony of Ida, Co. Kilkenny, or Carrickcloghan, barony of Orior Upper, Co. Armagh.

Deisel Temrach 'the sunwise, righthandwise direction of Tara'. The auspicious way to enter Tara was from the right and to follow the sun's course. A king of Tara was unlucky if he left Tara after sunset and nobody could visit him after sunset.

Carn na Macraide, Carn Macraide Uí Néill 'the grave of the youths (of the Uí Néill)'.

Ráith Cholmáin maic Caelchon 'the rath of Colmán son of Caelchú'. Colmán mac Caelchon or Colmán mac Faelchon belonged to the Domnainn, a people who were settled south of Tara along the coast and on a coastal strip in County Mayo.

Duma ind Luchdoinn 'the mound of the Luchdond'. The Luchdoinn was the canine guardine of the Otherworld.

Adlaic, Diadlaic '?pleasant, unpleasant'.

Further reading

Bhreathnach, E. 1995 *Tara. A select bibliography.* Discovery Programme Monographs 1. Dublin.

Bhreathnach, E. and Newman, C. 1995 *Tara*. Dublin.

Newman, C. 1997 *Tara: an archaeological survey.* Discovery Programme Monographs 2. Dublin.

Petrie, G. 1839 On the history and antiquities of Tara Hill. *Transactions of the Royal Irish Academy* **18**, 25–232.

Stokes, W. 1894 The prose tales in the Rennes Dindshenchas. *Revue Celtique* **15**, 277–89.

8

Tales from the Hill of Tara: the ghost of monuments past

Joe Fenwick

Mrs Maguire was somewhat bemused at the re-emergence of the archaeologists, one with laptop in hand, talking excitedly and transfixed by a series of grey blobs on the computer screen. Only moments earlier she had met the two of them at the door, long-faced and sodden, their dripping waterproofs and muddy boots discarded in the porch. It had become a daily ritual, after a week of fieldwork on the hilltop in the most inclement November conditions, for her to bring a pot of tea with warm buttered scones and delicious rhubarb jam to the front room on their return. There, in the warmth of the open fire, she would chat to her guests about the day's events and review, with as much interest as they, the latest results of the survey. In the excitement of this particular evening, the tea went cold.

Though Joan and Desmond Maguire, as B&B proprietors, had seen many strange pilgrims to the Hill of Tara — neo-pagans, white witches, New Age travellers, Celtic warriors in full battle dress, and even a bearded druid with rotating crystal on a chain who could 'pop' light bulbs at a glance — few would be daft enough to claim to see the secrets of the Hill on a laptop computer. We were making a magnetic map of the Hill of Tara. This claim won us instant recognition by the crystal-twirling druid as one of his own when he overheard us in conversation over breakfast. It transpired he was attempting to do something similar in mapping the energy lines on the Hill. Our credibility, however, evaporated on production of the fluxgate gradiometer.

This was not the first time Tara had been subjected to geophysics. During the early 1990s, while Kieron Goucher and I were undertaking the topographical survey, a no less important part of Conor Newman's research on the Hill (under the auspices of the Discovery Programme) included a geophysical survey. This involved a team of geophysicists from Durham, led by Mark Noel of GeoQuest Associates, conducting a large-scale magnetometer and electrical resistance survey over selected parts of the Hill with extraordinary success. A wealth of new subsurface archaeological monuments and features, which in most cases displayed little or no surface expression, were detected and mapped without so much as lifting a sod of grass.

Several years later, in 1998, the Centre for Archaeological Survey, NUI, Galway, in collaboration with the Discovery Programme, returned with the intention of mapping those parts of the Hill which had not previously been investigated. I found myself, yet again, back on the Hill of Tara.

The week before the evening of the tepid tea at Maguire's, Linda Shine, then an MA student of archaeology at NUI, Galway, and I had started the systematic geomagnetic survey of that part of the Hill lying immediately to the west of the earthwork called *Tech Midchúarta* (*Long na mBan*). We had established a grid of 10m by 10m squares or 'panels' aligned to the Irish National Grid, which served as the framework of the survey. Measurements were taken at 0.5m intervals along parallel lines set 0.5m apart within each of these panels. A total of 400 individual readings of magnetic gradient were therefore required for each completed panel, which accounts for the clarity of detail obtained in the resulting image. At the end of each day the data were downloaded to computer in the comfort of the guesthouse. A preliminary map of the day's work could be produced by arranging the panels, like tiles, in the correct order on the screen and then converting individual readings to an equivalent shade of grey (by effectively translating the range of numeric values to a range of tones from white to black) in order to produce a grey-scale image.

There would be little inkling of the results of each day's work until the return key was pressed and the new image scrolled slowly down the computer screen. Every evening we pored over the results and squinted at the screen searching for patterns and features of potential archaeological significance and, as the survey progressed, the results of each day were combined to make a composite map. Towards the end of the week, to our delight, a series of three conjoined circles, most likely ring-barrows, appeared, as if by magic, on the screen. We celebrated our success in Navan that evening and the following morning rang Brian Lacey, the Discovery Programme Manager, to tell him the good news.

Flushed by the success of the previous day and despite the worsening weather conditions, we started up the Hill, a spring in our step, with expectations of greater things to come — but nothing could have prepared us for the awaiting discovery.

As the image slowly scrolled down the screen I blinked in disbelief and then, remembering to breathe again, gasped in amazement:

'Henge … we've found a henge!'

The clarity and definition of the feature was astonishing. There was no need in this instance to adjust the contrast, squint at the screen or hold it sideways. There it was, in black and white, a broad white–black–white band curving its way along the right-hand side of the image with a series of black dots along either side — looking for all the world like the scar of a sutured wound (Fig. 12). In archaeo-geophysical terms, the feature manifests as a broad band of negative–positive–negative magnetic gradient, approximately 5m wide, on either side of which are a series of mutually opposed, regularly spaced, discrete circular anomalies of positive magnetic gradient. These discrete anomalies, roughly 1.5–2m in diameter, occur at approximately 4m intervals, centre to centre, along the entire length of the arc and 8m apart across the dividing lineament.

News was quick to spread. It was hard to keep secret our 'discovery', not least because we could not keep it to ourselves. The irrepressible Michael Slavin, broadcaster and local historian, seemed to know of our discovery almost before we did! Brian Lacey, Barry Masterson and Nigel McGuirk of the Discovery Programme were among the first on the scene to inspect, as much as one could, the new monument. There was, of course, nothing new to see on the Hill, as the monument existed only as a ghostly shadow in the computer's memory, but we

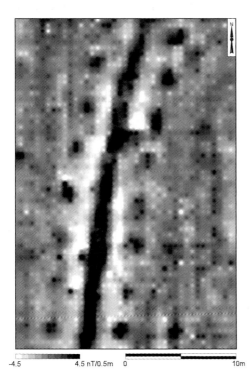

Fig. 12—A detail of the ditched pit enclosure (reproduced by kind permission of the Discovery Programme).

-4.5   4.5 nT/0.5m 0   10m

91

insisted they view it anyway. Because of its relatively strong magnetic response, it was possible to detect the line of the subsurface feature simply by scanning with the gradiometer and to mark its position with a series of bamboos. Only then was the enormous scale of the new enclosure brought home. At the time, we estimated it to be some 250m in diameter, second only in size to *Ráith na Ríg*, the great ceremonial earthwork which circumscribes the hilltop.

A meeting with Professor John Waddell and Conor Newman (then a newly appointed member of staff in the Department of Archaeology, NUI, Galway) was arranged for the following weekend — indeed, it was Conor's initiative and continued interest in the Hill of Tara that had prompted the collaborative research in the first instance. This time, however, the monument was brought to Galway and Christmas had arrived early.

Over the next two weeks Sinead Armstrong and Owen Kieron helped with the work, and with every passing day a little piece of the greater picture was revealed. It was intended at the outset to spend only three weeks on the Hill and so only about one third of the circumference was completed, to the west and south-west of *Ráith na Senad*, before, reluctantly, having to drag ourselves away.

Louise Finegan and I and later Conor Newman returned in the more favourable weather conditions of May of the following year, intent on tracing the remainder of the enclosure and investigating its interior. There was a renewed expectation and excitement every evening on viewing the latest piece of the puzzle. As the work progressed, the pieces, printed-out on paper, were literally stuck together with adhesive tape and this served as the basis of the following day's strategy (Fig. 13).

On completion, the enclosure turned out to be oval, not circular, and its dimensions were of a truly monumental scale, 210m north–south by 175m east–west, enclosing an area of some 3 hectares. With *Ráith na Senad* at its centre, it extends from the southern end of the ceremonial avenue or cursus known as *Tech Midchúarta* southwards to enclose most of St Patrick's churchyard and the passage tomb named *Duma na nGiall* situated on the hilltop. But what exactly had we found?

It may appear intriguing that some archaeological features exhibit magnetic properties, let alone that these can be detected or even mapped. The explanation for this extraordinary phenomenon lies not in the paranormal, as some would have us believe, but largely in the activities of those people, countless generations ago, who constructed these monuments. In essence, the distinctive magnetic signature is simply a by-product of past human activity, which is responsible, in many instances, for altering the physical and chemical properties of the soil and is also largely responsible for its subsequent distribution. Activities that involve intensive burning — for domestic, industrial or even ceremonial purposes, for

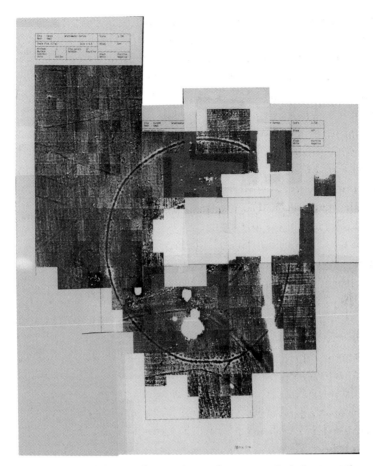

Fig. 13—The pieces of the puzzle were printed out on a daily basis and simply stuck together like a patchwork quilt to help formulate the survey strategy of the following day's work.

instance — can permanently alter the magnetic qualities of the soil. Other processes, such as the fermentation and decomposition of organic deposits, within, for example, a buried fosse, may also lead to an enhancement of magnetic susceptibility. The distribution of topsoil, which possesses an inherently higher magnetic susceptibility than underlying subsoil, may also have a bearing on the detection of archaeological features.

It is likely that the negative–positive–negative band and its accompanying series of discrete anomalies of positive magnetic gradient, which together define the enclosure, represent a broad fosse and a series of large pits to either side (perhaps post-pits for massive timber uprights). Supporting this interpretation is the almost imperceptible trace of the 'fosse' as a broad, shallow, curving depression to the west and north-west of *Ráith na Senad*, the significance of which was only realised after the event. This feature, and the 'pits' to either side, had been detected by the gradiometer by virtue of the fact that their fill contains a greater proportion, or volume, of magnetically enhanced sediments in contrast to that of the surrounding or 'background' soils. In view of the exceptional definition of these features, it is a distinct possibility that they may contain quantities of burnt material.

In keeping with archaeological tradition, we have given this extraordinary monument the rather uninspired but descriptively accurate title of 'ditched pit enclosure' and assigned it the code 31:33:71 to conform with the numbering conventions used by the Sites and Monuments Record for County Meath. It has proved difficult to classify the ditched pit enclosure into a convenient pigeonhole, as its plan is unique (as far as we know) in an Irish, or indeed British, context. We are further restricted by the fact that we are dealing with an incomplete geophysical image whose 'features' require an interpreted explanation in order for them to be translated, with a certain degree of subjectivity, to the physical reality of an archaeological monument. In this instance, we have neither the benefit of historical documents nor substantial visible physical remains. Furthermore, we do not have the advantage of stratigraphical relationships (layered sediments or overlapping deposits), absolute dating techniques (such as radiocarbon or dendrochronology) or recognisable and datable artefact types (for example pottery or stone tools) which one could expect through scientific excavation. Comparative archaeological analysis is further hindered by the fact that few diagnostic features are readily apparent in the image. There is, for instance, no obvious entrance or formal approach to the monument — but perhaps this lies under the churchyard, an area rendered unsuitable for survey owing to magnetic interference (from iron railings etc.) and other physical obstructions. Looking more closely at the image, an assortment of smaller, though no less important, circular, arcuate and linear anomalies can be observed, but it is all but impossible to affirm whether any of these are contemporary with the enclosure.

Despite these inherent difficulties, some interesting comparisons can be made between the ditched pit enclosure and the great palisaded enclosures and timber circles of Britain and Ireland constructed largely in the later Neolithic and early Bronze Age, some 4000 to 5000 years ago (and sometimes associated with a pottery type known as grooved ware). These monuments, along with associated earthwork types (embanked enclosures, internally ditched enclosures and embanked stone circles) are often referred to as 'hengiform' — in the broadest definition of the term. Some comparison can be made between the ditched pit enclosure and the great palisaded enclosures of Britain, most particularly those of Alex Gibson's type 1, which include, for example, Walton in Radnorshire,

Fortevoit in Perthshire and Dunragit in Dumfries, all of which are massively large, broadly elliptical in plan and composed of a perimeter of individual post-holes. Parallels can also be drawn with the timber circles of more modest dimensions (but whose constructional details are still on a massive scale) such as Woodhenge in Wiltshire. It should also be noted that the earliest phase of the latter's more famous nearby counterpart, Stonehenge, consists of a circular earthwork composed of a broad fosse with an internal bank within which are a series of 56 equi-spaced pits (the Aubrey holes) circumscribing its inner edge.

Still better comparisons can be found closer to home in some intermediately sized examples (which Gibson includes in his type 1 classification). The large elliptical enclosure (BNH5) at Ballynahatty, Co. Down, was defined by a double row of ramped, radially opposed post-pits, encircling a smaller ring (BNH6), both of which were composed of massive oak timbers. On excavation, Barrie Hartwell recovered foundation deposits including cremations in the post-pits of the smaller timber circle, the structure of which appears to have been deliberately fired. Equivalent ritual activity was recorded during investigation of the larger enclosure. Here too the posts were burned, the stumps extracted and the pits backfilled with charcoal and burnt stone. In addition to finds such as flint flakes and tools (many of which were burnt), polished stone axeheads and grooved ware, there was also evidence of feasting.

Similarly, David Sweetman's excavation of the great pit circle at Newgrange, Co. Meath, revealed a broad band of several concentric rows of pits, some of which appear to have held upright posts while others contained cremations and other ritually deposited material. Interestingly, the relatively diminutive timber circle at Knowth (*c.* 9m in diameter), again in the Boyne Valley, seems also to have had a range of material, including sherds of grooved ware, deliberately placed in a number of the post-pits. The occurrence of similar 'offerings' within the pits of other hengiform monuments suggests that this activity is by no means an unusual occurrence.

Though we have no artefactual evidence as yet from Tara's ditched pit enclosure, in assessing the evidence as a whole it would seem that it sits comfortably in the broad category of hengiform monuments along with Ballynahatty and Newgrange. It is likely, therefore, to date from the later Neolithic or early Bronze Age. The fact that all three of these sites are also associated with passage tomb cemeteries makes this comparison all the more compelling. This simple, or perhaps simplistic, hypothesis relies on the fact that all 'hengiform' monuments were constructed during this relatively limited time-period. It would appear, however, that the picture is somewhat complicated in an Irish context by the fact that some timber circles continued to be built up until the early centuries BC. Those excavated at Raffin, Co. Meath, or at the major royal centres of Navan Fort, Co. Armagh, and Knockaulinn, Co. Kildare, for example, have produced Bronze Age and Iron Age dates. In these cases, though, the monuments are considerably smaller in scale than the ditched pit enclosure and appear to have only a cursory resemblance (and no doubt an entirely different ritual function) to those earlier examples at Ballynahatty and Newgrange.

It is interesting to note that the circuit of the ditched pit enclosure is clearly truncated by the rock-cut fosse of *Ráith na Ríg* — itself an internally ditched 'hengiform' enclosure. Recent excavation of this feature by Helen Roche has confirmed that it was dug in the Iron Age, sometime in the last few centuries BC. It is likely, therefore, that the ditched pit enclosure was no longer a functioning monument by this time and perhaps remained only as a vague outline on the brow of the Hill. The *Dindgnai Temrach*, 'The landmarks of Tara' (see Edel Bhreathnach, Chapter 7), composed sometime around the tenth century, makes no mention of it, and perhaps by this time it no longer had a discernible topographical expression.

On the basis of our relatively meagre facts and inconclusive circumstantial evidence, it is difficult to date the ditched pit enclosure, let alone attempt to construct a plausible interpretation of its nature and its significance to those who built it without drifting into the world of conjecture and speculation. The complexities behind the religious and social motivation for such an undertaking can never be known for sure, and in attempting to understand it one quickly becomes bogged down in a mire of archaeological theory and opposing interpretations. At the risk of losing a wellie in the bog-hole of archaeological credibility, it is worth speculating, just a little, on the few shreds of evidence that we have at our disposal.

One can imagine that towards the end of the Neolithic the Hill of Tara had already assumed a degree of ceremonial and religious significance with the construction of one or more modestly sized passage tombs, including *Duma na nGiall* and, aligned to it, the cursus monument known as the *Tech Midchúarta*. The ditched pit enclosure was perhaps planned and built within a few centuries of these. Deliberately incorporated within its circuit were a number of pre-existing monuments, most notably *Duma na nGiall* and perhaps a monument of even greater significance at its centre — the place now occupied by *Ráith na Senad*, a multiperiod earthwork. Without doubt the ditched pit enclosure required considerable resources in labour and materials, and arguably involved as much ceremony and ritual in its construction, and subsequent destruction, as it did when serving as a completed, 'fully functional' monument. Offerings of grooved ware pottery, flint artefacts or cremation deposits may have accompanied the erection of huge timber posts. Opposing pairs of upwards of

300 mature oak trunks separated by a broad, deep, possibly rock-cut fosse would have presented a remarkable spectacle to pilgrims approaching the Hill from the east or north-east. Perhaps these massive posts, defining the sacred space, were elaborately carved and may have supported a planked façade, like the reconstruction proposed for the Ballynahatty enclosure, or a complex superstructure of lintels, similar to Stonehenge. Evidence from a number of excavated examples suggests that entry to the great ritual enclosures was strictly controlled, and even the view into the interior may have been restricted. Perhaps only a religious élite or those participants directly involved in the rituals were granted access. We can never truly know the nature of the rituals performed in these extraordinary structures but there is some evidence to suggest that they were related to mortuary practices. At Ballynahatty, for instance, it is speculated that a rectangular structure at the centre of the smaller timber circle, clearly the main focus of ritual activity, served as a platform for excarnation — the defleshing of bodies exposed to the elements and scavenging animals!

The remarkable definition of the ditched pit enclosure in the gradiometry image may reflect the fact that the posts, at the end of the monument's life, were not removed but ceremonially burnt *in situ*. Alternatively, the post stumps may have been removed and the post-pit carefully and deliberately backfilled with the charred debris of the ceremonially torched structure, along with the food remains of a great feast that marked this event.

The labour involved in the construction of a monument of this size suggests that it had a significance and symbolism on a regional scale and might have served as a religious focus for peoples well beyond the local community. The monument itself, its art and architecture, represented the physical manifestation of a sacred concept or set of religious beliefs, and as such transcended a purely utilitarian purpose. Such concepts may be difficult to reconcile with our purely functional perceptions of architecture today and, equally, many of their beliefs would be entirely alien to our understanding of the world. The remains of these extraordinary structures do, however, convey the sense of the deep-seated spirituality of our early ancestors, beliefs in which taboo and superstition may have played an ever-present and pervasive part in everyday life.

This ditched pit enclosure proclaims the possibility of an unbroken ritual continuum on the Hill of Tara over several millennia. With each new generation of monuments, the old appear not to have been discarded but were simply augmented and subsumed into the fabric of the new — and in a similar way, one might imagine, older beliefs and newly adopted customs could have been woven together in a series of seamless stitches over time. Perhaps with continued research on the Hill of Tara the monuments will, at last, tell the story for themselves.

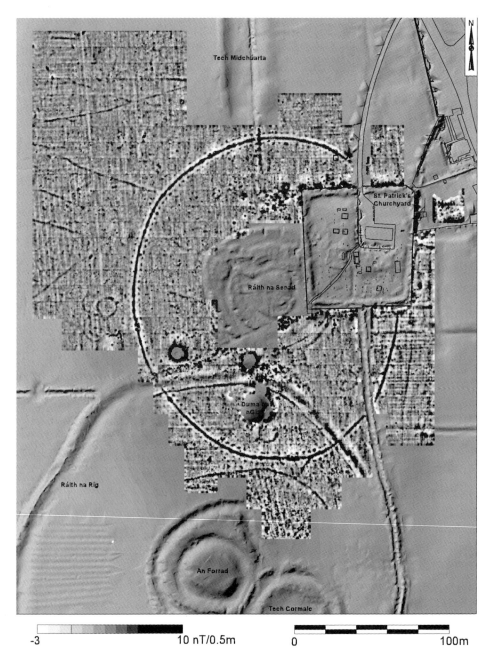

Fig. 14—The gradiometry survey, dominated by the remarkably clear geophysical signature of the ditched pit enclosure, draped over a topographical map of the hilltop (reproduced by kind permission of the Discovery Programme).

Acknowledgements

I am particularly grateful to all the people who shared my time while working on the Hill of Tara over the years, especially my former colleagues in the Discovery Programme, most particularly Conor Newman and Kieron Goucher (former Director of and Surveyor to the Tara Survey respectively). I am also indebted to the Maguires of Tara and the Tullys of Grange Bective for their kind hospitality during our time on the Hill. Thanks, too, are due to the Dúchas guides, especially Gerard Clark, for providing us with a refuge, entertaining conversation and a cup of tea on wet days, and Mrs O'Connell of Skryne for more entertainment and a pint on even wetter days.

I am most grateful to all those who assisted in the more recent survey of the ditched pit enclosure — Linda Shine, Sinead Armstrong, Owen Kieron, Louise Finegan and, of course, Conor Newman, who prompted the whole adventure in the first place. Thanks too to Brian Lacey, Discovery Programme Manager, for permission to reproduce the images and to Barry Masterson for his expertise in their production.

I would like to dedicate this essay to my parents, Jim and Elsie, who, against their better judgement, were brave enough to support and encourage me on my meandering path to a career in archaeology. I suppose things worked out okay in the end!

Further reading

Bhreathnach, E. 1995 *Tara: a select bibliography*. Discovery Programme Monographs 1. Dublin.

Clark, A. 1990 *Seeing beneath the soil*. London.

Darvill, T. and Thomas, J. (eds) 2001 *Neolithic enclosures in Atlantic Europe: Neolithic studies group seminars*, Papers 6. Oxford.

Eogan, G. and Roche, H. 1994 A grooved ware wooden structure at Knowth, Boyne Valley, Ireland. *Antiquity* **68**, 322–30.

Fenwick, J. and Newman, C. 2002 Geomagnetic survey on the Hill of Tara, Co. Meath, 1998–9. *Discovery Programme Reports* **6**, 1–17.

Gibson, A. 1998 Hindwell and the Neolithic palisaded sites of Britain and Ireland. In A. Gibson and D. Simpson (eds), *Prehistoric ritual and religion: essays in honour of Aubrey Burl*, 68–79. Gloucestershire.

Hartwell, B. 1998 The Ballynahatty complex. In A. Gibson and D. Simpson (eds), *Prehistoric ritual and religion: essays in honour of Aubrey Burl*, 32–44. Gloucestershire.

Newman, C. 1997 *Tara: an archaeological survey*. Discovery Programme Monographs 2. Dublin.

Roche, H. 1999 Late Iron Age activity at Tara, Co. Meath. *Ríocht na Mídhe* **10**, 18–30.

Sweetman, D. 1985 A late Neolithic/early Bronze Age pit circle at Newgrange, Co. Meath. *Proceedings of the Royal Irish Academy* **85**C, 196–221.

9

'Do you think you will find the Ark of the Covenant before Indiana Jones?'

Mairead Carew

'Do you think you will find the Ark of the Covenant before Indiana Jones?' my four-year-old son wanted to know when he saw me working on the text of my book *Tara and the Ark of the Covenant* for the Discovery Programme in Dublin. He had already told his teacher that his Mammy was busy looking for the Ark of the Covenant. Presumably, Teacher thought Mammy was daft. As an average four-year-old, the idea that his mother might be competing with the swarthy, whip-wielding, swashbuckling archaeologist, adventurer and stuntman, Indiana Jones, in exotic places such as deserts and jungles in order to recover a golden treasure such as the Ark of the Covenant caught his imagination. Funnily enough, the perception of the intrepid archaeologist on the trail of golden treasure is a popular one, in films at any rate. Nobody would think of making a film about a puny little archaeologist painstakingly digging a site and sending his soil samples and bone fragments to the lab.

My research on *Tara and the Ark of the Covenant* began at the Discovery Programme in Dublin in 1992. I was employed to compile the photo archive for *Tara: an archaeological survey*. During the course of my work I was given permission by the Royal Society of Antiquaries of Ireland to study their 'Tara' file. It was thought that it might contain some relevant photographs of Tara. Instead it was found to contain information on explorations carried out by 'British-Israelites' on Tara between the years 1899 and 1902 in their quest to find the Ark of the Covenant. There were a number of interesting newspaper clippings in the file. Unfortunately, most did not include the date or the name of the newspaper. There was also a letter from W.B. Yeats dated 25 June 1902 from Lady Gregory's house in Coole Park, Co. Galway, to Patrick Boylan of Tara, which intrigued me. On further enquiry it turned out that Patrick Boylan was the tenant of the lands at Tara which were being dug by the British-Israelites, and Yeats was trying to persuade him to put a stop to the explorations. However, apart from being fascinated by the material brought to my attention in the RSAI, I did nothing with it other than to photocopy it and type it into a computer file. It was to be another four years before I was invited back by the Discovery Programme to do some further study of the material about the British-Israelites' explorations with a view to, perhaps, publishing an article.

The 'Tara' file contained correspondence from the British-Israel Association of Ireland. Further computer research revealed that the British-Israel Association of London (to which the Irish organisation was affiliated) published a journal entitled *Covenant People,* housed in the Bodleian Library at Oxford. The association also published another journal, entitled *Banner of Israel,* that was housed in the British Newspaper Library at Collingsworth in London. I set off for London first, staying with friends, and hobbling (I had sustained a leg injury before embarking on this journey of discovery into the concrete jungles of London) onto trains and buses to get to Collingsworth. I was presented with many journals containing lots of interesting information on the Tara explorations, which I requested the Librarian to post to me. Then I travelled down to Oxford to go to the Bodleian Library. I handed my letters of recommendation from the Discovery Programme to a bespectacled man at the check-in desk, who looked at me suspiciously before grabbing a camera from somewhere under his desk and photographing me suddenly. I almost felt like a criminal and expected him to fingerprint me before issuing me with a card to allow entry. Then he asked me to repeat a phrase after him that involved stating that I would not burn down the library. I thought he was joking at first and had to resist the temptation to tell him I had a box of matches in my pocket. But then I realised, looking at his earnest face, that he was indeed serious and the probability existed that he did not have a sense of humour. In any event there was no need to resort to Indiana Jones-type tactics of somersaulting over his desk, running down the hall pursued by security men, and flooring the librarian to gain access to the Bodleian. No, the bespectacled man stamped my card and I walked sedately in the direction of the library.

From the dusty pages of the *Covenant People* I learned that the British-Israelites of the Tara story were from the British-Israel Association of London, which was founded in 1889. The British-Israelites believed that they were descended from the Lost Tribes of Israel and that the recovery of the Ark of the Covenant would prove this hypothesis. They also believed that it was buried at Tara and that Tara was the 'resuscitated' Jerusalem of a new Israel. They came to this conclusion from their studies of ancient Irish history, mythology, philology and the Bible. I also discovered that the British-Israel Association of Ireland was set up in Dublin in 1897 and that some of the same people were prominent in both organisations. These included Reverend Denis Hanan, rector of Tipperary, and Captain Joshua Fielding. Those who arrived at Tara to begin the explorations were named as Walton Adams and Charles Groom. They were given permission to proceed by the landlord at Tara, Gustavus Villiers Briscoe. I photocopied everything I could find on the Tara explorations between the years 1899 and 1902 from the *Covenant People* and came home laden with information. A few weeks later the photocopies from the British Newspaper Library arrived. The trip had been worthwhile. From the *Banner of Israel* I learned that there were connections between British-Israelism and Freemasonry.

The Ark of the Covenant was the symbol which British-Israelism and Freemasonry had in common (Fig. 15). In the *Covenant People* for the year 1901 it was noted that the Masonic ceremony in memory of the Ark could be discontinued when the Ark was recovered. A visit to the Freemason's Hall in Molesworth Street in Dublin proved very interesting. Its museum contains a model of the Ark of the Covenant in silver, made by Henry E. Flavelle, a prominent Freemason and jeweller silversmith (Pl. 23; Fig. 16). It was displayed in the Grand Lodge Room during the formal dedication of the Grand Lodge on 5 December 1877. It was later presented to the Grand Lodge by the artist's son, H.E. Flavelle, in 1898 and continued to be placed on the altar during meetings. A medallion with the words 'Knights of Tara 1885' engraved on the back is also on display in the museum. I was informed by the archivist that these knights were a select circle of the British-Israelites with a definite esoteric slant who believed that the Ark was buried at Tara. A tour of some of the other rooms in the Freemason's Hall was equally fascinating. I visited the Egyptian room, which has a throne-like seat covered in a red velvety fabric flanked by two smaller similar chairs under a marble arch. Two ornate sphinxes flank the front pillars of the arch. In front of the sphinxes is a marble altar on which an open bible lies on a red velvet cushion. Another room, known as the Knights Templar chapel, has its altar, floor and banners decorated with red crosses on white backgrounds. One wonders (unless, of course, one is a Freemason) what kind of rituals are carried out in these rooms.

The archivist provided me with information that those involved in the Tara explorations, including Hanan, Fielding, Adams, Groom and Briscoe, were all Freemasons. Hanan and Fielding had organised a trip for the British-Israel Association of London to Tara in April 1902. All of these people were also members of the Royal Society of Antiquaries of Ireland (RSAI). Fielding was a member of the Royal Irish Academy (RIA), elected in December 1900. He was also elected a fellow of the RSAI that year, having been proposed by Robert

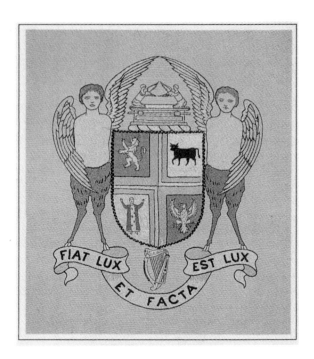

Fig. 15—The coat of arms of the Grand Lodge of Ireland with the detail of the Ark of the Covenant above the shield (illustration reproduced courtesy of the Freemason's Hall Archive, Dublin).

Pl. 23—The model of the Ark of the Covenant, made by Henry E. Flavelle, Freemason and jeweller silversmith, now housed in the museum of the Freemason's Hall in Molesworth Street, Dublin (illustration reproduced courtesy of the Freemason's Hall Archive, Dublin).

Cochrane, secretary of the RSAI and Inspector of Ancient and National Monuments at the OPW. Though Cochrane campaigned vigorously against the Tara explorations, he also subscribed to the journal of the British-Israel Association of London. From the RSAI file I learned that Charles Groom was displeased with Cochrane and the Society's attitude to the explorations. In a letter dated 4 July 1902 he asked why Cochrane as 'a mason of high degree' had forgotten his 'obligations to masonry'. Cochrane was a member of Prince Masons Chapter no. 9 in Dublin. However, his obligations to Masonry with regard to the Tara explorations were not elaborated upon in Groom's letter.

All this information led me to the interesting question of whether there was a connection between antiquarianism and Freemasonry, and whether the latter had influenced the former. This led me to some research at the Royal Irish Academy in Dawson Street, Dublin, where I discovered that Freemasonry played a part in the interpretation of archaeological monuments in the nineteenth century. There was a bitter controversy surrounding the interpretation of the round towers of Ireland, which resulted in a parting of the ways between speculative antiquarianism and the new subject of scientific archaeology. George

Fig. 16—Drawing of the Ark of the Covenant (illustration reproduced courtesy of the Freemason's Hall Archive, Dublin).

Petrie, the noted antiquarian, painter and musician, argued for the Christian origin of the towers and published his views (based on facts and evidence) in a book entitled *Ecclesiastical architecture of Ireland.* Henry O'Brien, a Freemason and member of the RIA, in contrast published his views in a book entitled *The round towers of Ireland or the mysteries of Freemasonry, of Sabaism and Buddhism for the first time revealed,* a speculative work whose title speaks for itself. This controversy was important in terms of the British-Israelite explorations at Tara as British-Israelites based many of their theories on the work of the noted eighteenth-century antiquarian Charles Vallancey (1721–1812). Vallancey too was a prominent Freemason. His writings on Irish history and philology were still being espoused by certain Freemasons within the RIA in the nineteenth century long after they had been discredited in scholarly circles.

Now that I had established who the British-Israelites were and the Freemason connection, it was time to find out what actually happened. It had been brought to my attention that there were two large files marked 'Tara' housed in the National Archives in Bishop Street, Dublin. Two dusty brown folders tied with twine can be as exciting to the archaeologist as the possibility of unearthing some golden treasure from a mud-filled trench. No athleticism with lassoes or other death-defying stunts were required in the recovery of some golden nuggets of information. A pencil and notebook were sufficient. My earth-coloured folders did not disappoint. They contained within their dusty leaves the correspondence between those who wished to carry out the explorations at Tara, including Rev. Denis Hanan, rector of Tipperary, and officials from the Office of Public Works, who refused his application. There was also correspondence between the OPW and the RIA about the explorations. Most valuable to the enquiring archaeologist was a report by a surveyor from the OPW dated 2 August 1899 which turned out to be the only official written record of the Tara explorations in progress which came to light.

There were, however, other written accounts, including newspaper reports of the activities of the British-Israelites on the site. In the Tara file at the RSAI I read a newspaper clipping from the *United Irishman* dated 9 March 1901 with an article entitled 'The Anglo-Israelite Destroyer of Tara'. This prompted me to go to the National Library to see if I could find any more articles on the subject. I spent many long, boring and tedious days in the library turning the handle of the microfilm machine and going through edition after edition of the *United Irishman* from 1899 onwards. Eventually the laborious work bore fruit, and I felt like jumping up and down and shouting '*eureka!*' when I found an article written by Maud Gonne in the edition dated 5 January 1901. I should have gone to my local bar and downed a whiskey in one gulp just to celebrate my discovery, as my fellow archaeologist Indiana would have done, but I decided that the Discovery

Programme would not appreciate the excess and that a more temperate approach to my research would be in order. Maud Gonne's article was followed by numerous articles on the Tara explorations in the editions of the paper for 1902. It began to emerge that Arthur Griffith, the editor of the *United Irishman,* had mounted a media campaign, the first of its kind in archaeological history, against the destruction of a national monument. Griffith (under the pseudonym Viking) wrote a series of eleven articles entitled 'Tara of the Kings — A sketch of the History of the Capital of Independent Ireland', which he published in the *United Irishman* between 26 July and 4 October 1902. It was also reported in the *United Irishman* that on 24 June 1902 Griffith, W.B. Yeats, George Moore and Douglas Hyde visited Tara to protest against the explorations. They were prevented from walking across the Hill by a man wielding a rifle. On foot of these articles I decided to go through the published correspondence of Yeats on the topic, and found that he corresponded with Maud Gonne. He also wrote to Wilfred Blunt, lover of Lady Gregory, about the 'Tempair Business' (a euphemism for the Tara explorations).

One of Maud Gonne's letters gives a humorous account of an Inginidhe na hÉireann excursion, including a number of schoolchildren, to Tara in July 1902. The landlord, Briscoe, had prepared a bonfire to light in honour of King Edward VII's coronation. The British-Israelites hoped to present the Ark of the Covenant to Edward VII as they believed him to be a direct descendant of the biblical king David. Maud Gonne commandeered his bonfire, lit it and organised the children to sing 'A Nation Once Again' in honour of a free and independent Ireland, much to the consternation of Briscoe. The constabulary danced with rage over this incident, which, according to Maud Gonne, 'added greatly to the fun'. These discoveries, apart from being interesting and humorous in themselves, placed the British-Israelite explorations firmly in the context of the Irish cultural revival. They also brought the events of the past to life as they unfolded. And that is what an archaeologist endeavours to do, to bring the past alive for the reader. While, unlike Indiana Jones, I may not have discovered the wonderful treasure that is the Ark of the Covenant, the thrill of the pursuit of knowledge about Tara and the Ark, in my opinion, is infinitely more interesting.

'Had the "Ark of the Covenant" dreamers even done so much as to record what they actually did find, much might have been forgiven them. But they made no such compensation for their offence against science and against reason' (Macalister 1931, 39).

'Several of the higher degrees refer to the ark, and without doubt it was first instituted to keep in mind its place of hiding. This accounts for masonry of this degree pointing to Ireland as the place of its origin' (Covenant People vol. 2 (1896), 109).

'The identity itself is so astounding, that we British-Israelites have often to witness a sarcastic smile; but when to the ordinary arguments we add that of the reappearance of the Ark, the smile turns to an open laugh' (Covenant People vol. 9 (1903), 70).

'That the Ark of the Lord is deposited in the Mound at Tara, there is in our mind but little doubt' (Covenant People vol. 9 (1903), 71).

Further reading

Bhreathnach, E. 1995 *Tara: a select bibliography*. Discovery Programme Monographs 1. Dublin.

Carew, M. 2003 *Tara and the Ark of the Covenant: a search for the Ark of the Covenant by British-Israelites on the Hill of Tara (1899–1902)*. Dublin.

Hamill, J. and Gilbert, R. (eds) 1993 *Freemasonry: a celebration of the craft*. London.

Macalister, R.A.S. 1931 *Tara: a pagan sanctuary of ancient Ireland*. London.

Newman, C. 1997 *Tara: an archaeological survey*. Discovery Programme Monographs 2. Dublin.

Wilson, J. 1968 British Israelism. *The Sociological Review* **16**, 41–57.

10

The Scotstown, Co. Monaghan, hoard:
a re-examination of the evidence

Aideen M. Ireland

In the very early spring of 1879 we must imagine a young man, John Murray, leaving his home in Killatten, Co. Monaghan, and travelling up the main road which led from Rosslea, Co. Fermanagh, to the nearby town of Scotstown. He probably travelled on through Scotstown, past the police barracks, across the main square and out the other side of the town. The rest is history.

The following article appeared in *The Weekly Irish Times* on Saturday 22 March 1879:

> A Curious Discovery. — A young man, while employed ploughing a field in a village called Scotstown, within a few miles from Monaghan, ploughed up some ancient ornaments which are evidently valuable. The articles which it was the fortune of this son of agriculture to unearth consist of two semicircular ornaments, about the size of a man's little finger. These ornaments are of pure gold, fluted and having small discs which turn upwards. Together with these, he found some bronze rings, perfectly whole, and some fragments of broken ones. The golden ornaments have the appearance of ladies' cloak fasteners used some centuries ago, while the appearance of the rings would suggest to one that a likeness existed between them and the ring money which formerly circulated in this country. The gold which is contained in the first-mentioned articles is worth £4.

On 24 March the Rev. Maxwell Close, treasurer of the Royal Irish Academy in Dublin, wrote to Thomas Henry Burke, under-secretary to the lord lieutenant, in Dublin Castle:

> The attention of the Museum Committee having been called to the recovery near Scotstown, Monaghan, of two Gold Fibulae, I am directed by them to say that they are desirous of obtaining them under the Treasure Trove Regulations; and to enquire what steps should be taken by them to this end.

Treasure trove was regarded by the administration in Dublin Castle as being 'Ancient Coins, Gold or Silver Ornaments or other Relics of Antiquity in Ireland', and such objects, if found, were to be handed over to the constabulary of the area in which they were found. The regulations were first published in March 1861.

Unfortunately there is no way of knowing how the Museum Committee heard of this find, though it is not impossible that a reading of the newspaper sufficed. The matter having come to the attention of the authorities in Dublin Castle, investigations were under way by 29 March.

It turned out that the finder of the objects was John Murray of Killatin, *recte* Killatten, in the parish of Tedavnet, Co. Monaghan. However, on 30 March Myles Blake Burke, the county inspector for the Royal Irish Constabulary for County Monaghan, reported that Murray had already sold the objects. This development was viewed with considerable alarm, since a matter of treasure trove was involved, and the name of the purchaser had to be ascertained as quickly as possible. While Blake Burke regarded the gold objects as '2 Gold Fibulae', to Wellington Colomb, an assistant inspector-general of the Royal Irish Constabulary, they were merely 'old ornaments'.

Yet the sub-inspector of the Royal Irish Constabulary, Andrew O'Brien Carleton of the Monaghan Sub-Inspector's Station, was able to report on 3 April that

> …John Murray has not up to a few days ago disposed of these articles to anyone not having been offered what he considered enough.
> He left home about the time above mentioned to plough in the Coy Fermanagh, taking the Fibulae & the Rings for the purpose of disposing of them — it is said, at Enniskillen. He is expected home tonight when I shall probably be able to ascertain where the ornaments are & in whose possession.

Blake Burke reiterated that Murray had not yet disposed of the items but Colomb was not impressed. In a furious memo he wrote:

> Inform the County Inspector that his reports about this simple matter are most unsatisfactory. His report of the 30th ult gave incorrect

information & as far as yet appears he took no steps between 30th ult and 2nd instant to ascertain the real facts. On the 3rd instant he submits imperfect information knowing that he would probably be in possession of exact information that evening or the following morning, & he has expressed no regret nor offered any explanation the latter is now required by the Inspr Genl.

Add that if the man in whose possession the articles are is willing to hand them over to the Constabulary let them be forwarded here at once.

Constable Patrick Cooney was dispatched to Scotstown so that a report could be made to the county inspector on 7 April concerning the present whereabouts of the objects. Constable Cooney was diligent, and in a report submitted to Sub-Inspector Carleton on 6 April he stated:

> I beg to state that at 9 o.C Pm on this day I saw John Murry of Killatten he refuses to give up the ornaments to the Constabulary (in Conditions of Code 1314) until he knows how much he is to get for them he says he has had several offers from persons anxious to purchase them and that he is not willing to part with the ornaments yet. He also told me tonight that he has found in the field where he got the first articles a peculiarly ornamented stone. He desires me to say he is willing to produce the articles for inspection if his train be paid to and from.

On 9 April John Monroe, the law adviser, wrote:

> As the man Murray has been fortunate enough to find these articles I think the Royal Irish Academy ought to offer him something for them. If he refuses to take a reasonable remuneration he should be informed that in concealing these articles he is guilty of a Criminal offence amounting to a Misdemeanour & that Criminal proceedings may be taken against him. Should he still refuse to give them up a Summons may be issued & Informations taken at Petty Sessions on a charge of 'unlawfully knowingly wilfully concealing treasure trove from the Crown'. If the facts are proved the case may be held for trial.

No doubt Monroe's advice had been obtained in the expectation that Murray would refuse to hand the objects over as he was required to do under treasure trove regulations. It was suggested by Under-Secretary Burke that the law adviser's opinion be conveyed to John Murray and that the local district inspector proceed to Scotstown to view the articles held by Murray and to ascertain from him whether he would part with them and for how much. Sub-Inspector Carleton went to Scotstown and reported on 12 April:

> I beg to say that I saw Murray today by appointment.
> He asked £20 for the articles found, but I think that £10 would be quite enough for them.
> However as I cannot pretend to be an authority on archaeological subjects and as I am aware that these articles have an aesthetic, quite apart from their intrinsic, value, I would suggest that they might be submitted to the V. Rev. Dr Reeves Dean of Armagh, himself an eminent Antiquarian & ex Member of the R.I. Academy, who in all probability will be able to give an authoritative opinion as to their value.
> Murray, who is only a lad of about nineteen, is not at all disposed to make a hard bargain, at least with me, and has entrusted the articles to me for submission to some competent authority and is willing to abide by the decision.
> I may add that he has been offered more than £10 by a lady in the neighbourhood and he would expect that at least, but of course I made him no offer as I was not authorized to do so.

Asked again for his opinion by Under-Secretary Burke, Monroe wrote:

> Let a letter be written to the Royal Irish Academy informing the Committee that Murray has placed the articles in the hands of Sub Inspector Carleton to be submitted to some competent authority & that if the name of some person acquainted with the value of such articles be mentioned by the Committee the Sub Inspector will submit them for his Examination. State that Murray has been offered £10 for them, & that probably they would be given up for a little more if the person suggested by the Committee considers the articles worth such a sum. State that proceedings of a criminal character for not giving up treasure trove are very unusual & that this should only be resorted to when no other course is fairly open.

Rev. Maxwell Close, the treasurer of the Royal Irish Academy, again wrote to Thomas H. Burke, the under-secretary, at Dublin Castle on 22 April, notifying him of a forthcoming meeting of the Museum Committee of the Academy and requesting that the articles be submitted for inspection by the Committee. Close noted:

> I may add that the prices offered by the Committee for Antiquities

generally exceed those obtainable from dealers.

The items in question were dispatched to the Royal Irish Academy on 26 April by Constable Edward Neeson. At a meeting of the Committee of Polite Literature and Antiquities and Museum on 28 April:

> Read letter from the Castle, from Sub Inspector Carleton referring to certain Gold Fibulae found near Scotstown.
> Resolved
> That the Treasurer be authorized to pay the sum of Eight pounds for the Gold Fibulae and bronze objects referred to in the letter.

On 29 April Rev. Maxwell Close again wrote to T.H. Burke in Dublin Castle, noting that the Museum Committee had examined the two gold fibulae and the bronze rings and that

> The Committee have authorized me to pay the sum of Eight Pounds for these objects and I have accordingly forwarded this amount to Sub Inspector Carleton for the finder.

Despite the drop in monetary payment to Murray, the matter was deemed closed on 2 May by the authorities in Dublin Castle. However, at a meeting of the Committee of Polite Literature and Antiquities and Museum in the Royal Irish Academy on 12 May:

> Read letter from sub-inspector Carleton acknowledging receipt by Murray of the same [*sic*] paid for the fibula [*sic*] as by Resolution of April 28th.

The objects then entered the museum collection of the Royal Irish Academy and are now in the Irish Antiquities Division of the National Museum of Ireland (Fig. 17). In all, 22 items or partial items were purchased. These consisted of the two gold fibulae, bronze rings or partial rings, some fragments of amber beads and some fragments of cord which had been attached to one of the bronze rings. The entry in the Royal Irish Academy register states:

> The forgoing objects numbered 6–18 inclusive were found when ploughing in a field near Scotstown, in a direct line between two ancient Raths, and adjacent to an old burying-ground, Co. Monaghan.
> Purchased under Treasure Trove regulations from Murray, April, £8.0.0.

So far the history — now the detail. One must assume from the evidence provided that John Murray was born about 1860. In 1881, two years after the finding of this hoard, Killatten, Co. Monaghan, boasted a population of 37 people living in seven houses with a total of 70 acres in the townland. It is clear from the printed census abstracts for 1881 that the population of the townland had been falling since 1841 (when it had been 52), as was the number of inhabited houses. The valuation of the houses and land in 1881 was put at £56.5.0. Yet Samuel Lewis in his *Topographical dictionary of Ireland* of 1837 writes of Tedavnet parish as being a populated and prosperous one, though no specific mention is made of the townland of Killatten.

While there is no knowing when John Murray was ploughing in Scotstown, it probably was not much before the newspaper article of 22 March 1879. Lewis tells us that Scotstown held a fair each seventeenth day of the month, so perhaps Murray had gone into Scotstown for the fair on the previous Monday and had undertaken some ploughing as well.

Neither is there any way of knowing where Murray was ploughing. The evidence from the Royal Irish Academy that the objects came from 'near Scotstown, in a direct line between two ancient Raths, and adjacent to an old burying-ground' cannot be fully proven on an Ordnance Survey map. Indeed, three ringforts are to be found in a direct line in the immediate vicinity of Scotstown. One is in the townland of Cussee, one is in the townland of Carrahata, *recte* Carrowhatta, and the third is in the adjacent townland of Coolkill West. Nowhere is a burial-ground to be found on the Ordnance Survey maps, and no reference to one appears in the *Archaeological inventory of County Monaghan*. However, since the report states that the items were found near Scotstown it is most likely that Murray was ploughing in the townlands of Coolkill West or Carrahata. The probability is that the hoard was found in Carrahata townland, as it lies closest to Scotstown itself. This, however, is not the only possible resolution, as a close examination of the Ordnance Survey sheets will show. Taken in conjunction with the evidence as presented in the *Archaeological inventory of County Monaghan,* many other possible direct lines of ringforts and/or earthworks (whether still present or vanished) present themselves. On the Ordnance Survey sheets the term *fort* is used for all circular enclosures (excluding what appear to be tree rings), though the *Archaeological inventory of County Monaghan* draws a distinction between an earthwork and a ringfort. However, if one abides by the Royal Irish Academy definition of 'Raths' and the *Archaeological inventory* definition of 'ringfort', the hypothesis of Coolkill West, Carrowhatta and Cussee remains.

Nor is there any indication in the reports as to how the hoard was found. Two alternatives are possible. A stone could have been hit and upset during

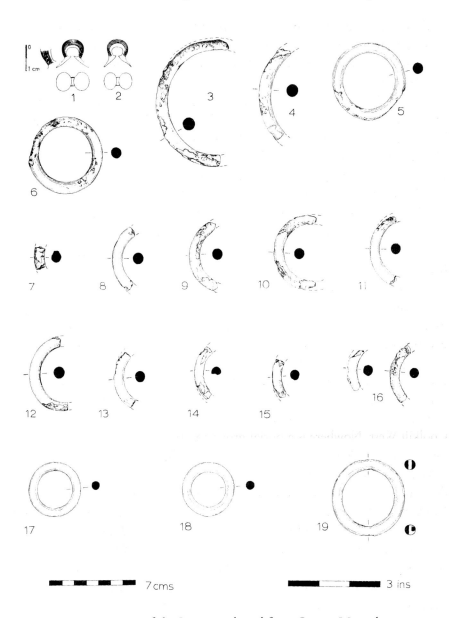

Fig. 17—Drawing of the Scotstown hoard from County Monaghan, showing two gold sleeve-fasteners and whole and partial bronze rings. Illustration reproduced courtesy of the National Museum of Ireland and Professor George Eogan (from whose book, Hoards of the Irish later Bronze Age, *it is taken).*

ploughing, revealing, perhaps, a hole into which the objects could have been consigned. Alternatively Murray may simply have seen a gold flash during the course of his ploughing when walking behind the horses. Either way, he must have bent down, dug out the items with his hands, probably scrabbling around in the clay to make sure that nothing had been missed, noted their unusual aspect and consigned them to his pocket or to a bag which he may have brought with him. One wonders what was going through his mind when he ceased his ploughing. One wonders whether he considered the curious fact of items having been consigned to the soil. Had they been deliberately hidden or had they been lost ? On returning home the items would have had to be cleaned, and only then would their true nature have been revealed — gold, brass or bronze, and some coloured beads which turned out to be amber. The sense of excitement in the house must have been extraordinary — made all the more intense as the finding of the objects could not be revealed for fear of detection, or even possible theft or seizure. One wonders how the reporter for *The Weekly Irish Times* came upon the story. Murray hardly boasted publicly of his find for fear of loss of the objects, since he was in breach of the law of treasure trove, so one must assume that he did not show them off outside his immediate family. For those anxious to experience this thrill of discovery for themselves a visit to the gold exhibition in the National Museum of Ireland is essential, for here the items are now on public display.

There is no way of establishing for whom Murray was undertaking this ploughing. Yet one must assume that he was ploughing on his own since the newspaper report does not state otherwise. What is interesting is that Murray held on to the objects and did not hand them over to his employer. Nor does he appear to have offered them to any of the large landowners in the vicinity of Scotstown. Another interesting fact is that Murray was reported to be selling the objects in Fermanagh, which lies just over the border from his home at Killatten, or, failing that, to a female purchaser in 'the neighbourhood'. Again it has not been possible to establish who she might have been.

By far the largest landholder in the immediate area had been Joseph C. Wright at Carrahor House in the townland of Carrahor, *recte* Carrachor, who owned more than 63 acres outright in 1860. Yet within less than twenty years the property had changed hands twice, and by 1879 the occupier was Joseph Mitchell. There is no indication as to whether he was a resident landlord or not. However, William Woodwright at Gola House in Killatten townland was a substantial landowner, owning more than 3000 acres in County Monaghan in 1876. Yet he held his land in Killatten from Henrietta Westenra, whose estate was in the Court of Chancery. The two immediate lessors of land (as opposed to occupiers) in the relevant townlands were Henrietta Westenra and Sir George

Forster. Forster lived in Carrickmacross while Henrietta Westenra lived outside the county altogether, though Woodwright lived locally. It may be that in this uncertain situation Murray turned to no one with his hoard but simply held on to it himself.

Nor did the matter appear to come to the attention of the constabulary based in Scotstown. Murray must often have passed by the premises and may well have seen the *Notice to Finders of Antiquities in Ireland*, a poster printed by the Royal Irish Academy explaining the nature of treasure trove and the rewards offered to finders, displayed inside. Murray was circumspect and returned from his ploughing mission presumably with the fibulae, amber beads and bronze rings on his person. Murray did recount that he 'found in the field where he got the first articles a peculiarly ornamented stone' but there is no indication of the fate of this stone. Probably it remained behind in the field. Once home, Murray must have faced the dual problem of disposing of the items profitably yet preventing them from being seized or falling into the wrong hands. While there is no hint that he attempted to defraud anyone, he was not prepared to part with the objects without some gain.

It is certain that Murray did not become rich on the basis of this treasure trove sale to the Royal Irish Academy. Sub-Inspector Carleton reported that Murray demanded twenty pounds for the objects but that Carleton himself felt that ten pounds would suffice. Indeed, Murray reported that he had been offered more than ten pounds by a local lady, while it was also reported that he had said that he had had several offers from persons anxious to purchase them and was not willing to part with the ornaments yet. In the end the hoard was acquired for eight pounds by the Royal Irish Academy despite the claim by the Rev. Maxwell Close that the prices offered by the Committee for Antiquities of the Royal Irish Academy generally exceeded those obtainable from dealers.

While it is pure speculation to consider the social circumstances of Murray or his family, they cannot have been very substantial. In the *Return of owners of land of one acre and upwards in the several counties…in Ireland*, printed in 1876, the only Murray returned as owning land in County Monaghan was resident in Beech Hill, Monaghan, and owned just over 330 acres. As we have already seen, the population of Killatten was falling. In the primary valuation of 1860 for the townland of Killatten we find a Thomas and George Murray holding over fourteen acres of land between them. Both rented from Arthur G. Lewis, an absentee landlord. By 1879 both Thomas and George were still occupying the same land. However, the lessor had changed and the land was now held by the absentee Henrietta Westenra.

It is pure speculation to consider the relationship between George, Thomas and John Murray. John, being born around 1860, probably figures in the 1901 census return for Killatten, Co. Monaghan. He would then have been aged about 41. While a John Murray (aged 41) is listed in the census return for Killatten, living with his sister and nephew, it is unfortunately not possible to establish whether he was the finder of the Scotstown hoard or not. A George Murray is also returned, aged 89, though in this case his son John is returned as aged 34. By the time of the 1911 census returns the first John Murray has married and returns his age as 53, while John Murray (son of the deceased George) is now a widower and aged 47. The identification of the finder of the hoard along with the place in which the hoard was found remain for the local population to discover.

On the basis of one newspaper story and a letter from the Royal Irish Academy to the authorities in Dublin Castle the story of the discovery of this important hoard has been revealed. Had the file of the Chief Secretary's Office not been preserved, our knowledge of the finder and the find circumstances and find-place would have been sorely incomplete.

Acknowledgements

The author gratefully acknowledges the permission of the Director of the National Archives of Ireland to quote from Chief Secretary's Office Registered Paper 1879/7202. This article could not have been written without the assistance of Mary Cahill, National Museum of Ireland, Brian MacDonald, Monaghan, and Steven ffeary-Smyrl, Dublin, whose help is gratefully acknowledged.

Further reading

Anon. 1876 *Return of owners of land of one acre and upwards in the several counties…in Ireland.* Dublin.

Anon. 1882 *Census of Ireland, 1881. Part 1. area, houses and population… Vol. III, Province of Ulster. No. 8, County of Monaghan.* Dublin. Stationery Office.

Brindley, A.L. 1986 *Archaeological inventory of County Monaghan.* Dublin.

Eogan, G. 1983 *Hoards of the Irish later Bronze Age.* Dublin.

Lewis, S. 1837 *A topographical dictionary of Ireland…with historical and statistical descriptions,* part ii. London.

11

Bogland surveys in Ireland: forty shades of brown

Cathy Moore, Cara Murray, Michael Stanley and Conor McDermott,
Irish Archaeological Wetland Unit

Coolnagun Bog

The bulldozers are in the bog today
destroying heather, lichen, furze and moss.
While walking down Coole Hill I see the loss
of purple panorama. Far way
the wide horizon, Derravaragh lake
(where once white feathers were the daily cross)
now blurred from view. Peat powder the new boss,
it peaks in mountains, spews into the air.

Old Phil Doran says developers will go
and this brown desert will become a marsh
and future generations will not know
the spring of turf like carpet, nor the glow
of Summer harvest in the Winter hearth,
the song of lark, bog cotton – globs of snow.

Breda Sullivan 1998
(by permission of the author)

In the beginning…

The quality of preservation and unique character of archaeological sites in our bogs make them one of the most exciting areas in Europe for new discoveries, with vast tracts of peatlands as yet unexplored. Pioneers of the peatfields, like Professors Etienne Rynne and Barry Raftery in Ireland and Professor John Coles in England, demonstrated this enormous potential by carrying out some of the first excavations and surveys in peatlands. Almost all of the sites and artefacts recorded in earlier decades were chance discoveries and it was recognised that a more systematic approach to peatland archaeology was required in order to fully realise this potential. In 1990 the Irish Archaeological Wetland Unit was established by Dúchas The Heritage Service (then the OPW) and University College Dublin to begin surveys of the some 80,000 hectares of midland bog in industrial production.

Discoveries in peatlands range from habitations of the earliest Irish peoples in the Mesolithic period to the footpaths and roads of prehistoric to recent centuries (Pl. 24). These sites testify to the continuous interaction between wetland and dryland in the past. Perhaps this is best exemplified by the many hundreds of smaller wooden structures which do not cross the bog, but rather show that the bogs themselves were a focus for people in the past.

Pl. 24—Excavation of a large plank-built trackway dating from c. 900 BC at Annaghcorrib, Garryduff Bog, Co. Galway (photo: IAWU).

Nearly all sites and artefacts found in our bogs are made of organic materials such as wood. The waterlogged conditions that prevail preserve these materials in almost pristine condition. This is what makes these finds so dramatic. Wood, leather, butter and even human bodies survive in their finest detail and retain the trace evidence of past human activity that rarely survives on dryland sites. Wood often retains its original bark, colour and every detail of each toolmark. A scatter of wood chips and a pointed stake can show the work of minutes at a very human level. As a site is sealed below the layers of growing peat so also is the surface of the bog environment on which it was built. Peatlands are one of the few stratified landscapes available for archaeologists to study. As the peat forms year by year and layer by layer, a record of changes to the bog and the surrounding dryland accumulates. Through the study of peat development, pollen, beetles and tephra (volcanic glass fragments), changes in climate, drainage and land use can be traced. Peatlands, therefore, not only give us a vital repository of archaeological sites and finds in their own right but also allow us to better understand the less well-preserved dryland sites.

The bogs, the people, the sites

The work of the IAWU and other organisations has uncovered large numbers of often dramatic sites and finds which have added greatly to our understanding of wetland and dryland landscapes in the past. In some cases, such as in County Offaly, surveys have almost tripled the numbers of known archaeological sites. These sites and artefacts can be found in both splendid isolation and dramatic density.

In order to make these discoveries it is necessary for a team of people to launch themselves into the vastness of our midland industrial bogs. While peatland survey depends on a coordinated and professional programme, its success is based on the individual archaeologist with a stout pair of 'wellies' and a keen eye. Many thousands of kilometres of bog drains have been walked and over 3000 sites are now known. In all likelihood many thousands of others remain to be found. Trudging through the all-too-yielding bog, you never know whether each footstep will be followed by many more or a stop to examine a stunning discovery. While there are abundant statistics for how many of each site type have been found, the golden rule is: expect the unexpected and you just might find it.

These sites can be very difficult for non-archaeologists to appreciate, as they do not get the opportunity to see them at first hand as they emerge from the peat. Within minutes, yellow wood can turn black as it is exposed to the air.

Wood must be continually watered to prevent it drying out, producing the strange picture of people pouring water into a hole in the bog. This is vital, however, as even a prolonged tea break can reduce perfectly preserved wood to desiccated fragments.

Archaeologists today rarely find many new archaeological sites, certainly not in the numbers remaining to be identified in peatlands. It is not unknown for a survey team to find over a hundred new sites in a day of bog-walking. The record of archaeological sites and artefacts for most areas is usually built up piece by piece over years of patient surveys, excavations and documentary research. Peatland surveys, by contrast, have the ability to rapidly fill areas of the landscape with archaeological sites. These can either augment the existing record by providing complementary site distributions with dryland sites or, perhaps more excitingly, highlight new areas with few previously known sites (Fig. 18). To date over 3000 sites have been identified in Irish midland bogs, and over double this number can be expected by the time the first surveys are completed.

Typically our survey team comprises twelve people, the IAWU staff and eight fieldworkers. Many of these are fresh from university exam halls, and finding themselves just days later in the middle of a bog can be something of a culture shock. Equipped with a handful of bamboos, a shovel and a backpack containing everything from sandwiches to sample bags, the team walks each bog in parallel runs about 30m apart. Each discovery is marked with a bamboo, and sometimes you stop suddenly on seeing a line of bamboos running across the bog and realise that you are standing on the line of a prehistoric trackway. On other occasions you see a sea of bamboos and realise that we are not the first people to spend a lot of time in this bog. At the end of each run the results are reported, with each bamboo inserted representing a potential new national monument or artefact. After finding the sites comes the more detailed recording stage, when we examine the sites and see the details of their construction. Even standing in a water-filled drain people never lose the excitement of working hands-on with such well-preserved remains.

When sites are found, an unofficial lottery starts as to what age they are. Unlike sites on dryland, most peatland sites cannot be dated by their general form. Instead, we rely upon indicators such as peat levels, toolmarks and, in some cases, associated artefacts. This is then followed by a more scientific approach whereby samples from selected sites are submitted for radiocarbon or dendrochronological dating. This latter method, which is based on oak tree rings, can be remarkably accurate, sometimes telling not only the year but also the season in which a tree was felled anytime up to 8000 years ago.

Sites dating from the earliest Irish human occupation in the Mesolithic period are relatively rare, and most of the midland examples come from lakeshores and

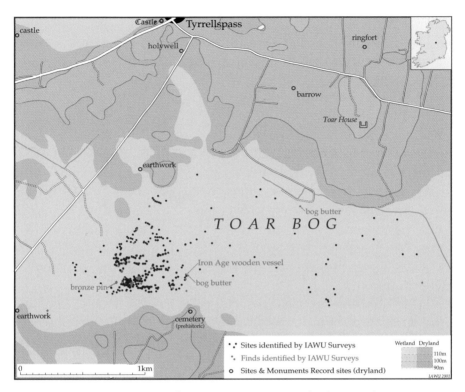

Fig. 18—Map of Toar Bog, Co. Westmeath, showing the peatland survey results 2000.

other wetland areas. With the advent of farming in the Neolithic period the number of sites increased somewhat but was still quite small. It was in the Bronze Age that sites started to be built in greater numbers across Irish bogs. The numbers declined markedly again in the Iron Age, but in the early centuries of the Christian era, around AD 600, the number of sites increased dramatically again. Peatlands continue to play an important role in today's landscape, with vast tracts used for fuel and being reclaimed for agriculture.

To highlight the quality and diversity of the archaeological record in our midland bogs a number of recent, less typical discoveries are presented below.

Corralanna Mesolithic site

Thankfully, the tradition whereby members of the public report chance discoveries in bogland continues. A keen eye and a firm knowledge of the past are to be thanked for a great number of finds throughout the country (generally, the full scope of such knowledge is masked by a gracious modesty and is never expressed). In April 2000, the IAWU was made aware of just such a discovery by Mr Michael Rainsford, a retired teacher, who had found two stone axes and a number of other stone tools in a bog in Corralanna townland, Co. Westmeath. What he had identified proved to be a large assemblage of material from the late Mesolithic period, when Ireland was first inhabited. Undoubtedly a discovery of both regional and national importance, yet none of this was apparent before the site visit.

The discovery was made between Lough Kinale and Lough Derravaragh. This is an area of Bord na Móna industrial peatland north of the Coole–Lismacaffry road and west of the River Inny. The margins of the bog are leased to a private operator who sells the turf locally. On one of his trips to buy turf, Mr Rainsford noticed two stone axes, pieces of worked stone, hazelnut shells and fragments of burnt wood strewn over a field surface and compacted into turf sods. The material was thought to have originated from below the waterline of a drain separating the peat face from the spreading surface, so its original location was not readily visible.

When Mr Rainsford, who had actually studied archaeology in college, started to describe this over the phone it caused a wave of excitement to run through the office. His first communication conjured tantalising images of what might have been found and what might yet await detection. As for the date and scale of the discovery, this also triggered excited speculation. Known sites in the area offered parallels and suggested a very early date. In the late 1960s, drainage lowered the level of the River Inny and adjacent lakes, exposing late Mesolithic finds in counties Cavan, Longford and Westmeath. A number of stray finds were identified at Lough Sheelin, Lough Kinale, Derragh Lough, Lough Derravaragh and Lough Iron, while undisturbed deposits were excavated at Lough Derravaragh (Fig. 19). Mr Rainsford also reported that the quantity of stone in the harvested turf makes it difficult to burn and noted that burnt wood and

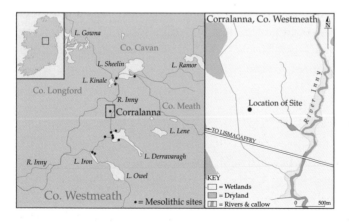

Fig. 19—Location of Corralanna in relation to known Mesolithic sites in the region and its immediate environment.

hazelnut shells had been recorded in the area for years. Taking everything together, we had ample reason to anticipate much from the site visit.

Before visiting the bog the IAWU, accompanied by Professor Gabriel Cooney and Aidan O'Sullivan of University College Dublin, travelled to Mr Rainsford's home to view the material he had collected. We weren't disappointed. Mr Rainsford led the way to his garage, where he produced a cardboard box containing a stone axe, 82 pieces of worked chert (a type of stone with properties similar to flint), fragments of charred wood, and four sods with chert and hazelnut shells compressed within them (Pl. 25). It was difficult to restrain enthusiasm or speed as we followed Mr Rainsford's car to the bog. On entering the field large quantities of disturbed material were immediately apparent. Worked chert, quartzite hammer-stones, miscellaneous stones, charred wood and hazelnut shells were everywhere to be seen (Pl. 26). A number of sods stacked along the field edge were also found to contain similar material. Even for experienced archaeologists there was still a definite thrill in seeing quality artefacts in such abundance. The conclusion that we were dealing with a site of considerable significance was now inescapable.

In reality, any surviving remains of the site could not be seen as the drain was filled with water, but this did not quash our enthusiasm. Unfortunately, we can only speculate as to the function of the site. The current evidence suggests that it was a late Mesolithic industrial site, specialising in the acquisition and working of chert, accommodating seasonal or perhaps long-term occupation. The local environment would have provided ample opportunities to gather food and raw materials and could have supported a range of activities. Given the quantity of artefacts in the area, it is highly likely that future investigations will identify traces of the original site. There is real potential for locating well-preserved organic remains, palaeoenvironmental evidence and possibly even habitations. The true significance of this discovery may be greater than is currently apparent. In the absence of archaeological surveys specifically designed to locate such sites we will continue to rely on an interested public to report these important, chance discoveries in the future.

Bowls, butter, and other finds

Aside from the discovery of hundreds of sites such as wooden trackways, the exceptional level of preservation in peatland areas means that many types of finds common to bogs are rare on dryland sites. Over the years the IAWU have discovered a large number of exciting finds and artefacts. Objects such as leather shoes, wooden vessels and bog butters have all lent an extraordinary dimension

Pl. 25—Material collected by Mr Rainsford (photo: Aidan O'Sullivan).

*Pl. 26—Approximate location of the Corralanna site. The photograph shows (from left)
Michael Stanley, Michael O'Neill, Professor Gabriel Cooney and Michael Rainsford
(photo: Aidan O'Sullivan).*

Pl. 27—Four leather shoes discovered in various bogs by the IAWU
(photo: David Jennings).

Pl. 28—The beautifully turned ash bowl discovered in Corhill Bog in 1996
(photo: David Jennings).

to the day-to-day work of archaeologists on the bog. Occasionally truly outstanding finds, like the hoard of silver coins discovered in 1996, have given all those involved the unique thrill of discovery.

Some of the most common finds in bogs are leather shoes, which generally date from the medieval period or later (Pl. 27). In Corhill Bog in 1996, amongst the disturbed remains of a small wooden track, a well-preserved leather shoe was found. Quite literally a case of someone losing their shoe in a puddle. The shoe was found close to the fragmentary remains of an exquisite turned and decorated wooden bowl made of ash (Pl. 28). In all, seven fragments of the bowl had been stacked on top of each other, presumably broken in antiquity and consequently thrown down during the building of the site.

While the IAWU have discovered a number of fine wooden vessels and bog butters in Bord na Móna bogs, similar finds have also been brought to our attention by both the staff of Bord na Móna and by private individuals. The practice of burying butter in bogs, apparently to preserve and protect it, has been carried out certainly since the Iron Age, with over 200 examples known from Ireland. In summer 2000 a beautiful example of bog butter in a wooden vessel was found by Bord na Móna employees, Eddie Dunne and Jim Kilmurray, in Clonad Bog, Co. Offaly (Pl. 29). The vessel, which was in superb condition, was carved from a single piece of wood with integral handles with rod-holes and a separate base and lid. It was cylindrical in shape and contained butter covered by an organic membrane, possibly the lining of a pig or sheep stomach. Comparisons with other vessels and bog butters suggest that this object was buried during the Iron Age, meaning that for the last 2000 years it had been secreted in Clonad Bog awaiting its chance discovery.

One of the most thrilling discoveries ever made by the IAWU was that of a collection of silver coins, found disturbed on a field surface in Corhill Bog, Co. Offaly, in 1996 (Pl. 30). On discovery fourteen coins were apparent, which alone were the cause of much excitement; however, further investigation with the aid of licensed metal-detectorist Mr Denis Lynch increased the total number of coins to twenty, making this one of our most unusual and exciting finds. Very few coin finds had previously been recorded in Irish bogs and this discovery added a new aspect to the history of the area. The coins date from the reign of Edward I (1279–1301), and while nineteen came from London, one was minted in County Waterford and can be dated to between 1281 and 1282 (Pl. 4). Interestingly the Annals of Clonmacnoise record a number of Anglo-Norman campaigns in the area during this time and, while we can only speculate, it is possible that these coins were lost during one of these conflicts.

Pl. 29—Bog butter in a wooden container. The butter was found in Clonad Bog, Co. Offaly, by Bord na Móna employees Eddie Dunne and Jimmy Kilmurray in 2000 (photo: IAWU).

Pl. 30—Fourteen of the twenty silver coins found in Corhill Bog in 1996, with inset showing the one minted in County Waterford. The coins date from the reign of Edward I (1279–1301) (photo: David Jennings).

The discovery of the Toar Iron Age vessel

In the summer of 2000 during field-walking of Toar Bog, Co. Westmeath, a spectacular discovery was made by Dr Gill Plunkett and John Powderly in one of the drain faces (Fig. 18; Pl. 31). Unlike most of the brushwood and roundwood sites we encountered in this bog, it first appeared as a large carved object with slightly concave surfaces dressed with fine toolmarks. The industrial cutting of the drain had damaged part of a squared projection on the outer surface. It was clear from their examination that more of this object extended back into the drain face. At first it was thought to be a small vessel of the kind that might have been found on any prehistoric dinner table, or at best a wooden cauldron. We had to be patient, however, until the field-walking was completed and a proper strategy was devised before we could begin work on the find.

Imagine our surprise when we finally came to excavate and realised that the vessel extended back over 1m from the drain edge and was over 60cm in depth! Once the top of the vessel was completely exposed it was seen to be even more spectacular than we had first thought (Pl. 32). It was rectilinear in shape with a curved base and sides, and at one of the ends there was a beautifully carved, perforated wooden block handle, extending below the rim. The piece we had first seen was all that remained of the handle and rim at the other end. In all our years spent working in Irish bogs, rarely had we seen anything as beautifully preserved as this. Almost the entire surface of the vessel was dressed with very fine toolmarks that would have cracked if allowed to dry out, and all of this fine detail would have been lost. The sun and the wind were equally dangerous. To help reduce the drying out we had to keep most of the wood under protective cover and only expose the area we were working on.

The vessel was made from a single piece of alder tree trunk that, at over 56 years of age, was an unusually mature specimen. Part of one side of the vessel had been displaced and had collapsed inwards. There was a thin, carved, wooden repair panel in place over a crack that had developed during the use of the vessel. With one on the outer surface and one on the inner surface, these repair panels were secured with slight wooden ties stitched through six perforations in the side of the vessel. Overlying the damaged side were the remains of a wonderfully preserved wooden withe (a piece of twisted hazel rope). There were three lengths of withe in all, one below the base of the vessel extending up the sides and one through the handle at either end. Although these withes appear very fragile, they would have been very strong and pliable when first made and would have been perfectly suited to moving the vessel. The vessel was secured in an upright position by three stakes placed along each of the intact sides, one of which was a trimmed forked branch. This originally hooked over the rim. Each of the stakes

Pl. 31—(above) The
wooden vessel as found in
the drain face, with a
proud John Powderly
watching over it (photo:
IAWU).

Pl. 32—(left) Fully
exposed, the top and
collapsed side of the Toar
Iron Age vessel with the
associated stakes and
withe (photo: IAWU).

was over 2m in length and a portion of one of these, sent for dating, returned an Iron Age date around 75 BC. The only materials found within the vessel were three small pieces of cut brushwood, additional fragments of withe and some very small stone chips and silt in the base.

It is the piecing together and recording of the vessel as it was found that helps us to determine more about how and why it was made and placed in the bog. After we removed it, we examined the body of the vessel and noticed that a second and earlier repair had been made during its construction. Close to the intact handle a very fine split had developed from the centre of the tree, and four very small wooden wedges were driven in across the split to prevent it developing further. Examination of the woodworking indicated that at least six tools were used, including five possible axes/adzes and at least one gouge.

The vessel may have been used for a variety of functions, which could have changed after it had been damaged. There was some scorching on the sides that occurred before it was deposited, as the withes around the vessel were unburned. Four similar vessels are known from Northern Ireland, all of which were recovered from peatland environments, and it is believed that these were small lake-navigable crafts, or slipes, used for transporting materials and towed behind larger boats. From the fine woodworking and its form it seems more likely that this was a large domestic vessel which may have been used for salting, curing, cooking, tanning or dyeing. Most of the Iron Age wooden vessels from Ireland are small, flat linear troughs, carved tubs or stave-built containers, making this vessel quite unique in an Iron Age context. As work on this find continues, more details are revealed and new questions are posed.

And finally…

Our awareness of past activity in the bogs of Ireland has been substantially increased through the systematic work of professional archaeologists and the chance finds made by Bord na Móna workers and members of the public. All have made significant contributions. The number and sheer scale of recent peatland discoveries have been both exhilarating and overwhelming. Much work lies ahead as archaeologists struggle to bring some understanding to these enigmatic landscapes before they disappear. Each new discovery, large or small, adds something to the picture. Inevitably, the discoverer's tale often goes untold. It can be all too easy to forget the human element unless given an opportunity such as this. The work of the IAWU is low-tech and labour-intensive. To detect bogland sites means operating at the same human scale as those responsible for constructing the sites and depositing the artefacts. As a result, the labour and skill of a large number of people are imperative. We dedicate this article to all those who have contributed to the IAWU's work over the last twelve years of discovery.

Further reading

Cooney, G. and Grogan, E. 1994 *Irish prehistory: a social perspective*. Bray.

Earwood, C. 1993 *Domestic wooden artefacts in Britain and Ireland from Neolithic to Viking times*. Exeter.

IAWU 1993 *Survey of the raised bogs of County Longford*. Transactions of the Irish Archaeological Wetland Unit 1. Dublin.

IAWU 1993 *Excavations at Clonfinlough, County Offaly*. Transactions of the Irish Archaeological Wetland Unit 2. Dublin.

IAWU 1995 *Blackwater survey and excavations; artefact deterioration in peatlands; Lough More, Co. Mayo*. Transactions of the Irish Archaeological Wetland Unit 4. Dublin.

Raftery, B. 1990 *Trackways through time: archaeological investigations on Irish bog roads, 1985–1989*. Rush.

Raftery, B. 1996 *Trackway excavations in the Mountdillon Bogs, Co Longford, 1985–1991*. Transactions of the Irish Archaeological Wetland Unit 3. Dublin.

12

Once upon a time in the west

Barry Raftery

For me archaeology was always simply a fact of life. My father, Joseph Raftery, was Keeper of Irish Antiquities and in my home archaeology was an all-pervading presence, in the many shelves bending with books on archaeological topics, in the frequent visiting archaeologists and, as I got older, in the field trips which I made with my father. There was never any attempt to influence me in my career choice but I cannot remember a time when I did not aim to be an archaeologist. It never occurred to me that there might *not* be a job available in archaeology (how different from today) and, as it happened, in 1970 I was offered jobs almost simultaneously in the National Museum and in UCD. With my father as Keeper in the Museum, there could only have been one choice: I went to UCD.

I have an older brother called Olaf, actually christened Eoin Olaf because of my father's admiration and respect for Eoin MacNeill. Olaf, though growing up in the same environment as myself, never felt the call of archaeology. He did take part in some of my father's earlier excavations but he chose to enter the real world and joined Lufthansa, the German airline.

Olaf has, however, one great archaeological achievement to his credit. This was on the occasion of Joe's excavations in 1943 at Cairn H, one of the Lough Crew passage tombs in County Meath. The tomb is 274m above sea-level and, as is well known, the climb to the summit is steep and tiring. The site office on the summit was a bell-tent, as was normal in those days, which, more often than not, had blown away when the excavators reached the summit in the morning. This danger, as well as the obvious lack of any security, made it clearly impossible to leave any cameras, surveying equipment, drawing-boards, plans, finds or anything of value overnight. Everything had to be brought down at night and brought up again in the morning. As my mother took part in the excavation, along with Olaf — a strapping lad a year or so in age — there was the extra burden of one infant to be carried daily to the summit.

Eamon de Valera, who was taoiseach at the time, had a deep and genuine interest in archaeology and had always been friendly with Joe. Thus on one occasion he came to visit the site (Pl. 33). He met the excavation party in the morning at the foot of the hill as they were about to commence the climb to the summit. Joe, burdened with cameras and other equipment, had the additional weight of Olaf in his arms. Dev, however, as an experienced family man, would have none of this and insisted on carrying the baby to the summit.

In those days things such as disposable, padded nappies had not been invented. Thus when the taoiseach reached the summit there was a large damp patch on his coat where he had been carrying the baby. Needless to say, Joe was aghast and utterly mortified. He tried to stammer some apologies, but Dev, not noted for his humour, turned to Joe with a twinkle in his eye, stating that Olaf had only done what his political opponents had been trying unsuccessfully to do for years! Thus did Olaf enter the political Hall of Fame!

Pl. 33—Lough Crew, Co. Meath, 1943, Cairn H.
'Long fellow, short fellow'—left to right: Joe Raftery, Eamon de Valera, Olaf Raftery,
Lotte Raftery. Olaf is standing on one of the kerbstones. The excavation is in progress in
the background.

My own early archaeological experience was not in any way as distinguished as that of my elder brother! But it was my time spent at Lough Gara in County Sligo, about ten years after the fateful event at Lough Crew, which stands out most vividly in my early memory as an incipient archaeologist.

The deepening of the Boyle River in County Sligo, and the subsequent drop in the level of Lough Gara in 1952/3, virtually overnight revealed hundreds of crannogs, which appeared as circular rings of posts, or as mounds of stones of varying sizes, on the newly exposed lake mud (Pl. 34). In addition, on the freshly revealed muddy foreshore it was possible to pick up a quantity and variety of artefacts of almost all periods which was nothing short of astonishing.

These dramatic finds obviously led to considerable media interest. The newspapers of the day gave extensive coverage to the discoveries and I remember being with Joe — I cannot recall why — when he was interviewed in the Russell Hotel (long since demolished) at the corner of St Stephen's Green by the then internationally prestigious American magazine *Life*. Inevitably, of course, the National Museum became involved. Extensive survey of the new discoveries and the excavation of two sites took place in the three years between 1953 and 1955.

As a young schoolboy I spent two full summers at Lough Gara. Even then (in 1953 I was nine) I had, as noted above, firmly settled on a career in archaeology, and I took a deep interest in all that was happening on the lake in those exciting years. I remember on numerous occasions walking along the foreshore with Joe as he pointed out to me the newly emerged crannogs. I have a clear memory of seeing, on several occasions, zigzag causeways of spaced stepping-stones leading to a crannog from what must have been the original foreshore.

Strolling around the edge of the lake it became routine (today I am tempted to use the word surreal) to pick up items of all kinds, and of virtually all dates (of course I had little knowledge of the latter in those days). As I recall, out of the mud we picked up flints, tools and weapons of bronze and iron, a variety of dress-fasteners, quernstones and numerous other artefacts. A large number of log-boats also appeared, simply resting on the newly exposed mud where they had presumably foundered, or been abandoned, a millennium or more before (Pl. 35). There were so many finds that mapping their distribution became a major problem, apart from those that could be associated specifically with a numbered crannog.

On a sadder note was the appearance at the site most mornings for several successive days of a young boy, perhaps twelve years of age. Each day he had a galvanised bucket filled to the brim with artefacts — mainly, as I recall, Bann flakes and other chert objects, but also some bronzes. The finds were the excuse to meet my father and the presentation of the bucket of material invariably led to the poor boy pleading for a job, as his widowed mother had a large family and

Pl. 34—Lough Gara, Co. Sligo, 1954. Typical crannog as first revealed (Ardsoreen townland).

Pl. 35—(left) Lough Gara, 1954. Newly revealed logboat with the author in the foreground, Olaf behind.

little means of support. I think my father arranged for a small honorarium to be paid to the boy for the finds but unfortunately, within the system as it then was (the boy was not registered at the local labour exchange), despite his best efforts at official level, Joe was unable to take the lad on in any capacity, and this led to bitter tears on every occasion. I remember how upset Joe was at the poor boy's plight. Now looking back it is evident that this distressing occurrence was one symptom of the severe rural poverty (and urban too) that prevailed in many parts of Ireland in the 1950s.

Joe was supplied by the army with a Bedford jeep, which proved extremely suitable for transporting finds, samples and of course people. We also had a rowing-boat of aluminium in which Joe and I used to row around the lake looking at the various crannogs. I remember him pointing out to me wooden piles underwater that were projecting from the bed of the lake, and I have a very vivid memory of landing on a small crannog in the townland of Killnagranshy (for some reason I always remembered that name) where a circular mound of flakes and broken fragments of chert could be clearly seen. I cannot recall what his comments were on the site (though I think he spoke of a manufacturing centre) or whether he hazarded a guess as to its dating. I think he spoke of a possible Mesolithic date and, more recently, G.F. Mitchell did indeed propose a late Mesolithic date for the crannog.

A full survey of the newly discovered crannogs was carried out by, among others, the late Paddy Healy and somebody called, I think, Jack White. To walk on the treacherous mud the surveyors created things that they called 'skootches'. These were, as I recall, objects resembling tennis-rackets, which were attached to the boots and which effectively supported the weight of a man on the extraordinarily treacherous mud. The splendid distribution map of the Lough Gara crannogs which they produced is eloquent testimony to their surveying skills, and indeed their dedication, for my memory is of continuous rain and mud with the consistency of clinging glue.

Joe selected two sites for excavation, Crannog 124 in Tivannagh townland and Crannog 61, one of the largest of all the crannogs, in Rathtinaun on the Sligo side of the lake. I did not help at Tivannagh. It was at Rathtinaun that I cut my archaeological teeth.

In the first year my parents, Olaf and I lived in a prefabricated wooden hut erected for us close to the lakeshore. I think we were reasonably comfortable and I remember we were presented with fresh milk (I was told it was unpasteurised but had no idea what this meant), eggs, fish and eels by the generous local people. As regards the last I still have a vivid memory of my mother receiving a brown package tied with binder twine from one of our workmen (a fisherman) called Paddy Hayden. When opened, the package disgorged a writhing mass of

Pl. 36—Lough Gara, Co. Sligo, 1954. The author engaged in planning at Rathtinaun, Crannog 61.

Pl. 37—Two stick-in-the-muds? The young Etienne Rynne (right) with unidentified companion in 1954 experiencing the problems of the newly revealed mud at Lough Gara, Co. Sligo.

fresh eel, which instantly wriggled in all directions across the table and onto the floor. I seem to remember that dispatching the creatures for the pan presented considerable problems for my poor mother, and I have to confess that this has given me a lifelong aversion to the consumption of eel. The hut may not have been deemed a success, however, as in the second year at Gara we stayed at the Royal Hotel in Boyle.

From the very beginning I was completely immersed in the work. I recall many happy days cleaning brushwood. Who would have thought that more than thirty years later, as a seasoned archaeologist, I would be doing the same thing on trackways in the middle of a County Longford bog!

I remember, when the time came, that I was taught to plan using a plane-table (Pl. 36). Today this would be seen as a primitive method of planning which is virtually obsolete. In those days, however, the sophisticated surveying instruments of today were unknown and, in fact, on a small scale such as at Gara, this was a highly accurate method of planning. Personally I planned hundreds of posts and other features. Many years later Joe admitted to me that he had (unknown to me) checked my plots — but, thankfully, had found them to be in order!

In those days excavation was funded through the State Relief of Unemployment scheme (which was to continue for many years after Gara). This meant, in effect, that the funding was made available primarily to employ local labourers. The bulk of the work was thus carried out by an unskilled workforce. I remember many of the men, and some, indeed, became expert diggers under my father's instruction and vigilant supervision. He always carried a pearl-handled dagger at his waist and when anything puzzling appeared during digging he would leap into the cutting and investigate with this lethal weapon! I still possess this implement as a souvenir of happy days.

But I remember these as fine men who were initially puzzled by the nature of the work but who soon became extremely interested. These were poor men, in financial terms, but they were friendly, honest and hard-working and were especially kind to me, the funny little boy with shorts who spent his day scratching in the mud rather than playing cowboys or doing what little boys are supposed to do! As the site was prolific in finds, every day brought a new excitement in which we all shared.

There were no professional assistants in those days (how different today) but many volunteers worked with us. I remember some of the names. The distinguished Professor of Irish at Trinity, David Green, spent time at Gara and I recall him, a man of ample proportions, swimming naked in the muddy waters of the lake. This was not a pretty sight! Harold Leask, author of the seminal three-volume work on early Irish architecture, also spent time at Gara. My memory of him is as a meticulous draughtsman, and I can still see him engaged laboriously in the scale-drawing of a large wooden ox-yoke which seemed to take forever to complete! Percy Le Clerc, an architect with the then Office of Public Works, was with us too, and he drew many of the sections through the crannog. He devised a method using white tapes strung along the section faces to differentiate between the various layers. I have a feeling my father was not too impressed with this technique. A scruffy, bearded Englishman also helped at Gara, one David Trump. He was a penniless student at the time and he lived in the site office. He is today one of the leading specialists in Maltese archaeology.

There were many visitors, colleagues of my father. I can recall only a few, including Máire and Liam de Paor, Seán P. Ó Ríordáin and, of course, Frank Mitchell. A young, very junior assistant in the National Museum named Etienne Rynne visited the site (Pl. 37). Nattily dressed in jacket and tie, and wearing gumboots, he braved the mud of the lake with commendable fortitude. Joe always felt that this young chap had a bright future in archaeology — how right he was! The distinguished German scholar Gerhard Bersu also visited, as did Gordon Childe. As an aside I might mention that, when Childe visited my parents at home, some time before this when I was a small child, I am told that I actually sat on the great man's knee. I have no memory of this but I must be the only living archaeologist who can claim such distinction!

A young lady, Anne Stafford King-Harmon, worked with us as a volunteer. She was the daughter of Sir Cecil, who lived in Rockingham, the local Big House (since burned down). She was a quiet, gentle girl as I recall, of no small artistic talent. She did a number of watercolour paintings of the crannogs on the lake, including several views of how they might have looked in early times. I wonder what became of these paintings? Even then I could see that her health was delicate, and subsequently, alas, she succumbed to TB.

On one occasion Joe and I were invited to dinner at the Big House. A uniformed butler greeted us at the door and at dinner we were served by a suitably obsequious maid in a short black dress, with white cap and a white apron, who frequently curtsied at the appropriate moments. I have no memory of what we ate but I do recall my puzzlement as to the purpose of a small bowl of water at each place! Here indeed were relics of auld dacency!

I also remember an elderly lady visiting on more than one occasion with an equally elderly female companion. She often brought chert flakes and other items which she had picked up on the lakeshore. She carried a stout walking-stick and took an almost vicious pleasure in decapitating thistles, which she did regularly, followed by a cry of victory! She often stayed for a cup of tea.

The lady, I was later told, was Miss Gwendoline Clare Stacpoole, a niece of the great Thomas Johnson Westropp. Her friend, who was her constant companion for many years, was Miss Primrose Neville. Miss Stacpoole, who was a dedicated antiquary all her life, died in 1966 at the age of 80.

I have little memory of the finer archaeological details of the excavation. I remember the extensive brushwood, the numerous, beautifully preserved wooden posts and the many finds, particularly the wooden objects, mainly potstaves, which caused such problems of conservation. One find stands out — a small, beautifully carved wooden animal's head with transverse perforation which my father viewed as part of the handle mechanism of a tankard of some sort. Looking at this splendid object today I am convinced that this is the carving of an otter's head, entirely appropriate in such a lacustrine environment.

I was at all times conscious of the sheer volume of finds recovered every day. Miss Eileen Johnson of the National Museum was present and she carried out the drawing of the artefacts. There were, however, far too many for her to complete on site but I have a very clear recollection of the exquisite quality of her work. Present also was Paddy Morrissy, a technical assistant in the Museum, with whom I was very friendly. In those days there were chocolate bars called 'Big Five' bars, more or less the equivalent of today's Mars Bars. Paddy used to get me one on most days and for some reason, I'm not too sure why (was there a parental veto?), this was always a secretive and conspiratorial process.

While work at Gara progressed, the very fine portal tomb at Drumanone, several kilometres distant from the site in County Roscommon, was being excavated by a jolly English lady, Mrs Celia Topp. She later published an important nineteenth-century find of gold artefacts from Newgrange. I have no idea how, or why, she came to be digging at Drumanone. At any rate, I occasionally accompanied Joe on his frequent visits of inspection, though I have to admit that apart from the impressive architecture of the tomb, and, of course, its prodigious dimensions, I found the work at Gara far more exciting. However, I recall, on one such occasion, how excited Mrs Topp was when she produced a large, white, beautifully made Bann flake, I think the only find from the excavation.

I have no memory of any precautions being taken to ensure the safety of those digging underneath the huge capstone. There were no timber supports to prevent the capstone from collapse and nobody wore helmets. In those days the health and safety procedures were somewhat less stringent than those of today! How things have changed, indeed changed for the better. At any rate, I think Joe became increasingly nervous at the prospect of digging under a stone many tonnes in weight for he very soon called a halt to the excavation, which, I seem to recall, was never fully completed.

One of the most exciting days for me at Gara was the discovery of the well-known hoard of personal ornaments of the later Bronze Age (Pl. 38). As well as a pin and tweezers of bronze, rings of bronze and tin and a series of boars' tusks, the find contained three penannular rings of decorated gold foil wrapped around cores, which are probably of lead. The hoard had been buried in a wooden box and the site had been clearly marked by the owner with upright wooden pegs. I remember that there was much speculation as to whether this was a votive deposit or whether it had been buried for safe-keeping in advance of the rapidly rising lake waters.

I remember clearly that it was late in the season, late August, I think, and had been pouring for days. The excavation had reached the basal layers of the crannog and a mechanical pump was in continuous use in an attempt to enable the diggers to operate. One of the best of the workmen (I clearly remember that he was called Tom Doherty) suddenly called Joe, and there was the hoard *in situ* in the sticky mud. In the subsequent recording and excavation I was only a spectator, but I can still feel the palpable sense of excitement that I then experienced.

I remember crying bitterly when I had to leave Gara for school in the autumn of that year with the dig still in progress. I pleaded to stay on but to no avail! After Gara, however, there was not the slightest possibility that I could ever pursue any career path other than archaeology.

Pl. 38—The Rathtinaun hoard as first revealed in the mud. Note the way the rings are stacked, and the boars' tusks encircling them. The three gold-plated lead rings are visible in the upper left, immediately above the larger bracelet.

Further reading

For the Rathtinaun hoard, see G. Eogan, *Hoards of the Irish Later Bronze Age* (Dublin, 1983), 151–2, fig. 132. The hoard, drawn *in situ*, is illustrated in B. Raftery, *Pagan Celtic Ireland* (London, 1994), 34, fig. 19.

For the Newgrange hoard, see C. Topp, 'The gold ornaments reputedly found near the entrance to Newgrange in 1842', *University of London Institute of Archaeology, Twelfth Annual Report* (1956), 53–62.

For Drumanone, see C. Topp, 'The portal dolmen of Drumanone, Co. Roscommon', *Bulletin of the University of London Institute of Archaeology* **3** (1962), 38–46.

Publication of the excavations at Lough Crew and Rathtinaun is pending. A description and overview of the Lough Crew tombs can be found in M. Herity, *Irish passage graves* (Dublin, 1974), 41–55.

Good general outlines of the relevant phases of Irish prehistory can be found in J. Waddell, *The prehistoric archaeology of Ireland* (Galway, 1998), and in G.F. Mitchell and M. Ryan, *Reading the Irish landscape* (Dublin,1997).

13

Old letters and new technology — the Ballyrashane gold hoard

Richard Warner

In 1999 I was invited to inspect two gold ornaments in private possession in England. They were found, the owner told me, over a century ago in Northern Ireland and had since been in the possession of his family. My first opinion, following the telephone description, that they were ornaments of the kind known as ribbon torcs was confirmed when I saw them in an office in central London. Although, in their battered cardboard box, under the office lights, they looked decidedly uninspiring, they were nevertheless of particular interest as they belonged to a very rare class of ribbon torc of which type the Ulster Museum had no example. I shall explain this statement by digressing briefly from the story of these particular torcs.

A digression on Irish gold ornaments

Ireland has produced an enormous wealth of prehistoric gold objects dating from various times between the early Bronze Age and the Iron Age (between about 2300 BC and the fifth century AD). The majority of these gold objects seem to be personal ornaments, although it has to be said that their mode of use is often very unclear, and a matter of some contention. For example, one type of object is like a circular 'pill-box' and has accordingly been given the archaeological name of 'box' — archaeologists being very literal people. Recently Mary Cahill suggested that these boxes were actually ear-ornaments — worn as inserts in prehistoric ear-lobes. In some cases tiny balls of gold inside them made them rattle as they moved — the Bronze Age hippies who wore them had musical ear-lobes.

Most of the Irish gold ornaments can be assigned fairly confidently to one of

151

the well-dated phases of Irish prehistory. There was a strong use of gold ornaments during the early Bronze Age, around 2000 BC, and a revival in gold use (with quite different ornaments) in the middle Bronze Age, around 1500 BC. In the late Bronze Age, around 1000 BC, there was an extraordinary obsession with gold in Ireland — hundreds of ornaments of this date have been found. Then in the Iron Age, around the time of Christ, new gold ornaments briefly appeared. While my description of all these objects as 'Irish' correctly implies that they were almost all *Irish-made*, it does not follow that they were made of Irish gold, for, despite intensive research, we still have no firm idea as to where the source of the gold lay — whether it was native or imported.

I have said, above, that most of the ornament types can be assigned to a dated cultural phase. One class — the ribbon torc (Fig. 20) — is rather more difficult than the rest to pin down, and I shall explain why this is so. Though quite distinctive, a ribbon torc is a rather unsophisticated type of ornament, being a thin ribbon of gold, twisted about its axis and turned into an open circle. At the ends a pair of hooks, which lock simply together, allow it to be fixed rigidly into its circular shape to be worn, presumably, on the neck or wrist. Although the vast majority of gold ribbon torcs from the British Isles have been found in Ireland, especially in the northern part, they are known also from Scotland and Wales. The problem is that few have been found with other objects, and those that have tell conflicting stories. One was found with a larger and more complex flange-twist torc at Coolmanagh, Co. Wicklow. The larger Coolmanagh ornament is certainly of middle Bronze Age date and this association appears to provide good

Fig. 20—Class 1 torc from Coolmanagh (left, diameter 25cm, drawing courtesy of the National Museum of Ireland and G. Eogan) and class 2 ribbon torc from Inishowen (right, diameter 8cm, drawing D. Crone) (not to scale).

evidence for the date of ribbon torcs — a date favoured by the majority of archaeologists. On the other hand, a ribbon torc was found with an Iron Age gold collar at Knock, Co. Roscommon, and another, curled up in a bronze box, formed part of a hoard of Iron Age objects found at Somerset, Co. Galway. These examples, contradicting the first, appear to place ribbon torcs firmly in the Iron Age. There are about 1500 years between these two periods, and this time includes the phase during which most Irish gold hoards were deposited (many in bogs and lakes). In not one of these hoards is there a ribbon torc.

The most recent archaeologist to write in detail about Irish ribbon torcs, George Eogan, has noted this chronological ambiguity and suggested, pragmatically, that ribbon torcs were developed twice in Ireland, independently. It must be said that this hypothesis has found little favour amongst archaeologists (not a notably pragmatic race). Even though they are relatively simple objects, Irish ribbon torcs come in two different forms. Most are fairly tightly twisted,

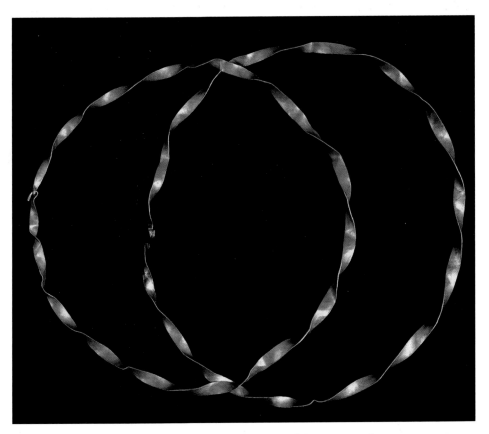

*Pl. 39—The two Ballyrashane torcs. Each is 20cm in diameter
(copyright: Trustees of the Museums and Galleries of Northern Ireland).*

often tapering from the middle towards each end, and having knobs on the turned-back terminals. The two referred to above with certain Iron Age associations belong to this class, which I shall call class 2. A few ribbon torcs, on the other hand, are loosely twisted, of unchanging width, and have simple hooks without knobs on. To this class (which I shall call class 1) belongs the middle Bronze Age torc from Coolmanagh. It is, therefore, possible to put forward a variation of Eogan's dual-tradition hypothesis — that the ribbon torcs in each tradition were subtly different, especially in the form of their terminals. Unfortunately archaeologists need better evidence than I have thus far adduced if they are to accept what still appears to be an unlikely hypothesis. Fortunately science comes to the rescue. First, however, I will return to the pair of torcs in the London office.

Some old letters

The 'London' torcs were of the rarer, knobless, form (class 1) that I have suggested is the middle Bronze Age type, which was why they particularly excited me. They are each 20cm in diameter and the ribbon is about 0.75cm wide. One is complete, but a terminal is missing from the other. The owner of the torcs was not familiar with the geography of Northern Ireland and was quite amazed, when he told me the name of the find-spot as it had survived in family tradition, that I had actually heard of the place. It was near the small village of Ballyrashane, which, although it lies east of the River Bann near Coleraine, is in County Derry. The owner told me that, again according to the family tradition, three torcs had been found in a bog in 1884 and one had been sold to a tinker (interestingly the only ribbon torcs from Wales, three in number, were of the same type and were also found together in a bog). The owner of the 'London' torcs was unable, at the time, to give me any further information, and left me with the task of attempting to unravel the history of these torcs, which were apparently unknown to the archaeological world.

The National Museum in Dublin has a useful 'historical file' in which correspondence on items reported to, but not necessarily acquired by, the Museum is preserved and this was my obvious first port of call. Mary Cahill, curator of the gold collections in that museum (and the proposer of the 'ear-lobe' hypothesis), searched the files on my behalf and sent me transcripts of a number of letters referring to ribbon torcs that had since disappeared. Two of these letters seemed promising.

Fig. 21—The complete Ballyrashane torc (diameter 20cm, drawing D. Crone).

Fig. 22—The Ballywindelland torc (diameter 20cm, taken from Armstrong).

Robertson, Leslie, Ferguson & Co. Ltd.
The Bank Buildings, Belfast
22 October 1915

Dear Mr Armstrong,

I wrote the man who has the Gold Torc. as well as I recollect it is a Ribbon
of bright yellow gold about ½ an inch broad twisted spiral and would go
round the waist of a young woman with hooks at each end and as well as
I mind one of the hooks was missing — I wrote him I could probably get
him double the weight of it in sovereigns and he replied that the person
who had it was not in need of money that they would not part with it for
that. He is a Presbyterian Minister & he wishes it to be understood that it
is another person has it. He would want more for it. If I could get him to
meet me with it in Coleraine I might be able to buy it from him for
perhaps 2 ½ its weight in gold. I would have to go & see & would like you
to give me an idea of the uttermost you would give — he is a very wary
sort of man as he says it belongs to a neighbour who is well off & who likes
it & is not caring to sell it.

from [?] Milligan

The recipient of the letter was E.C.R. Armstrong, curator of the National
Museum and author of a superb catalogue of the gold in the Museum's
collection. Armstrong's reply is not preserved (so we do not know how he reacted
to the fascinating idea of a 'young woman with hooks at each end'), but there is
no evidence that the Museum acquired this torc. The next letter of interest, again
to Armstrong, is from the historian Henry Morris, then living in Derry.

Melrose Villa
Springtown, Londonderry
17.6.1920

R. C. Armstrong Esq.
Curator National Museum
Dublin

Dear Sir,
Excuse pencil. I had in my hands about half an hour ago two twisted gold
torques. Three of them were found together in a bog: the third is lost and

cannot be traced. They are like the torques you got at Horn Head but not so twisted. The gold is very soft: they are about 24 or 27 inches long each. Owner unwilling to part with them, but a good figure might tempt him. He appears to be a rather rabid Unionist; questioned me closely was I a Roman Catholic from all which I think he would hardly let them go to Dublin — bad repute in north. I proposed to buy them for Derry museum but I really mean them for Dublin. What should I offer for them. Could you come to Coleraine on Saty 26th June and I'd go with you to the place, but we'd both have to say we were buying for Derry or you might represent Belfast. Please reply as early as possible.

Yours ffully

H Morris.

Finally, the National Museum's Antiquities Committee Minute Book of November 1920 quotes the following missive from Morris:

Two gold torques found circa 10 years ago in a bog near Coleraine are still in the possession of the finder William James Sterling of Knockeera.

We cannot assume that the Milligan and Morris letters refer to the same discovery, but let us hold this as a working hypothesis and see where it gets us. We may summarise as follows.

From the Morris letters we learn that three gold ribbon torcs were found in about 1910, in a bog, presumably near Coleraine; that two were, in 1920, in the possession of William James Sterling of 'Knockeera'; that the third was lost. The Milligan letter tells us that one, let us suppose either the 'lost' one or one of the Sterling pair, was in the possession of (though not owned by) a Presbyterian minister in 1915.

Morris's 'Knockeera' is the townland of Knocknakeeragh (or Knockinkerragh) on the edge of Ballyrashane village and within Ballyrashane parish. It was from Ballyrashane, it will be recalled, that the pair of torcs I saw in London reportedly came. The descriptions of the torcs in the letters exactly match the 'London' torcs, and the Morris reference to the 'three found, one lost' is strikingly like the tradition I heard in London. We can hardly doubt that our 'London' torcs are those seen by Morris. I have discovered that William Sterling (or Stirling) lived at Knocknakeeragh. He was a Presbyterian tenant farmer (whose family had once been prominent local landowners), and treasurer of the

Ballyrashane congregation until 1916. He was, of course, Morris's 'rather rabid Unionist', and he died in 1921. The minister of Ballyrashane was the Reverend Charles Hunter, whom I take to be the subject of Milligan's letter. After I came up with these names it was confirmed by the London owner that it was from one of these people that the two torcs passed into his family — I am not at liberty to give further details. We may be quite sure, therefore, that both letters refer to the same find and that the 'London' torcs are those seen by Morris.

There are, of course, apparent contradictions for which I have, as yet, no answer. For instance the dates '1884' and 'about 1910' are difficult to reconcile. Again, was the torc that was in Hunter's possession in 1915 one of Sterling's pair

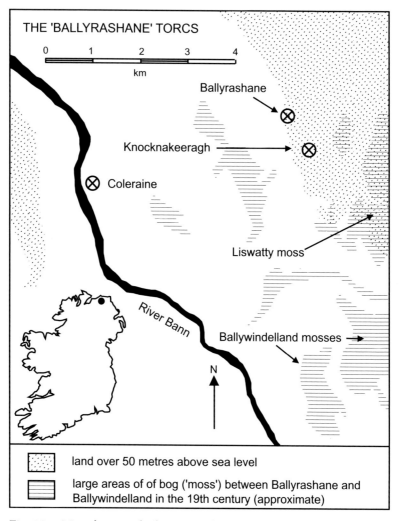

THE 'BALLYRASHANE' TORCS

Ballyrashane

Knocknakeeragh

⊗ Coleraine

Liswatty moss

River Bann

Ballywindelland mosses →

N

land over 50 metres above sea level

large areas of of bog ('moss') between Ballyrashane and Ballywindelland in the 19th century (approximate)

Fig. 23—Map showing the locations of Ballyrashane, Co. Derry, and Ballywindelland, Co. Antrim.

or the missing one? I will explore these questions when I discuss the find in more detail in the future. There is, however, a high possibility that the missing torc can be identified. In the National Museum in Dublin there is a ribbon torc whose similarity to the 'London' pair (we may now call them the Ballyrashane torcs) is striking. Indeed, when the Ulster Museum finally obtained the pair I was able to place them alongside the Dublin torc and was impressed by the fact that they were identical in every respect. The Dublin torc has a diameter of 20cm, as do the Ballyrashane torcs, and a weight of 28g, which compares closely with our weights of 29g and 30g. According to the National Museum register their torc was:

> Purchased 1919 by RIA from Mr Stringer of Belfast, who purchased it in 1908 from G Cochrane of Ballymoney, who purchased it from Robert Adams whose servant man found it in Ballywindland Bog, probably before 1903.

Ballywindelland, Co. Antrim, is a mere 5km south of Ballyrashane (Fig 23). The closeness of date of discovery, the closeness of place of discovery and the identity of form all give weight to the idea that this is the missing torc (Figs 21 and 22). Furthermore, I have been able to discover two persons called Robert Adams who were alive at the right time and had Ballyrashane connections (the wife of each was a native of Ballyrashane). One was a draper in Portrush. The other lived at the Loughan — a settlement on the eastern bank of the River Bann, lying almost midway between Ballyrashane and Ballywindelland. But can we reconcile the conflicting details of the reports of the two discoveries? Three torcs were found by a tenant farmer, Sterling, presumably on one of the bogs in the Ballyrashane area on which he had right of turbary. One torc was reportedly found by the servant of Adams 5km to the south. I have to admit that while there are obviously many possible scenarios that might solve the puzzle none is better than the others and none, therefore, recommends itself as especially likely. It is, however, my opinion (I can put it no more strongly) that the 'Ballywindelland' torc is the missing 'Ballyrashane' torc, and this opinion is strengthened by the evidence of modern science, as we shall see.

Science to the rescue

In all Irish prehistoric gold ornaments the gold content is between about 75% and 95%. The next most abundant metal in the objects is silver, which varies between about 5% and 25%. After that comes copper, from about 0.1% to

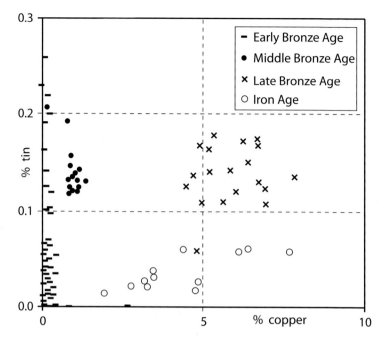

Fig. 24—*Values of tin and copper, as measured by Hartmann, for the key Irish gold objects belonging to the four prehistoric metal-using phases.*

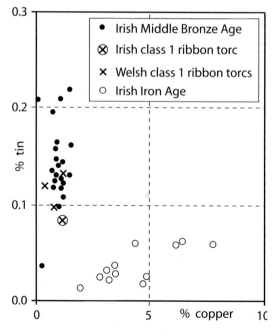

Fig. 25—*Hartmann's measurements for tin and copper in the class 1 ribbon torcs, plotted alongside Irish middle Bronze Age and Iron Age objects.*

about 10%, followed by tin at less than 1%. Thirty years ago a German analytical chemist, Axel Hartmann, analysed thousands of European prehistoric gold objects, including most of the Irish ornaments then in public collections, for these four elements plus elements that were present in even lower concentrations. The results were extremely interesting, for they showed that the proportions of these elements varied chronologically. In other words, it was possible to distinguish the objects from each of the main Irish cultural phases on the basis of the amounts of copper, tin and (to a lesser extent) silver in them. In Fig. 24 I show Hartmann's values of tin and copper for the main objects of early, middle and late Bronze Age date, and of the Iron Age. The distinctions are very clear, and the Iron Age objects are further distinguished from those of the Bronze Age by their much higher level of silver (about 15% for the former compared with up to 30% for the latter). Furthermore, in common with Iron Age objects on the Continent, many of the Irish objects of that date contained detectable traces of platinum, never found in Irish Bronze Age objects.

In Fig. 25 I have plotted the class 1 ribbon torcs (including that from Ballywindelland), whose form, I have suggested, puts them into the middle Bronze Age. On the same figure I show Irish objects of certain middle Bronze Age and Iron Age date. The position of the torcs on this chart confirms the suggested middle Bronze Age date (look also at Fig. 27). Similarly in Fig. 26 I show the class 2 ribbon torcs (those with knobbed terminals), and it will be noted that these are analytically indistinguishable from the Irish Iron Age objects (the torcs also contain high levels of silver and traces of platinum). These charts clearly confirm the two distinct classes and their quite different dates. While there is no reason to doubt the reliability of the tin and copper measurements made by Hartmann, the rather different methodology used by him to assay the silver level has caused several scientists to doubt the reliability of the silver values given by him. This is of particular concern because geologists who have been working with archaeologists in an attempt to locate the sources of the gold used by prehistoric Irish goldsmiths believe that reliable measurements of the levels of silver are crucial to this study. Accordingly Ms Cahill, Ms Harnett and I have been re-analysing as many as possible of the ornaments analysed by Hartmann, and many that were not (including the Ballyrashane and Coolmanagh torcs), on a state-of-the-art spectrometer in the National Museum in Dublin. For practical reasons we have confined our measurements to silver and copper, confirming the reliability of Hartmann's copper measurements but also confirming the doubts regarding his silver values. The new values determined by us show that the amount of silver also varied with the date of the object. This work confirmed the middle Bronze Age date of the class 1 torcs and the Iron Age date of the class 2 torcs (Fig. 27). Additionally it showed, as seen in Fig. 28, that the Ballywindelland and

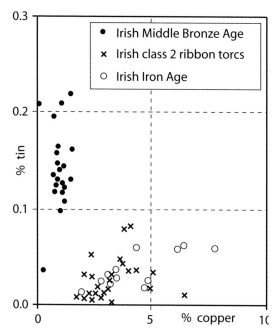

Fig. 26—Hartmann's measurements for tin and copper in the class 2 ribbon torcs, plotted alongside Irish middle Bronze Age and Iron Age objects.

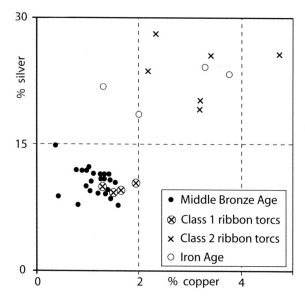

Fig. 27—Recent results for silver and copper values for ribbon torcs of classes 1 and 2, plotted alongside middle Bronze Age and Iron Age objects.

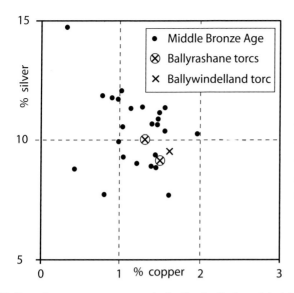

Fig. 28—Detail from Fig. 27 showing the Ballyrashane and Ballywindelland torcs plotted alongside middle Bronze Age objects.

Ballyrashane torcs are analytically indistinguishable — indeed, were probably made from the same gold stock at the same time.

There are three lessons to be learned from the 'case of the Ballyrashane torcs' and the work described above. The first is that carefully preserved records can bring unexpectedly helpful information to the archaeologist many years later, and the simple tasks of preserving and searching old files should be a primary tool in archaeological research. The second lesson is that, despite the confidence of many archaeological writers, orthodoxies can be quite wrong and there is still much to learn about the past. The third is that archaeology is not all about excavation and classification — modern technology offers tools for research that can, and will, revolutionise the way archaeologists study the past.

Acknowledgements

I am grateful to Mary Cahill, Lucia Harnett and Anthony Read of the National Museum for their help in this study and for access to their analytical facilities, and to the National Museum generally for allowing me to publish the Milligan and Morris letters. I am also grateful to the local historian the Reverend T. H. Mullin (a successor of Charles Hunter as rector of Ballyrashane), who has supplied me with detailed information on the local personalities involved in the case. The Trustees of the Museums and Galleries of Northern Ireland are grateful to the National Heritage Lottery Fund, the National Arts Collection Fund and the Esme Mitchell Fund for their generous financial support towards the acquisition of the two Ballyrashane torcs by the Ulster Museum. The

Ballyrashane torcs are registered as A25814 and A25815 (Ulster Museum) and the Ballywindelland torc is RIA:1919:10 (National Museum of Ireland).

Further reading

Armstrong, E.C.R. 1933 *Catalogue of Irish gold ornaments in the collections of the Royal Irish Academy*. Dublin.

Cahill, M. 2001 Unspooling the mystery. *Archaeology Ireland* **15** (3), 9–15.

Eogan, G. 1983 Ribbon torcs in Britain and Ireland. In A. O'Connor and D.V. Clarke (eds), *From the Stone Age to the 'Forty-five*, 87–126. Edinburgh.

Eogan, G. 1994 *The accomplished art*. Oxford.

Taylor, J. 1980 *Bronze Age goldwork of the British Isles*. Cambridge.

Warner, R. 1993 Irish prehistoric goldwork: a provisional analysis. *Archaeomaterials* 7, 101–13.

14

On the trail of an ancient highway: rediscovering Dála's Road

Elizabeth FitzPatrick

The early medieval literature of Ireland is rich in place-names evocative of the natural and man-made landscapes of the country. Many of these place-names still survive in one form or another and offer the archaeologist and historian alike clues to understanding and reconstructing the appearance of the more ancient geography of Ireland, with its medieval settlements, boundaries and roads.

Irish place-names preserve a variety of words for roads of different construction, quality and status. Among these are *bóthar*, a cattle track, *bealach*, a passage, gap or road, and *tóchar*, meaning a causeway or path which, as archaeological excavations have shown, was more often a timber construction. Footpaths are denoted by the words *casán* and *ceis*, which specifically refers to a path made of wattles. The term *slighe* is given to a high road, an important and perhaps more travelled national route.

The most visible expression of the modernisation of Ireland is the ongoing improvement of old roads and the construction of new ones, a process which, like most changes, has both positive benefits and negative consequences. Tracks, paths and roads are the result of the enduring human need for forward movement and greater mobility and the desire to reach distant places in the quickest time and with the most ease. The five great roads that radiated out from Tara in ancient Midhe (Meath), reaching deep into the Irish countryside, were to early travellers what the N1, N4, N6 or N7 represent for the modern commuter. The Slighe Mór followed the route of the gravel ridge known as the Eiscir Riada between Dublin and Clarinbridge, Co. Galway, and the Slighe Dhála was the road from west Munster to Tara and formed part of the boundary of north Munster. Slighe Assail connected ancient Midhe with Connacht, Slighe Mhidhluachra linked Tara to Emain Macha in Armagh, and Slighe Chualann led from Tara to the south-east. The tradition that the five great roads of Ireland ultimately led to and from the symbolic capital of Tara finds its modern counterpart in the confluence of our superhighways at the capital of Dublin.

How did the five great roads from Tara originate? Did they emerge as the result of the growing together of minor routeways in the many early Irish kingdoms through which they passed, or were they conceptualised and created under the authority of different kings at different times? Like so many of the more conspicuous early monuments on the Irish landscape, the five roads are attributed with supernatural origins. The story goes that various legendary heroes discovered the roads as they travelled to Tara to celebrate the birth of King Conn Céadcathach at the Feast of Tara in the first century AD. Surprisingly little research has been done on this road system. In the only comprehensive enquiry into the subject, Colm Ó Lochlainn in 1940 suggested that Cormac son of Art and grandson of Conn Céadcathach could have been the king who instigated the road-building programme. What Cormac undertook was perhaps the construction of link roads connecting Tara with a long-established countrywide road system.

My encounter with what I now believe to be a section of the Slighe Dhála, the road from Tara to Munster, happened in the autumn of 1995. It was accidental and, like most archaeologists who recover or bring back into view a landmark of the past, my understanding of the discovery was not immediate. The story of the finding of Dála's Road began at Clonfert-Molua — an early medieval church reputedly founded by St Molua, who was born *c.* 554 and died *c.* 605. Amicably and enthusiastically assisted by two friends — Hugh Carey and Karen Cronin, a fellow archaeologist and an illustrator — I had set myself the task of recording and interpreting what remained of Molua's church and graveyard nestling in pastureland at the foothills of the Slieve Bloom Mountains near Borris-in-Ossory, Co. Laois. Our immediate concern was to make sense of the ruined foundations of the church itself and to search the graveyard for early medieval graveslabs and stray architectural fragments which might help to piece together the complex building history of the site.

St Molua's church has a very long history of use from its foundation in the late sixth or early seventh century through to its decline as a parish church in the seventeenth century. It was the parish centre of an Anglo-Norman manor granted *c.* 1200 to the knight Adam de Hereford. After the collapse of Anglo-Norman control in this part of the midlands Clonfert-Molua continued to serve the parishioners of Kyle well into the seventeenth century. As late as 1622 a royal enquiry into the state of the diocese of Killaloe reported that William Duignan, the coarb of Clonfert-Molua, was harbouring a 'popish priest' there. The word coarb or *comharba* literally means the 'heir' of a founder saint — an abbot or churchman who succeeded to the authority and income of the founder of an early monastery. The Duignan family, associated with nearby Cloncourse Castle, held that position for centuries, and in that capacity they were also keepers of the 'Mionn Molua', St Molua's bell-shrine.

Our labours in the graveyard over several days were rewarded by the recovery of an early medieval pillar stone, crudely decorated on one face with overlapping circles and a cross (Fig. 29), along with a cross-inscribed graveslab, a large bullaun stone, and the site of a founder's tomb. The ever-helpful local people pointed to a small sandstone container — possibly a reliquary without its lid — at the nearby RC church, which had been removed from the graveyard for safe-keeping. By chance, a richly ornamented Romanesque capital, which had once graced the church doorway and had long since tumbled into the graveyard, showed up in the long grass under the late autumn sunshine (Pl. 40). This, together with two decorated window stones lodged in an early nineteenth-century family vault, told us that the church had been refurbished in the fashionable Romanesque style in the twelfth century, or perhaps when Adam de Hereford had been granted the manor of Clonfert-Molua *c.* 1200. But the most exciting discovery was yet to be made in the environs of the church and graveyard.

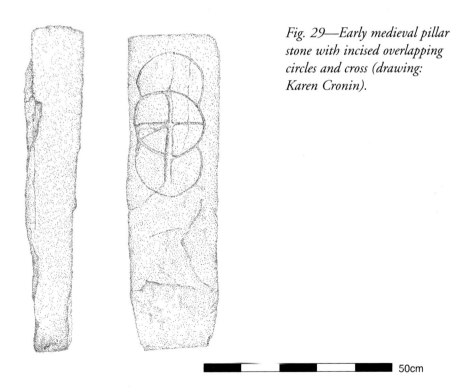

Fig. 29—Early medieval pillar stone with incised overlapping circles and cross (drawing: Karen Cronin).

50cm

Pl. 40—Romanesque scalloped capital with decorative scrollwork.

Pl. 41—Aerial view of Clonfert-Molua, showing the church and graveyard at centre right (1). The tree-clad banks at the bottom of the field south of the church delimit the hollow way or road (2). Note the linear soil-mark of the northern bank of the road running in the field to the east (3), and the interesting alignment of field banks further west (4), to the left of the picture (photo: Con Brogan, Dúchas The Heritage Service, 1996).

A maxim worth embracing for an adventurous life as an archaeologist is *Solvitur ambulando* — 'It is solved by walking'. There seemed no better conditions in which to pursue that belief than at that time, in the ochre light of autumn, with the whole range of Slieve Bloom etched in purple against the northern skyline. And so we went walking. Knowing that parish churches served a community of people, researching the church itself was not enough. We ventured out into the broad fields around it in order to see if there were any further traces of the ecclesiastical establishment, and perhaps the remains of a village settlement associated with the manorial phase of the site or with its later use as a centre of spiritual care. Being aware that the Slighe Dhála passed this way between Ballaghmore and Borris-in-Ossory, the matter of communication between the church site and the main artery between Tara and the south-west also occupied my thoughts. We first discovered that the road running immediately south of the church and graveyard had split it in two and that the remains of the southern extent of the graveyard lay in the field south of the road. Local people, who had witnessed human bone appearing on the surface of the field during ploughing, corroborated the field evidence. Walking further south I picked up a number of curious banks that were clearly part of an earlier field system. At the end of the large field that stretched south of the graveyard boundary the critical find was an 82m length of a sunken or hollow way — an earlier road running in an east-north-east/west-north-west direction, delimited by two banks. Initially I thought that this could have been a surviving portion of a monastic *vallum* or enclosure, or a ditch around Adam de Hereford's manorial settlement. Conversation with the landowner ruled out any possibility of it being the remnants of a more recent field boundary. The proportions of the construction were simply too large to be anything other than a road. The hollow way itself was almost 4m wide in places and lay *c.* 1m below present ground-level. Aerial photographs taken by Con Brogan of Dúchas in the spring of 1996 showed still more remains of this ancient way in the form of linear soil-marks running eastwards in the field immediately adjacent to the surviving stretch. The curious arrangement of field boundaries one field over to the west also pointed to the preservation of the line of a further portion of the road there.

The full name of the Slighe Dhála is Slighe Dhála Meic Umhóir — the Road of Dála, son of Umhóir. On its south-west course, which took it as far as Tarbert, Co. Kerry, it passed through what are now the modern counties of Dublin, Kildare, Laois, Tipperary and Limerick. Its route in the Laois area took in Ballyroan, Abbeyleix, Shanahoe, Aghaboe, Borris-in-Ossory and Ballaghmore. Créa, after whom is named the Tipperary town of Roscrea through which the Slighe Dhála passed, was the wife of Dála. The road is also known as Bealach Muighe Dála, a name that partly survives in the name Ballaghmore — 'Great

Pl. 42—The author (left of picture) with fellow fieldworkers Hugh Carey and Karen Cronin at Clonfert-Molua, autumn 1995.

Road' — given to the two townlands of Ballaghmore Upper and Lower which lie just a mile and a half west of Clonfert-Molua. At the beginning of the twentieth century two surviving parts of the Slighe Dhála in Laois were noted by the Reverends O'Hanlon, O'Leary and Lalor and by the antiquary Canon Carrigan, and both are marked on the 1909 edition of the Ordnance Survey six-inch maps. All trace of the stretch located a short distance south-east of Ballaghmore Castle is now unfortunately erased from the landscape. The second portion of the old road is preserved in the line of a laneway running past 'Brandybush Fort' in the townland of Cashel, which lies several miles south-east of Ballaghmore.

Most of the more significant monastic sites of early medieval Ireland were sited close to major routeways, whether roads or navigable rivers, and Clonfert-Molua was no exception. Like the neighbouring church sites of Aghaboe and Roscrea, proximity to the Slighe Dhála must have been a key factor in the foundation and development of Molua's Christian church. The discovery in 1995 of what is probably a further portion of the road at Clonfert-Molua, between Ballaghmore and Borris-in-Ossory, adds to the jigsaw puzzle of evidence for the route of the Slighe Dhála in the Laois area. The circumstance of its finding is a reminder that any field study of an ancient monument can be greatly enhanced by an energetic walkabout combined with aerial photography.

Further reading

Carrigan, W. 1905 *The history and antiquities of the diocese of Ossory*, vol. 2. Kilkenny.

O'Hanlon, J., O'Leary, E. and Lalor, M. 1914 *History of the Queen's County*, vol. 2. Kilkenny.

Ó Lochlainn, C. 1940 Roadways in ancient Ireland. In J. Ryan (ed.), *Essays and studies presented to Professor Eoin MacNeill*, 465–74. Dublin.

Lost and found

15

Discovery and early days in the excavation of the Lisleagh ringforts

Michael Monk

Every archaeologist will be aware of the inverse relationship between the amount of careful research, preparation and expectation prior to excavation and the productivity of the site when eventually excavated. Conversely, development sites, often excavated under extreme constraints of time and weather, produce more than can be handled with the resources available. There are, however, the rare occasions when the sites you choose, through a process of systematic fieldwork, produce evidence to challenge and stimulate — the two ringforts situated in Lisleagh townland (Lisleagh I and II) in north Cork certainly fall within that category.

As I write, it is twenty years this year since we began our excavations in Lisleagh I, and I am indebted to this publication for affording me the opportunity to share the story of the beginning of the project, and the story of some of the people involved. I would like especially to pay tribute to those people who worked on the project and the people of north Cork for their kindness and support, not least the landowners, the Burke family, as well as the Corbetts, from whom we rented the 'dig house' for nine seasons, and other individuals in the area, particularly Ned Roche, whose hostelry we frequently visited.

If one takes to heart the recent criticisms of current practice in fieldwork and excavation by the likes of Ian Hodder, Alan Chadwick and Gavin Lucas and their call for a more 'reflexive' interpretative archaeology, then I, like many colleagues, could argue that we have been practising a semblance of this for many years; it is just that we did not 'dress it up' in the terminology now being used. We were always aware of the broader issues raised by our fieldwork and its impact on the people of the area. For this reason I took every opportunity to explain our work to the local community and to hear their views. We lectured locally, and my wife Judith and I contributed to the Ballindangan community magazine, *Ogham*.

Articles also appeared in the local newspaper, *The Avondhu*, during every season of the excavation. I have said on many occasions that the archaeology of north Cork, while it holds considerable interest for archaeologists like myself, is the archaeology of the people who live there; it is part of their cultural landscape and inheritance. I hope, in relating the story of the beginning of our research at Lisleagh, to demonstrate that fieldwork is not just a cold, clinical, form-filling exercise devoid of any real experience. It clearly concerns more than just those who supervised the project or participated in the excavation. This is 'reflexive' archaeology as it has always been and should always be.

Background

Before I ever came to Ireland to take up my current position, ringforts had already attracted my interest. When I was working on plant remains and researching my MPhil on the agricultural economy of the Anglo-Saxons in Britain, I discovered, via Bruce Proudfoot's article 'The economy of the Irish rath', that these broadly contemporaneous settlement sites in Ireland had produced significant evidence for farming practices — in many cases better evidence than was coming from the very few rural Anglo-Saxon sites excavated up to that time.

When I was appointed to the lectureship in Cork in 1978 it was at a time when there were relatively few excavations taking place in Ireland on which students could gain excavation experience. In University College Cork, M. J. O'Kelly had 'hung up his trowel' to write up Newgrange, Elizabeth Shee-Twohig was also out of the field, and Aidan MacDonald, like me, was a new appointee to the Department. For the following two years, while I began research on Irish material, I encouraged students to join other excavation projects — for example Wroxeter Roman city (where I was the site environmentalist). Another of these projects was at Carrowmore, Co. Sligo. In 1980 Judith and I, with several of my students, joined the Swedish-run expedition as volunteers. Despite the appalling weather, Carrowmore was an experience in more ways than one, not least because of the interesting living conditions and the eccentric Swedes! Discussions in the evening, often over drinks in the Riding Stables bar, convinced me that in the following year I should initiate a long-term field project in Munster to address early medieval settlement. Significant in these discussions was a certain Redmond Tobin, whose boundless enthusiasm for archaeology and humour is legendary.

174

Discovery

In the autumn of 1980 and spring of 1981 we organised and executed a systematic programme of field visits to decide on a study area. We had identified three potential areas and during almost every weekend for eight weeks we visited these in search of the ideal site. One area was in south Tipperary, around Caher, but — as I saw it then — had too much 'contamination' by Anglo-Normans (I would think very differently now!). A second location was in east Cork, centring on Tallow, an area that had many grouped ringforts on the maps, but on the ground many had been destroyed. Then there was the third area around Glanworth, near Fermoy, which Red, being from the area, was promoting heavily. Red's jovial persuasion apart, the area had grown in significance in my mind because of the high survival of well-preserved sites, as well as its convenient closeness to Cork and the relative ease with which many of the sites could be accessed. Furthermore, the ringforts under consideration demonstrated an interesting variety of topographical location — the geographer in me was surfacing periodically! It was our first visit to Lisleagh, however, that decided it for me. While we had been systematic and reasoned in our fieldwork up to that point, the first visit to those sites proved to be something special — the site, its location, the people we met and my sixth sense told me that this was the right place!

Although Red had known of their existence, and despite his own extensive site-visiting in the area, he had never seen the ringforts before that day in late October 1980. The three of us walked down an unpaved boreen that led to a traditional house with its white plastered walls and galvanised roof. We were met by the inevitable dog, 'Phil', whose barking attracted Mary and John Reardon's attention. At that time, not being tuned into the north Cork accent, I could not understand a word they were saying but Red, 'interpreting', asked them the whereabouts of the two forts marked on the map. They pointed further down the boreen, where its surface turns into a grassy track. Turning into a field, we saw the two forts — Lisleagh II in front of us, its enclosure now part of a field fence, and standing proud to the west, only 40m from the first, Lisleagh I, one of the best-preserved sites that we had seen during all of our fieldwork (Pl. 44). Their position was impressive, having panoramic views to the south and west. Like all good archaeologists we walked over to Lisleagh I first, attracted to the biggest and the best preserved. The sound of a tractor and another barking dog drifted from the field between the two forts. On approaching the gate between them 'Rover' ran up to us, wagging his tail (a good sign!) and barking a greeting — this was the beginning of a great relationship with the Burkes' sheepdog.

John Burke stopped his tractor and we went over. Although he and Red knew of each other, they hadn't met before. We talked. Up to that point neither Red

Pl. 43—Red Tobin getting to grips with the theodolite.

Pl. 44—Lisleagh I prior to excavation in 1981.

nor I had spoken about the ringfort but both of us evidently had the same feeling independently. These were the sites we had been looking for! The conversation eventually got around to our research and, plucking up courage, I asked John the million-dollar question — how would he and his father feel about us excavating these sites? John, I think, had partly anticipated the question. He was immediately taken with the idea, not least because of his interest in the history of his local area but also, I guess, partly because of an almost instant rapport between us. He felt that his father would also be favourably disposed to the idea but that we would need to talk to him first. When we rang Mike Burke later that evening John had him well primed. He said he would give his permission, provided we would talk to him further — which we did.

Then began the whole process of applying to the Royal Irish Academy's National Committee for Archaeology for funding. At that time this was the only source of finance available for research archaeology. Although they would not commit themselves to a multi-year project, we decided to go ahead on a year-by-year basis. We then had to find a 'dig' house in the area for that first year — therein lies another tale that brought the persuasive talents of Ned Roche, proprietor of the local hostelry, to the fore. A regular customer and friend of Ned's, George Mansell, card player extraordinaire, had been working steadily on building his own house on the Ballindangan road. It was felt that some sort of spur to completion was required and that our need would provide a sufficient catalyst (we only found this out subsequently!). Our concerns over the completion of the house in time proved ill founded. On the Sunday before our planned start to excavations (June 1981) the unfinished house was a hive of activity. Various neighbours were in around the place assisting George in all manner of ways — providing furniture, carpets, tables and chairs, fitting taps and sinks, and screwing in light fittings. It was a complete community effort, masterminded by Ned. This was to be our first introduction to the many people we got to know in the area. The bathroom was finally installed on the day we moved in!

The first season

We had spent several days in the weeks before the excavation making an accurate survey of the site and laying out the grid. For this purpose Professor O'Kelly had entrusted us with the Department's prize piece of equipment at the time — a state-of-the-art Wild T-series theodolite. While I was not without surveying skills, this instrument was like driving a Rolls-Royce after riding a bicycle. With much-appreciated advice from Pat Casey, Red Tobin, Colin Rynne, Denis Power, Judith and I managed the task. John Burke had kindly sprayed the area where we had decided to lay out the trenches with herbicide to prevent the bracken establishing a foothold. In the heat of that June, one of the hottest Junes on record, the excavation crew and ourselves de-sodded the entire area we had set out for excavation within just three days. Several of the locals, who at that stage would only come and see what these mad people from Cork were up to after we left in the evening, remarked to John and Ned that we were 'fierce industrious'. They became less impressed by progress when they saw us on our hands and knees scraping the ground with mason's trowels and using paintbrushes to clean the increasingly dusty surface in advance of photographs and drawings (Pl. 45).

But by that stage they were coming to visit us by day and I made it my business to take time out to show everyone around the site, explaining the various features that were appearing. Many of the farmers could appreciate the evidence of the post-holes we were beginning to find, having had experience in setting up wooden posts themselves and packing stones around them to keep them in place.

While the surface vegetation had been burnt off, the bracken roots continued to be a curse. It was some task to cut them out as we progressed. One useful thing we noticed from observation of the roots, however, was that their direction often helped to identify surfaces and the location of dug features such as post-holes. Trowelling is an art form once you get the hang of it. Most of our student crew took a few days before they could get a good clean surface and see the point of the exercise — to identify context edges and the relationship between them. John Burke, however, who joined us for the first season of the excavation, was a natural from the start. He got the point on the first day and could clean the surface quicker and more neatly than anyone I had had the pleasure to work with on any excavation. Unfortunately for us, he had to withdraw his services all too soon, as working on an excavation and managing a farm was one job too many! Sorry we were to let him go. We owe him a debt of gratitude for his assistance and his continued help over the years in facilitating the project.

Another great supporter of the project, in his own particular way, was the late Professor M. J. O'Kelly. In many ways the results of his speculative interpretation of the paired ringforts at Garryduff in east Cork were a touchstone for the project. However, it was the discovery of the large dump of iron slag in the outer ditch of Lisleagh I that really took his interest. This discovery was completely unanticipated and demonstrates a particular 'sod's law' in archaeology — that is, wherever you decide to put a pit for the contents of the chemical toilet, you will inevitably find archaeology. In some ways it was a poor decision on my part to

Pl. 45—Digging in progress on Lisleagh I.

put this pit in the outer ditch of the fort but I did not want to take up even more of the farmer's ground than the acre the ringfort already covered. Our intention was, of course, to fully record the ditch fills in the pit before it was used but we were not prepared to find what we did. We hit upon an expanse of iron slag and the 'die was cast'. We had to excavate and, in the process, recovered a metric tonne and a half of slag that had been dumped into the ditch from elsewhere. The dump, the greatest quantity of iron-working debris from an early medieval site to date, produced numerous furnace bottoms as well as four tuyeres. Colin Rynne was delegated to excavate it, and, arguably, this began his subsequent involvement in industrial archaeology.

At one point during the excavation O'Kelly required Colin (whose interest in horizontal water-mills was also just beginning) to go off to west Cork and undertake a rescue excavation of the horizontal water-mill at Cloontycarthy near Macroom. In his briefing O'Kelly (who at this stage had not visited us but had heard some reports) impressed on Colin that there was only a short time within which to do the job and not to treat it 'like the Pyramids of Egypt', as he felt we were treating the Lisleagh I excavation!

Needless to say this gave us an idea for his visit, so from a newly de-sodded area we built a turf pyramid. When he finally did visit, with the inevitable six-packs and biscuits, he hardly noticed the irony of our pyramid, but he certainly noticed the huge amount of iron-working evidence and from that point onwards his support for our excavation methodology was unconditional. The study of early iron-working was an abiding interest of his ever since his work at Ballyvourney in the early 1950s, which initiated his subsequent experiments in the area.

The first round house

With the bracken roots, topsoil and the late-dated spade-dug furrows finally cleared, we had post-holes galore, but five weeks on we could not convincingly form a house out of them. An area of burning had been staring us in the face for a few weeks. It had first appeared just under the sod so I thought it was simply the remains of a bonfire. One day, however, four weeks into the excavation, the renowned Red, whose skills as a photographer were also coming to the fore, was taking some overall shots from the photo tower. We had just sprayed the site down with water and were beginning to do so again when he noted the classic indicator of residual humic material, a strip of moisture retention continuing the curving edge of the burnt area, revealing what turned out to be the former wattle wall line of a burnt round house.

'We've got a [insert suitable expletive] round house!'

I still have the photograph that Red took in his excitement, which has the edge of the photographic tower in the frame (Pl. 46). It was a magic moment. The house had been staring us in the face all along but, like many things in archaeology, it only appeared when the time was right for it to do so. That was the beginning. From then on, we all became very tuned in to the subtleties of the archaeological sediments and the extremely shallow stratification at Lisleagh.

Getting serious — the problems of recording

At that time our recording system was not in fact geared up to cope with the subtlety of the strata at Lisleagh. It was based on experience gained while working for Phil Barker at Wroxeter and was very dependent on the multi-context plans and photographs. We had developed a context sheet for the written recording of undisturbed 'features' but, as with the Wroxeter system at the time, it was up to the supervisors, principally Denis Power (another unsung veteran of Lisleagh) and I, to fill them in (Pl. 47). To be honest, we spent too much of the time training those with less experience than us, making decisions for them in terms of what to dig next and making decisions as best we could to help them excavate the very subtle archaeology. We inevitably fell behind with the paperwork.

Pl. 46—Red Tobin's photograph of the burnt round house at the moment of discovery.

Pl. 47—Lisleagh I under excavation — Denis Power (right) and the author.

By the second season of the excavation I was becoming increasingly concerned that we were losing a lot of the evidence and that our record was not really picking up the sequence of contexts that we knew were present. With this concern as a background, and thinking back to a major discussion that we had had with Phil Barker at Wroxeter in 1980 (spearheaded by Steve Roskams), I got in contact with a former Wroxeter colleague and good friend, Tim Williams, who was working in London at the time for the Department of Urban Archaeology. In previous years, those working for the DUA had begun to develop a system of recording called single-context planning. Although the idea was first mooted and experimented with in Winchester in 1974, it was first fully implemented only in 1975 on the General Post Office site in London. Tim Williams — who, as it turned out, had also worked with our supervisor in 1983, David MacLeod — said that he would come over for a busman's holiday and would go over the system with us at the beginning of that season. This he did. Basically we had an ongoing on-site seminar about all aspects of the single-context methodology. Our adoption of the system after some days of debate and discussion with Dave and Tim was conditional on our insistence that we continue to draw multi-context plans at the end of each season. Gradually, having a drawn record for each identified context in addition to a recording sheet enabled us to appreciate the incremental nature of the evidence. It also allowed us to demonstrate the stratigraphic sequence as it revealed itself, constructing what I call the 'formation history' of the site and representing it in a shorthand way on the Harris Matrix.

Apart from this, this system also facilitated the delegation of recording, under supervision, to the excavation crew. At last the people who were at the cutting edge were now carrying out the recording. This required an important investment on our part in training, but that was a key objective of the excavation project from the very beginning. Trusting in your crew to be part of the process has to be a main tenet of any excavation and it certainly guaranteed considerable commitment from all the crews we had for the subsequent eight seasons of excavation at Lisleagh. In more ways than one, our adoption of single-context recording was an experiment. It was one of the first occasions that it was adopted outside the deeply stratified deposits of urban sites like London. It was a great learning experience for all of us and especially those of us who had spent a good few years working on sites with supervisor-led recording systems. It worked very well for us and for all those people who worked with us over the years. If anything, it ensured that the excitement of discovery now continues into the post-excavation phase of the project when we can, with the thorough record made on site, make stratigraphic and spatial connections that we did not fully appreciate during excavation. In hindsight we can see how our knowledge and the interpretation of the site evolved as the archaeology revealed itself — and in some cases continues to do so in the post-excavation work.

Learning and legacy

Judith and I were loath to call Lisleagh a training excavation, partly because of our experiences of training excavations in Britain, which left a lot to be desired. In several cases they were a useful exercise in learning how not to dig! Lisleagh, however, did perform an important training function in parallel with its research focus. Over the years many people have worked for us, some with prior experience while others were novices to archaeological excavation. Among those who contributed were Denis Power, Maurice Hurley, Red Tobin, Dave MacLeod, Tim Williams and Craig Spence, to name but a few. I would hope that, for all concerned, it was an experience that they can look back on with satisfaction, fondness and a smile. I thank them, one and all, for their hard work and dedication, and I am proud to say that many of them still remain in the archaeological profession and continue to contribute to our knowledge of our collective past.

Acknowledgements

Thanks to all our friends in north Cork, particularly the Burkes, the Corbetts and Ned Roche. Thanks to all our crews and supervisory staff over the years on both excavations. Thanks also for the support we had from the Office of Public Works/Dúchas The Heritage Service (especially the Mallow depot), the Royal Irish Academy, the National Museum of Ireland, and my colleagues on the staff of the Department of Archaeology, University College Cork.

Further reading

Barker, P. 1993 *Techniques of archaeological excavation* (3rd edn). London.

Hodder, I. 1997 Always momentary, fluid and flexible: towards a reflexive excavation methodology. *Antiquity* 71, 691–700.

Hodder, I. 1999 *The archaeological process: an introduction.* Oxford.

Lucas, G. 2001 *Critical approaches to fieldwork.* London.

MacLeod, D., Monk, M. and Williams, T. 1988 The use of single context recording on a seasonally excavated site in Ireland: a learning experience. *Journal of Irish Archaeology* 4, 55–63.

Monk, J. and Monk, M.A. 1998 Lisleagh revisited. *Ogham Magazine: Ballindangan and District Review* 4, 49–51.

Monk, M. 1984 Excavations at Lisleagh ringfort. *Ogham Magazine: Ballindangan and District Review* 1, 33–4.

Monk, M. 1985 Excavations at Lisleagh 2. *Ogham Magazine: Ballindangan and District Review* 2, 18–19.

Monk, M.A. 1988 Excavations at Lisleagh ringfort, north Cork. *Archaeology Ireland* 2 (2), 57–60.

Monk, M.A. 1995 A tale of two ringforts, Lisleagh I and II. *Journal of the Cork Historical and Archaeological Society* 100, 105–16.

Proudfoot, B. 1961 The economy of the Irish rath. *Medieval Archaeology* 5, 245–77.

Roskams, S. 2001 *Excavation.* Cambridge.

Spence, C. 1993 Recording the archaeology of London: the development and implementation of the DUA recording system. In E. C. Harris, M. R. Brown III and G. J. Brown (eds), *Practices of archaeological stratigraphy*, 23–44. London.

16

Early metalworking and myth
on the lakes of Killarney

William O'Brien

From Schliemann's search for ancient Troy to the discovery of the Minoan
civilisation, archaeologists have long pondered the historical basis of early
myths and legends. This is true also for Ireland, where legends offer a
window on an ancient 'Celtic' world populated by great heroes and supernatural
beings. These stories, though fanciful and embellished over time, may contain
elements of historical truth, testifying to the strength of the oral tradition in early
Ireland. This is illustrated by the results of excavations at 'royal' centres like Tara
and Emain Macha where history, mythology and archaeology converge.

The first steps towards written history in Ireland began with the introduction
of Christianity in the fifth century AD. The following centuries were a Golden
Age of metalworking. National treasures such as the Ardagh Chalice, Tara
Brooch and Derrynaflan hoard bear witness to the extraordinary skill of the
craftsman in the pre-Viking era. The early law-tracts and annals record the
special position of the *cerd* or smith in this society. There is also a supernatural
dimension to metalworking, as seen in the story of the legendary Battle of
Moytura, where the god Lugh was assisted by the three gods of craftsmanship:
Goibniu the blacksmith, Luchta the wright, and Credne the bronze-worker.

The early literary sources also mention mines where copper, lead, iron, silver
and gold were extracted in ancient Ireland. Though it has proven difficult for
archaeologists to identify these mining locations, important discoveries have
recently been made in the Killarney area.

Lakes of Killarney

Renowned for its scenic splendour, it is hard to imagine that the Killarney lake

185

Pl. 48—A gilt-bronze penannular brooch of eighth–ninth-century AD date from Kilshanny, Co. Clare (courtesy National Museum of Ireland).

area was the setting for mining enterprises at various times over the past 4000 years. Several mine locations, most notably Ross Island and Muckross, were worked for copper, lead, iron and possibly silver (Fig. 30). Most significantly, Ross Island is one of the first places where metal was actually made in Ireland, as the Stone Age ended around 2400 BC.

The metal mines of Killarney lie on the junction of two great rock formations, with Old Red Sandstone mountains to the south and west, and limestone lowlands to the north and east. The mines at Ross Island and Muckross are located on metal ore deposits in the Carboniferous limestone, which are locally rich in copper, lead, zinc, silver and cobalt. While of no economic importance today, these ore bodies were attractive to early miners as they contained quality metal that was easily extracted.

De mirabilibus Hiberniae

The Welsh monk Nennius, writing in the ninth century AD, listed the mineral wealth of this area as a wonder of the known world:

> 'There is a lake called Lough Lein. Four circles are around it. In the first circle, it is surrounded by tin, in the second by lead, in the third by iron and in the fourth by copper...'

It is clear from this passage in the *Historia Britonum* that the Killarney metal mines had a wide reputation in the Early Christian era. The mining record for Killarney confirms that copper and iron were worked here, while Ross Island is also likely to have been a source of lead and possibly silver. The only discrepancy with the Nennius account is that this area is unlikely to have ever produced tin.

Recent archaeological research at Ross Island has shed exciting new light on mining and metalworking in this area around the time that Nennius was writing.

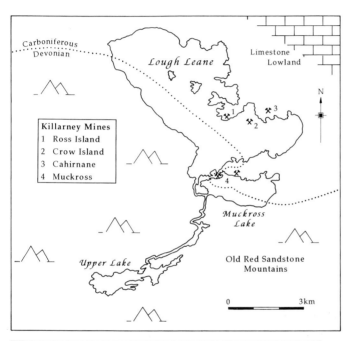

Fig. 30—The metal mines of Killarney.

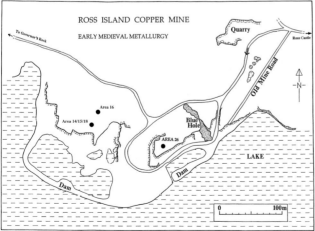

Fig. 31—Location of Early Christian period furnaces and plate slag deposits in the Ross Island mine.

187

Ross Island mine

The Ross Island mine is located on the eastern side of Lough Leane, the lower lake in Killarney (Pl. 49). Mining for copper and possibly other metals like lead and silver took place here periodically over the past 4000 years. The focus was a copper-rich horizon within the local limestone geology that extends to a maximum depth of only 13–16m along the southern lakeshore. There are two separate areas of mining here. The first is a bed of mineralised limestone called the Western Mine that contained a rich deposit of chalcopyrite ($CuFeS_2$), tennantite ($Cu_{12}As_4S_{13}$) and bornite (Cu_5FeS_4) ore. This is bordered on the eastern side by a vein-type structure called the Blue Hole, which held an abundance of copper, lead and zinc ore (Fig. 31).

The most recent mining at Ross Island occurred in early modern times when this location was part of the Kenmare estate. Sporadic working during the eighteenth century led to industrial operations between 1804 and 1829 (Pl. 50). Records show that some 5000 tons of quality copper ore were extracted and sold to smelters in England in that period. The mine was finally abandoned in 1829 owing to poor ore returns and operational problems caused by lake flooding.

*Pl. 49—Ross Island, Killarney. Location of copper mine marked;
Ross Castle in foreground.*

Pl. 50—Aerial view of Ross Island copper mine, showing nineteenth-century dam embankment.

The Danish mines

'It is not above thirty years since a very rich copper mine was discovered on the borders of this lake, and worked with very great profit to the proprietors for many years; but what is greatly to our purpose, is, that on pushing on their works, they found shafts had been regularly sunk, and implements of mining were found. These works were ignorantly imputed to the Danes...' (Sylvester O'Halloran, 1772).

This mining at Ross Island uncovered older primitive workings, described as the 'Danish Mines' in the antiquarian tradition of the time. Visitor accounts recall 'chambers of rudely vaulted form', worked by '...kindling large fires on the limestone, thereby reducing it to a caustic state'. Numerous stone tools or 'Danish hammers' used in this mining are also recorded. Though badly damaged by mining in early modern times, some of these ancient workings survive to the present (Pl. 51).

The Ross Island Project was established in 1992 by the National University of Ireland, Galway, to investigate the history and archaeology of metal-mining at this site. The research involved many specialists from Ireland and abroad working in the fields of geology, archaeology and the environmental sciences. It

189

also included a programme of archaeological survey and excavation, which has shed much light on what we now know to be a unique mining landscape.

The initial focus of the archaeological excavation was a large cave-like opening in the Western Mine area. The broken rock deposits and discarded tools here reveal something of the techniques used by the early miners. The discovery of an adjacent work camp provides an insight into the organisation of this activity and the production of copper metal. Radiocarbon dates now place the early phase of mining here between 2400 and 1800 BC, making Ross Island the oldest copper mine presently known in north-western Europe. The discovery of Beaker pottery links this mine to the very beginning of metal production in Ireland during the final Neolithic period.

Archaeological excavation at Ross Island also uncovered evidence for metal production from around the time of Nennius. Two copper-smelting furnaces and associated slag deposits have been dated to the seventh and eighth centuries AD. This is the first evidence in Ireland for primary copper production dating from the Early Christian period.

Pl. 51—Archaeological excavation of the 'Danish Mines' at Ross Island.

From the fiery furnace

The investigation at Ross Island uncovered two small furnaces in the western part of the site (Areas 14/15 and 16) (Fig. 31). These comprised bowl-shaped pits, measuring 0.4–0.5m in diameter and 0.12–0.15m deep, filled with charcoal ash sediments and surrounded by a spread of thin slag fragments (Pl. 52). The plate slag, as it is termed, created a localised magnetic anomaly that was first detected in a pre-excavation geophysical survey carried out by Mr Fergal Gavin. The location of a third furnace is suggested by a separate spread of slag in the adjacent Area 18. This distinctive slag was also discovered at another location (Area 26), close to the Blue Hole working in this mine.

Some 12,000 fragments of plate slag were found at these four locations, together with a smaller quantity of vitrified ceramic and slagged sandy soil. The ceramic fragments derive from short tuyeres or clay nozzles used to protect the end of a bellows or blowpipe where it was inserted into the furnace. These furnaces had low shaft walls, probably less than 1m in height, which were dismantled after smelting and survive only as fragments of slagged soil. An adjacent small pit was used to collect molten slag, which was tapped off from these furnaces during smelting.

Samples of charcoal taken from these furnaces and plate slag deposits have been scientifically dated by the radiocarbon method. The results obtained confirm that this furnace technology was being used at Ross Island between AD 650 and 770.

The metallurgy of these furnace operations is currently under research in the Institute of Archaeology, London. The microstructure of the plate slag has been analysed using optical and electron microscopy, with other analyses to examine chemical composition. The results confirm that these furnaces were used to smelt a rich sulphidic copper ore, probably chalcopyrite ($CuFeS_2$). This appears to have been a three-stage process, where the ore was first roasted in an open fire to expel as much of the sulphur as possible. The roasted ore was then smelted in a low-shaft furnace to produce matte, a copper-iron sulphide, which was reduced to copper metal by further smelting. This was achieved by adding crushed sandstone to the smelt as a flux, which separated the iron content off as plate slag.

To smelt the copper ore to metal, temperatures of 1100°C would have to be reached in the furnace. This was achieved by using a bellows or a blowpipe to create a forced draught, as suggested by the discovery of clay tuyere fragments. The smelting fuel used was oak charcoal. Professor Rehren, who is studying this process in London, believes that one of these small furnaces could have produced around 5kg of pure copper.

Pl. 52—Early Christian period smelting furnace at Ross Island.

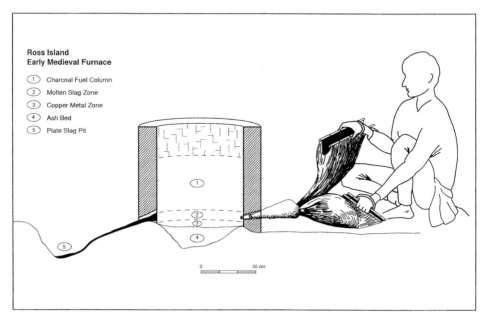

Ross Island
Early Medieval Furnace

1. Charcoal Fuel Column
2. Molten Slag Zone
3. Copper Metal Zone
4. Ash Bed
5. Plate Slag Pit

0   30 cm

Fig. 32—Reconstruction of Early Christian period copper-smelting furnace from Ross Island.

The wider landscape

The cultural background of the early medieval metallurgists at Ross Island is unknown; however, there are several indicators in the surrounding landscape. Lying off the north-eastern side of Ross Island is the island monastery of Inishfallen. Established as early as the seventh century AD, this monastery grew to become an important centre of learning by the tenth century, when it was linked to one Maelsuthain O'Carroll, a friend of Brian Boru. Despite Viking raids, the monastery flourished in late medieval times, before finally being abandoned in the sixteenth century. The Annals of Inishfallen, an important historical source, were partly written here around 1215.

Evidence for metalworking has been discovered at many early church settlements in Ireland. These include the crucibles and tuyeres found at Reask near Dingle, Co. Kerry, and similar finds from St Gobnet's House at Ballyvourney, Co. Cork. While no archaeological excavation has been carried out on Inishfallen, it is possible that the early monks who lived there engaged in metal production and fabrication. Copper ore could have been obtained at Ross Island, either by mining or by searching the rock spoil left behind by earlier miners.

There is also much evidence for secular settlement from the Early Christian era in the Killarney area. This takes the form of numerous earthwork enclosures, which are distributed across the limestone lowlands to the north and east of the modern town. These ringforts were farmstead settlements that may also have contained workshops where metal objects were made. While there is no direct archaeological evidence from this area, it is likely that many larger ringforts were centres of non-ferrous metalworking where objects were made using metal from Ross Island.

In 1996 archaeological monitoring in advance of a housing development at Scrahane, on the edge of Killarney town, exposed an extensive early metallurgical complex. Pit furnaces and slag deposits were uncovered in the vicinity of a large ditched enclosure. Regrettably, this metallurgy has not been dated, but the plate slag found is identical to that from the Early Christian furnaces at Ross Island. Scrahane is 2.5km east of the Ross Island mine, which is the most likely source of the metal produced there.

Elsewhere in Ireland there is considerable evidence for Early Christian period metalworking in ringfort settlements. These include the important tribal centre at Garranes, Co. Cork, only 60km from Killarney. Excavations here uncovered bronze ingots and scrap, together with crucibles, tuyeres, clay and stone moulds, and a range of iron tools used in casting and fabrication during the fifth and sixth centuries AD, and possibly later. Settlements like this provide clear evidence of craft specialisation under the patronage of tribal leaders. Genealogical sources for this Early Christian period identify occupational caste names that include several groups of *Cerdraige* ('smith-folk'). The metalworkers of Ross Island and Scrahane probably belonged to one such group of *Cerdraige* based in the Killarney area.

Lén the Smith

The importance of Killarney as a metalworking centre in the Early Christian era is also indicated by the name Lough Leane itself. This derives from a mythological character, Lén Lín-fíaclach ('Lén of the White Teeth'), a famous artificer who had his forge on the shore. His accomplishments are recalled in an early medieval poem that includes the following passages:

'I have heard of Lén with hammers in plenty,
as being under the marge of its blooming bank,
where he shaped by no feeble forceless work
the shining vessels of Fainne daughter of Flidais...

Were it chariot or helmet of gold,
were it cup or well-made instrument of music,
justly Lén won good fame therefrom,
it was finished work ere night.'

Lén the Smith appears in one modern folk legend as a giant who dwells in Lough Leane and jealously guards the mineral treasure of Ross Island, leading modern miners astray. The latter are called the *Fir Gorma* ('Blue Men'), a wild breed of Cornish miners brought in during the mid-eighteenth century to work this mine. The legend relates how Lén deliberately led the manager, Captain Read, astray, causing the mine to flood and two miners to drown. This story has a historical basis in the eighteenth century, when there was a major accident in the Ross Island mine.

Local tradition attributes the name of the lower lake in Killarney, Lough Leane ('Lake of Learning'), to the island monastery of Inishfallen, where around the tenth century there was an important school. This etymology is doubtful and it is more likely that the name of this lake derives from its association with early metalworking and the mythical Lén. This is now supported by the excavation evidence from Ross Island and nearby Scrahane.

Pl. 53—Lough Leane, Killarney.

Conclusions

It is now apparent that the Killarney area was an important source of copper, and possibly other metals, during the Early Christian period. Recent archaeological discoveries, supported by the Nennius record, suggest that these mines were an important part of the 'Golden Age' of metalworking of this era. The use of chemical and isotope analysis may some day make it possible to scientifically link these copper and bronze objects to mine sources like Ross Island. This would allow us to examine the movement of metal in this period and thus the organisation of production and supply. Further research may also shed light on the society of the *Cerdraige* in Killarney who made metal at Ross Island under Lén's watchful eye.

Further reading

O'Brien, W. 2000 *Ross Island and the mining heritage of Killarney*. Department of Archaeology, National University of Ireland, Galway. Also: www.nuigalway.ie/ross_island

Ryan, M. 1993 *Metal craftsmanship in early Ireland*. Dublin.

17

The Moylough Belt-shrine

Raghnall Ó Floinn

'This is the spot where the Moylough Belt was found in 1943 or '44 and I'm the one that found it. I was cutting turf here and I went down about four feet from the top when I hit an iron or stone, I thought, or something with the turf spade. So I stopped and dug it out and it happened to be the Moylough Belt. So I didn't know what to do with it, so 'twas left in the house for some months and our local postman, Lord rest him, was on to make a visit to Dublin. So I sent it at the finish up to Dublin, up to the Museum and Doctor Raftery came down and he said it was the second-best find in Ireland at the time. So he bought it off me. I suppose, I don't know, if I was paid for it enough or not or too much or what. I've seen it several times since and gone inside the Museum and had a talk to them there. I suppose I'm glad I was the one that found it.'

Thus, in modest fashion, did Mr John Towey, the finder of the Moylough Belt-shrine, one of the major treasures of Early Christian Irish art, describe his discovery in a video made at the find-spot to record the fiftieth anniversary of the object's discovery (Pl. 56).

It is an unfortunate fact that first-hand accounts for major archaeological finds are relatively scarce. It is also the case that the finders of such objects are often unknown to us and, indeed, that finders are often overlooked and not given due credit for their discoveries. The finders of major pieces such as the Tara Brooch, the St John's (or Athlone) Crucifixion Plaque or the Petrie Crown remain anonymous, and it is often the case that little is known about when, by whom and exactly where these discoveries were made. In many cases this is due to the fact that the objects made their way into public collections through dealers, collectors or other third parties.

On the other hand, there are cases where the finders were known but their testimony was overlooked. This is the case with the Moylough Belt-shrine, found in a bog in County Sligo in 1945. In this case there was a lapse of time between the object's discovery and its transfer to the National Museum of Ireland. The matter was further complicated by the fact that although the site was visited, the finder interviewed and samples of peat taken for pollen analysis, no report appears to have been placed on the Museum's object file. As a result the precise find-place was not recorded, and varying accounts of when the object was found and the depth at which it was found were to be found in the National Museum's file on the object.

I therefore took the opportunity while on fieldwork in County Sligo in October 1994 to contact the finder, Mr John Towey, who was still living at the family farm on the outskirts of Moylough, a small village about 4km south-east of Tubbercurry. I established from him the precise circumstances of the find, which offer an insight into how such finds are made and reported. It will be noted that the account below is at some variance with Mr Towey's own words above.

Mr Towey told me that he had made the discovery about four weeks before he contacted the National Museum at the end of May 1945. This placed the date of discovery sometime in late April or early May 1945 (and not in 1942 or 1943 or June 1945 as recorded variously in the Museum's own file and in subsequent publications by Professor M. Duignan of University College, Galway, and Professor M.J. O'Kelly of University College, Cork). Mr Towey was about 21 years of age at the time and he told me that he was in England from September 1942 until January 1944 working on the land in Gloucestershire and Lincolnshire. He then returned to Ireland to work on the family farm.

The find was made during turf-cutting on Mr Towey's father's land. Mr Towey recalled how the turf spade hit something hard and, thinking that he had hit a stone, he removed the surrounding peat with a garden trowel. The belt was resting in an upright position and lay slightly open in the peat, forming a diamond shape when viewed from above. There was no sign of a container or covering of cloth, leather or wood, and nothing unusual was noticed in the bog surrounding the find. Mr Towey estimated that the belt lay at a depth of about three and a half feet in virgin bog — the total depth of peat in the area at that time being about six feet. When he lifted it out of the bog, the sections of the belt were moveable, that is, the hinges which join the various parts of the belt were not stuck or corroded. Mr Towey told me that he saw the belt in the National Museum some years later but that he felt it never looked as good as the day when it was found!

The object was kept at the family home at Moylough for some weeks until it was seen there by the local postman, Mr John Nicholson of Tubbercurry, who recognised the object as being of archaeological importance and advised Mr Towey to contact the National Museum. Mr Towey was adamant that there was no truth in the stories that the belt had been used either to hold a gate in place or as a horse-collar (both stories were in circulation in the area after news of the find became public).

The subsequent history of the object can be reconstructed from correspondence on the Museum file. Mr Towey wrote to the National Museum on 28 May 1945 as follows:

> I have found in the bog on the fourth spit of turf what appears to be a belt. It's round in shape and has four separate pieces with celtic crosses and it's made of iron. I would be much obliged if you could let me know what it is.

The object was brought to the Museum by Mr Nicholson on or around 9 June. It was described by Dr Joseph Raftery, then Acting Keeper of Antiquities at the National Museum, as 'an exceedingly fine specimen of Early Christian metal, glass and enamel work of the 8th century A.D.' and as being 'easily one of the finest things that have been acquired by this Division in the last 50 years'. Dr Raftery elsewhere compared the decoration on the object to the Book of Durrow and the Ardagh Chalice. From the beginning, then, it was recognised that this was a significant find. Dr Raftery visited the site sometime between 14 June and 12 July 1945. He interviewed Mr Towey and took peat samples from the surrounding area.

At the time of the discovery, the collections of the Museum had just been returned from Athlone, where they had been stored during the Second World War. The Museum's resources were stretched to the limit and from early on it was apparent that the conservation of the belt-shrine was beyond the Museum's resources. As early as 20 July 1945 it was decided to approach the British Museum to see if it could undertake the necessary work, as it had undertaken the conservation of St Manchan's Shrine in the early 1930s. However, the British Museum's resources were also fully stretched as a result of disturbance and bomb damage during the war.

Meanwhile news of the discovery was made public in the newspapers on 26 June. The *Irish Press* published a brief note under the heading 'Gold Belt for Museum' (Fig. 33). The following day the *Irish Press* printed a correction to the effect that the belt was of bronze, not gold. The *Irish Times* report of 12 July 1945 was more expansive, stating that the find was 'one of the finest pieces of art metalwork discovered in Ireland during the past 50 years'. Neither report contained any reference to the finder or to the find-place, presumably to protect the find-place until any further Museum investigation was finished. The *Irish*

Pl. 54—The Moylough Belt-shrine. View of front (photo: National Museum of Ireland).

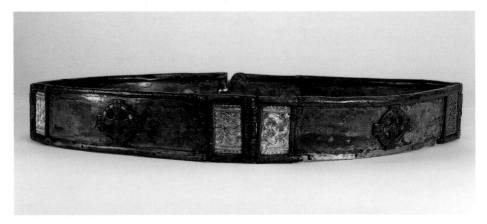

Pl. 55—The Moylough Belt-shrine. View of back (photo: National Museum of Ireland).

Press report of 17 August under the heading 'Bronze Belt, A Unique Find' included an interview with Dr Raftery and was accompanied by the first photograph of the belt-shrine. It also named the finder as Mr John Towey, jnr and the find-place as Moylough, and acknowledged the role of Mr John Nicholson who had advised Mr Towey to write to the Museum. Dr Raftery was reported as saying that he could give no information regarding its purpose but suggested that the object might possibly be a belt-shrine or the belt of a statue.

The belt-shrine was finally forwarded to the British Museum for examination in May 1946 and was exhibited at a meeting of the Society of Antiquaries of London. It was conserved in the British Museum and returned on 26 February 1947.

Since its return, the Moylough Belt-shrine has occupied a prominent position in the Museum's exhibition of Early Christian metalwork. It was displayed as

Pl. 56—Mr John Towey, finder of the Moylough Belt-shrine (image captured from Rev. Fr Martin Jennings's video recording).

The attached cutting appeared in our issue of...... 26 JUNE 1945 ....

Fig. 33—Press cutting from the Irish Press *for 26 June 1945 announcing the discovery of the Moylough Belt-shrine.*

Gold Belt For Museum

A find of outstanding archaeological importance to reach the National Museum is an 8th century gold belt found by a Co. Sligo bog worker.

The find is being examined by Dr. S. Raftery. M.A.. of the Irish Antiquities Division.

There is always some item of interest to you in "THE IRISH PRESS" part of an exhibition of Irish antiquities in Australia in 1988 and as part of the 'Work of Angels' exhibition in London, Dublin and Edinburgh in 1989–91. It currently forms part of the centrepiece of the Treasury in the National Museum, where it is exhibited alongside the Ardagh Chalice, the Tara Brooch and the Derrynaflan Hoard.

The belt-shrine consists of four bronze segments hinged together so that the components are flexible (Pls 55 and 56). Each segment consists of two strips of sheet bronze which were originally tinned to give the appearance of being made of silver. These enclose strips of plain leather and are held together with bronze bindings riveted along each edge. The outer face of each segment bears additional ornament. In the centre of each is a medallion, which takes the form of a ringed 'Celtic' cross of cast bronze inlaid with glass and enamel. Two of these medallions have in addition sheets of silver foil on which spiral patterns have been drawn. The ends of each section have further panels of stamped silver foil or panels of openwork bronze backed by thin sheets of mica, a type of glittering rock found in granite, which can be removed as thin scales.

The most elaborate decoration is found on the two front segments of the belt and takes the form of a false buckle and buckle plate richly decorated with silver foils, glass and enamel. The tongue of the buckle is formed of a pair of birds' heads while the ends of the buckle and buckle plate are formed from animal heads, which grasp coloured glass studs with silver inlays. The significance of these studs is that they are very similar to studs on the Ardagh Chalice and are one of the elements that enable us to date the Moylough Belt-shrine to the eighth century. All the other design elements — the cast-bronze medallions, the glass, enamel and stamped silver inlays, the animal and bird heads, and the interlace and spiral ornament — suggest a date in the eighth century.

What, then, was the function of this eighth-century metal belt? The object could not have functioned as a true belt as its size was fixed and could not be adjusted. Its internal circumference is fixed for a waist size of 90cm or 35.5 inches. Also, the buckle is non-functional and purely decorative. Other examples of buckles, such as that from excavations carried out at Lough Gara in the 1950s, show that in eighth-century Ireland functioning buckles were known and used.

The rich ornament of the Moylough belt indicate that it was used for some ceremonial purpose. It has been suggested that the belt may have been an item of secular regalia, used perhaps in the inauguration of a king. It has also been suggested that it was a liturgical girdle or that it was a votive offering to some sacred image. These theories have been discounted on the basis that the evidence for considerable wear and the repairs made to the object indicate that it was in continuous use and not simply produced for special occasions.

One thing is certain. There is no doubt that the metal fittings were made to enclose the leather strips which otherwise serve no useful purpose in the structure of the piece. Therefore it has been argued that they are the reason for making the object in the first place and that the metal plates were made to protect them. The object is therefore a protective reliquary or shrine that was made to house a relic — in this case the remains of a leather strap or belt. This reliquary is made in the shape and form of the relic it encloses in the same way that a crozier or bell-shrine takes the form of the sacred object it contains.

In early medieval Ireland, as elsewhere, the cult of relics was well developed by the eighth century. In Ireland, more than elsewhere, objects regarded as the possessions of early Irish saints have survived in large numbers. The most important of these were bells, croziers and books, but other objects such as shoes and cloaks were also preserved and venerated. There is also evidence in the literature that belts or girdles associated with saints were known. These are mentioned in the early Lives of the saints and, as with other saintly possessions, some of these belts were thought to have miraculous powers. The girdle of St Crónán of Roscrea, for instance, was placed around the waist of a king of Munster, thereby curing him of a terrible ailment. Another girdle belonging to St Brigid of Kildare would heal any disease or illness. In another instance, one of the properties of the sacred girdle of St Mobhí was that 'it was never closed around lies', meaning that it was used in the swearing of oaths, as were many other Irish relics. The common theme running through all these accounts is the fact that the wonder-working belt or girdle was placed around the waist, whether to effect a cure or to establish truthfulness. This, then, would account for the extensive wear seen on the hinges and buckle of the Moylough belt.

There is a reference to the existence of a jewelled girdle similar to that from Moylough in a Life of the Galway saint Colmán mac Duach. It is recounted how the saint was advised by God to build his monastery on the spot where his belt fell. The place was Kilmacduagh in south Galway, where the remains of Colmán's foundation still stand to this day. The author of the Life then goes on to describe how the saint's girdle was afterwards treasured in his honour. It was adorned with gold and jewels and was preserved down to the present day by the O'Shaughnessys. It was famous for many wonderful cures, but was particularly celebrated as a test of chastity. Unfortunately this belt no longer survives, but a crozier associated with this saint does and it is now preserved in the National Museum of Ireland.

We can imagine, therefore, that the belt found at Moylough 50 years ago was another of these belt-shrines — the only one to have survived to the present day. It has suffered somewhat through wear and use. In particular, most of the tinned surface has worn away, but originally the contrast between the bronze panels set with inlays of yellow and red enamel and blue and white glass and the silvered appearance of the side plates would have been striking. It must have been associated with an early Connacht saint, but unfortunately the find-place gives us no clue as to who this was or where it might have been kept in medieval times. From what we know of other reliquaries, however, it seems likely that the unknown saint may have been local. There is no reason to suppose that the object was not made locally, and indeed the mica plates used on the end panels could have come from the granite of the Ox Mountains.

On this basis, given the fact that Moylough lies only 6km south of Achonry, which gives its name to the parish and diocese, one could speculate that it was perhaps associated with the ancient church of Achonry or Achad Conaire. This church was founded by St Finnian of Clonard and its patron saint is St Nathí. Nathí was buried at Achonry and his feast-day falls on 9 August according to the early ninth-century 'Martyrology of Oengus'. Little is known of the early history of Achonry, however, and the first recorded bishop was Máel Ruadáin Ua Ruadáin, who was present at the Synod of Kells in 1152. He was accorded the title 'easpog Luigne', that is 'bishop of the Luigne', after the territory in which Achonry is located and which gives its name to the modern barony of Leyny.

There is no way we can establish when and why the belt-shrine ended up in the bog at Moylough. From the evidence of its repairs and the amount of wear, it appears to have been of some considerable age before being buried. This

Pl. 57—Members of the Towey family, the Curry Moylough community and Sligo County Council at the unveiling of the monument on the site where the belt-shrine was found, July 2001 (photo: Brian Cahill/Sligo Champion).

suggests that it might have been buried during the later Middle Ages. It is unlikely that the object was lost casually in the bog, but on the other hand it would seem from the finder's description of its discovery that the object was not protected in any way, as might be expected if it had been placed there for safety.

The Moylough Belt-shrine is artistically a very beautiful object showing a high degree of technical skill in its manufacture, and its techniques are comparable to those found on some of the best pieces of eighth-century Irish metalwork. In recognition of the importance of the find to the local community, the National Museum of Ireland agreed to the exhibition of the belt-shrine in the parish church at Moylough on 1 July 1995 as part of the celebrations marking the fiftieth anniversary of its discovery. Sadly, Mr Towey had passed away some three months previously. The people of Moylough themselves marked the discovery of the find in July 2001 when a small monument was unveiled close to the site where the shrine was found (Pl. 57). It bears an engraved image of the belt-shrine with an inscription which reads 'Moylough Belt. Found nearby in 1945 by John Towey.'

Acknowledgements

I am grateful to Rev. Fr Martin Jennings, P.P., Moylough, for providing me with a copy of the video recording of Mr Towey's account of the finding of the belt-shrine from which the picture of Mr John Towey is taken. The photograph of the unveiling of the monument on the site where the belt-shrine was found, taken by Brian Cahill, was kindly provided by the *Sligo Champion*.

Further reading

Duignan, M. 1951 The Moylough (Co. Sligo) and other Irish belt-reliquaries. *Journal of the Galway Archaeological and Historical Society* **24**, 83–94.

Duignan, M. 1953 Early Irish belt-reliquaries. In E. Vogt (ed.), *Actes de la IIIe Session Zurich 1950*, 308–10. Zurich.

O'Kelly, M.J. 1965 The belt-shrine from Moylough, Sligo. *Journal of the Royal Society of Antiquaries of Ireland* **95**, 149–88.

Harbison, P. 1981 The date of the Moylough belt-shrine. In D. Ó Corráin (ed.), *Irish antiquity*, 231–9. Cork.

Ryan, M. 1989 Belt-shrine. In S. Youngs (ed.), *'The Work of Angels' — masterpieces of Celtic metalwork, 6th–9th centuries AD*, 58–9. London.

18

A 'Danish' legacy

Brian Lacey

Archaeology in Ireland is a thoroughly professional activity which is, of course, becoming ever more 'professionalised' all the time. The requirement that all those directing excavations should be licensed by the state has been an important backbone of that system since the 1930s. However, amateurs (in the literal and best sense of that word, i.e. as 'lovers' of the subject) have also been (and are) at the heart of Irish archaeology as long as the subject has existed. Like many others I have benefited personally on numerous occasions from the enthusiasms and knowledge of those who do not make their living from archaeology — not least during the archaeological survey of County Donegal which I had the privilege to direct from the summer of 1979 until the publication of the survey volume in the summer of 1983.

That 'professional' survey had been preceded by an 'amateur' survey which had been established in 1972 by the Donegal Historical Society and carried out by its volunteer members. This survey had been inspired by and was at first under the direction of Mairéad Dunlevy of the National Museum of Ireland, as well as the late Mr E. W. Steadman, the then principal of the Royal and Prior School in Raphoe. In 1975, shortly after I moved to live in Derry, Mairéad asked me if I would take over in her place; thus began an association with the many people interested in the archaeology of the marvellous and beautiful County Donegal.

Among the people I met in this connection was Miss M.R. ('Mabel') Colhoun of Derry or, as she might have preferred, Londonderry. In fact Mabel was one of the first persons I met on taking up a post as a 'local studies' lecturer at Magee College in Derry late in 1974. If anything was going on connected, however vaguely, with the archaeology, history or natural history of the north-west of Ireland Mabel was in the thick of it. She was a member and, indeed, a

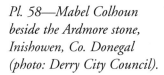
Pl. 58—Mabel Colhoun beside the Ardmore stone, Inishowen, Co. Donegal (photo: Derry City Council).

founding member of several societies involved with these matters, and a long-standing member of the Royal Society of Antiquaries of Ireland, serving as its Vice-President for Ulster from 1978 to 1980. Although Mabel came from a thoroughly Northern Ireland unionist background (several of her relatives had been involved in the municipal politics in the city of Derry), since the 1930s she had taken a particular interest in the field studies of the Inishowen Peninsula, Co. Donegal, and had been encouraged by Dr A. T. Lucas and Dr J. Raftery of the National Museum to apply a standardised scientific method to her work there. The result was a lifetime's collection of detailed field notebooks which were accompanied by meticulously and beautifully marked-up 6in. maps. Although it became an increasing ambition of Mabel's to publish this material in book form, she was incredibly generous with her knowledge to anyone who showed any interest in the material she had collected.

In 1979 the professional survey of the county was established, based to some extent on the previous voluntary work but largely driven from the Donegal Regional Development Organisation as a means of capitalising for tourism purposes on the archaeological resources of the county. I became director of that survey and had reasons to consult with many amateur enthusiasts from all over the county. Invariably I had occasion to consult with Mabel, and although, to some extent, we were the brash young newcomers who were 'stealing her thunder' (we had the money not only to carry out the survey but, crucially, also to publish it) she could not have been more helpful. On one occasion I went to see Mabel's records about a site in the townland of Roosky in the north-west of Inishowen. The site, which seems to have been a cashel, had been destroyed for the most part in 1966 when a dwelling-house was erected there. I was hoping that Mabel had recorded the site prior to its destruction. During the house construction a hoard of four Viking silver bracelets had 'fallen, apparently, from the surrounding wall when it was being removed'.

The site had been further investigated and the hoard described by Dr Joseph Raftery in 1969, although he made no reference to Mabel's notes. However, as I expected, Mabel had made a detailed record of the site in 1946, a long time before its destruction and the dramatic Scandinavian find. What was most surprising, however, about her notes was that Mabel had recorded a local tradition that 'A Dane was buried in the enclosure'. I am fully aware that beliefs of this sort were commonly associated with ancient monuments in many parts of Ireland. No actual evidence of a burial of any kind was recorded during the destruction of the site at Roosky, although that is not to say that such a burial didn't actually exist. Notwithstanding this, is it possible that Mabel had preserved some sort of genuine tradition about the site, originating 1000 years earlier and preserved down to the twentieth century when she visited it, twenty years before 'evidence' of any Scandinavian connection actually came to light?

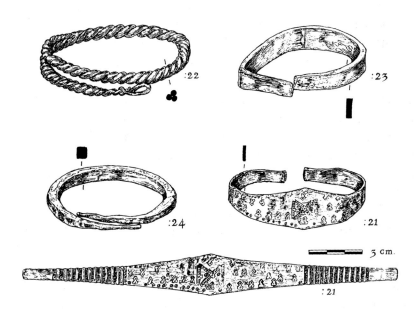

Fig. 34—Viking silver bracelets, Roosky, Inishowen, Co. Donegal (after Raftery 1969).

Despite the publication of the *Archaeological survey of Donegal* in 1983, efforts continued by Mabel and others, including this author, to have her work published. I remember on one occasion trying to explain to Mabel the benefits of transferring her text on to that new invention of the time, the personal word processor. As an example of the wonders of this new technology I explained to Mabel that, at 'one flick of a switch', if she wished, all the 'Derrys' could be changed to 'Londonderrys', or vice versa for that matter!

Like many amateur archaeologists around the country, Mabel did not see her work published. Unfortunately she died in 1992, but a group of people continued to work on her text, which was published posthumously in book form on 16 November 1995. A large group of Mabel's relatives and acquaintances gathered for the occasion, among them her nephew David Trimble, leader of the Ulster Unionist Party, who flew home specially from London, where he had been taking part in important discussions relating to the Northern Ireland peace process.

Further reading

Colhoun, M.R. 1995 *The heritage of Inishowen: its archaeology, history and folklore.* Derry.

Lac[e]y, B. 1979 Archaeological survey of Donegal. *Donegal Annual* **13** (3), 445–6.

Lac[e]y, B. 1983 The archaeological survey of County Donegal. In T. Reeves-Smyth and F. Hamond (eds), *Landscape archaeology in Ireland*, 9–23. British Archaeological Reports, British Series 116. Oxford.

Lac[e]y, B. *et al.* 1983 *Archaeological survey of Donegal.* Lifford.

Raftery, J. 1969 A hoard of Viking silver bracelets from County Donegal. *Journal of the Royal Society of Antiquaries of Ireland* **99**, 133–6.

19

Discovering Versailles in the smallness of my own experience

Tadhg O'Keeffe

What draws us towards archaeology? Many of us can vaguely remember, as some childhood epiphany, the wonder and excitement of a visit to an ancient site or an encounter with some old object. I have a very clear recall of my own 'first encounter'. I can put a date on it: summer 1971. I was very young then, but I worked it out when I was in my early teens by calculating backwards from other events in my life. The moment we fall under archaeology's spell for the first time is the moment that we make our most important discovery: we discover ourselves. I don't mean this in terms of a vocation, a finding out of what we want to be when we grow up, but in terms of our own identity, our own sense of being and of belonging. It is the one discovery shared by every author in this book.

This chapter is largely about the castle at Ballymoon, Co. Carlow, even if the title makes no allusion to that. It contains no startling revelation of fact or interpretation — it's simply a ramble through a fascinating building, reflecting on who was here and what happened to them. There is, however, a central idea which I wish to develop. As archaeologists we are constantly looking for dry facts about the things that we study. How old is this axe? What things are inside this mound? Where was this manuscript made? What did people do with this flint tool? But the answers to such questions are pit-stops, not finishing lines. Our reconstructions of the past are communicated as narratives or stories, which means that we are not laboratory scientists who *know* the parameters of our experiments and *know* then when the solutions are found, but storytellers, even historical novelists, and the accounts of the past which we offer our audience are most convincing when the plots seem plausible and the protagonists are recognisable.

But I don't want to start with Ballymoon. Instead, I'm going to take full advantage of the spirit of this book and begin this chapter by writing about my discovery of archaeology in 1971. And, in a further shameless exploitation of the book's spirit, I'm going to write the entire chapter in a conversational style, which means that I'll use personal pronouns and contractions!

* * * * *

That summer my father, a schoolteacher with a passion for Cork hurling, brought my brother and me to see a particularly well-preserved castle in the Moore Park estate in north Cork, close to his home village of Kilworth. Motorists will probably know the castle quite well: it's on the Mitchelstown side of Fermoy and rises out of a magnificent spread of trees on the banks of that most onomatopoeically-titled of trout rivers, the Funcheon. The castle was simply the most special element in a landscape which I grew to know and love. While for much of its history it stood, like many of Ireland's castles, in a kind of adversarial relationship with the people of its locality, the passage of time had made it a familiar and friendly face, a quintessential feature of the locale by any reckoning. Anyway, what I remember particularly about that first castle-visit is the large stone-floored room inside. My father held us back in the stairwell and gingerly stepped into the room, tapping the floor with his foot to see if it was safe to stand on. And when he established that it was safe we all ventured in. Of course it was safe: there's an intact barrel vault underneath. I now know that floor-tapping, to coin a phrase, is not needed (and, anyway, no insurance company would accept it as a reasonable test of safety!), but I still do it every time I enter a ruined castle which I haven't previously been in, and every single time I do it I remember my father.

There is something fascinating about a castle which ends its life in ruins. Why are some castles allowed to fall more and more deeply into decay? Why are other castles spared this? If my father was proud of his local castle, and his home village proud of it as well, what does the abandonment or pulling down of a castle somewhere else say about memory and identity in its locality? These are not scientific questions, but they touch upon important issues, so we should not be afraid to ask them and to think about their possible answers.

It is an unfamiliar feeling, all these years later, to be writing about this for a book which is about archaeology, which contains articles by colleagues and friends within archaeology, and which will — we all hope! — be bought in copious amounts in bookshops around Ireland, including in north Cork. Archaeologists are not accustomed to writing about themselves in any autobiographical sense, at least not before retirement age, and even then it is only the most senior figures with the most distinguished careers who are spared the accusation that autobiography is an utterly narcissistic enterprise! We're not supposed to be a part of the story. Should I have told you about myself? Were this book an academic publication in the, eh, 'conventional' sense of the word I wouldn't have told you about myself, nor would I have been allowed to tell you. Why? Standing beside me is an imaginary referee; I'll let her answer that question: *it has nothing to do with the castle in Cork*. It is a fair point, but to return to the point I made at the start, every chapter in this book is about the archaeologist as well as the archaeology. Every chapter here has its origin in some moment of self-discovery, and every idea and mode of expression presented here says something about the personal as well as the professional journey which the archaeologist has taken from that first discovery. So we are a part of the story. This typically reflective quote from Henry Glassie (taken from his 1999 book *Material culture*, with emphasis added) surely applies as readily to the writings of archaeologists as it does to the things which are produced by builders, potters and poets:

> Buildings, like pots and poems, realize culture. Their designers rationalize their actions differently. Some say they design and build as they do because it is the ancient way of their people and place. Others claim that their practice correctly manifests the universally valid laws of science. But all of them create out of *the smallness of their own experience.*

Versailles and Ballymoon

Now we can turn to Ballymoon Castle (Pl. 59). This is in Carlow, not in Cork, and is a less familiar but better-known structure. Anybody who has ever written anything scholarly or popular about Irish castles has written something about Ballymoon, which puts it in the same exalted company as castles like Trim and Carrickfergus, or Cahir and Bunratty. If we wish to make lists, then Ballymoon certainly belongs in that company, but it is worth pointing out, even at this stage of the paper, that it is also the odd-man-out — and as a castle it has to be a 'man', hasn't it? — in any such pantheon: we don't know when it was built, we don't know for whom or by whom it was built, we have no documentary references to its medieval occupation, and we have no exact parallels for its architectural form. Ballymoon may feature in all the published histories of castles in Ireland, but it does so rather uncooperatively. What makes it truly remarkable to my mind is that there are no obvious buildings against which to judge quite how remarkable it is! It's the best of its type in Ireland because it's the only example of its type.

Most of Ballymoon's visitors today probably reach it via Bagenalstown; some carry on towards Bunclody via Fenagh, and some might venture a little deeper into rural Carlow to see Ballyloughan, another castle of about the same date. Bagenalstown is a small River Barrow town several miles to the west of Ballymoon, and is the quintessence of a granite-cut landlord town of the Blackstairs region. It was founded by Walter Bagenal just over 200 years ago to bear the name Versailles! It is not intended to be disrespectful to Bagenalstown to say that we would see the reality as falling rather short of the ambition. In some ways the reality is less relevant than the idea. Bagenal's very conceit is intrinsically interesting, and the proximity of his town to Ballymoon, another ambitious project in Leinster granite which appears to us unfulfilled, seems entirely appropriate if fortuitous.

The walk up to the castle from the main road brings you among and past old earthen banks which are identified by some scholars as the remains of an abortive or long-abandoned settlement. If they are settlement earthworks they are rather unusual. Perhaps it is better — unless and until geophysical or excavation evidence eventually suggests otherwise — to think of these as features of landscape gardening intended to enhance visual perspectives of the castle; given the increasing volume of evidence that water was an important feature of thirteenth- and fourteenth-century castles in England, we should perhaps extend this interpretation to the moated site which sits several hundred metres from the castle within a different field but within the same relatively open landscape.

The castle is entered today through a modest gate-opening (Pl. 61) which was originally protected by a portcullis if not also by some external pit-and-drawbridge. Inside is a large empty courtyard, but it is clear that there was originally a much smaller courtyard and that the circuit of inner walling is missing (Pl. 60). Facing you on the side opposite the entrance are cross-loop windows, fireplaces, and small doorways leading into toilets (Pl. 61). Over to the right the same arrangement is also apparent, but here there is a tall tower halfway along the wall. On the opposite wall there is a canopy-less double fireplace and the plunging sills of large windows, features consistent with a great hall (Pl. 62). These are all indicators that this is a colonial or English castle, no earlier than the mid-1200s but not likely to be later than the mid-1300s.

Standing at the entrance you can see immediately why everybody agrees that Ballymoon is unfinished: the outer walls all rise to about the same height, and you can easily interpret that as the height at which the builders stopped. The alternative is to see the incomplete walls as evidence of destruction, but that would involve visualising some intrepid stone-robbers clambering along the top and dismantling the fabric with pickaxes and spirit-levels! While we can work out some of the intended functions of some parts of the castle, no floors may ever have been put in place for people to walk on, and no rooms may ever have been

216

formed for those functions to take place inside. We have all been inside ruined castles, but I find the effect of being inside an unfinished castle, even one left unfinished seven-odd centuries ago, strangely unsettling, as if I am trespassing and a ghostly site-foreman might appear to reprimand me at any moment. It's that type of place. Something happened very suddenly here in the Middle Ages.

Now, I have described Ballymoon only very briefly, not according to its plan and elevations and details, which is how archaeologists conventionally describe buildings, but according to the experiences of approaching it and of looking around it from the vantage point of the entrance. Why this particular strategy? Well, were we attempting a comparative analysis of the castle we would talk about those plans, elevations and details. Indeed, implicitly underpinning so much archaeological literature is the notion that establishing the comparative context of a site is tantamount to understanding it. So, our desire to find context not only leads us to privilege certain recording techniques — plans, elevations and details — over other, more experiential, ones, but it makes us feel that lingering on the intrinsic interest, even beauty, of a site is closer to dilettantism than to scholarship.

Plans, elevations and detail-drawings are somewhat abstract things, reduced from (or, in the case of details, extracted from) the physical realities of sites. This is absolutely not to deny the importance of this type of record but instead to suggest that, whereas I find it difficult to think about Ballymoon without conjuring up a mental image of a drawn plan, the medieval world did not necessarily see it that way. We negotiate our own lived-in spaces by using cognitive maps rather than measured plans, even though measured plans do exist for so many elements of our world. So, perhaps the nearest the medieval builders of Ballymoon got to making a plan was when they marked and dug out the lines of the foundations on the ground; perhaps no proper scaled plan of Ballymoon existed until Harold Leask drew one seventy-odd years ago. All of this is worth reflecting on, given the problem of locating a stylistic context for Ballymoon: other castle-builders of the Middle Ages may have found inspiration in Ballymoon and may have undertaken to reproduce something from it in other buildings, but if they conceptualised Ballymoon differently from us then we might not identify those reproductions; they might not be exact formal replicas. By the same token, Ballymoon may itself have been inspired by some other building and yet that inspiration might not be detectable to us in the building's formal character. Our problem at Ballymoon is that we're not privy to the intellectual processes involved in the architectural imitation and innovation which led to it and then led away from it.

Pl. 59—A general view of Ballymoon Castle, taken from the Bagenalstown–Bunclody road.

Pl. 60—The moated site to the north-west of Ballymoon, viewed from the castle walls.

Pl. 61—The main entrance and, in the background, a window, a fireplace and a doorway for a toilet.

Pl. 62—The great hall at Ballymoon.

Life on the frontier

The apparent lack of formal comparanda is only a small part of Ballymoon's intrigue. The real mystery surrounds its qualities as a castle and its location in an area which is regularly assumed to have been unsafe around the time it was constructed.

Let's take the latter point first. The road which leads from Bagenalstown to the Ballymoon/Ballyloughan area continues on towards the Blackstairs Mountains and into a land which is commonly assumed to have harboured Gaelic-Irish groups antagonistic to the medieval Anglo-Norman (actually English) settlers in the Barrow Valley. There is comparatively little settlement archaeology between Ballymoon and these mountains which could be attributed indisputably to colonial families, and for archaeologists that reinforces the impression that this was mainly a Gaelic-Irish area. Armed with this model of the English and Irish facing each other across the rolling foothills of central Carlow, it is easy to stand at Ballymoon and tell a bunch of students — as I admit to having done in the past — that they should imagine a scene something like this:

The new century — the fourteenth — is barely under way. The castle is still a building site, busy with stone-cutters and carpenters. Nothing has been roofed yet. Cold winds swirl around its half-finished courtyard; the ground, hardened by the trampling of feet, has scattered pools of stagnant, white lime-stained water. There is rickety wooden scaffolding here and there around the walls, and it's creaking under the strain as men operate pulleys and hoists to raise large stones up to the wall-head.

Suddenly, somebody on the scaffolding spots trouble on the horizon. It's the Irish. Like horse-riding Apache warriors in a 1950s Western, or the Zulu warriors at Rourke's Drift, they are lined up side by side on the low granite rises to the north, perfectly silhouetted against the sky. There are weapons in the Ballymoon courtyard, and there are men here who know how to use them, but most of the people here are really just builders, and they are just doing their labour service — today the lord has them cracking open yellow granite for the castle, and tomorrow they might be back on the demesne, cracking open the soil and planting seeds for next season's cereals. Had the architect followed the conventions of most castle-architects of the period and designed circular corner towers for flanking defence, or a twin-towered gate-building at the entrance, the place could be defended, even with the parapets left unfinished. Instead, the castle is very vulnerable to attack, and today its moment has come. Maybe the workmen run; maybe they are overrun. The Irish dismantle the scaffolding and make off with it; they have no need for the cut stone — it's too heavy to transport and, anyway, what would they do with it? They could, of course, stay around Ballymoon now that it's been wrested away from the English, but they're not keen; they don't want the English here, but they don't particularly want to be here themselves either. Ballymoon is left as an isolated ruin in an isolated countryside. With the dismantling of the scaffolding the English aspirations in central Carlow are also dismantled.

This is quite an easy flight of imagination. Ironically, it brings to life Ballymoon's death. But it is also a very twentieth-century story. The imagining is cinematic and the protagonists are stereotyped: we see the Irish as if looking through the eyes of a John Wayne or a Michael Caine, and they have all the gestures, all the posturing, which we associate with the 'native' and dispossessed. It is very difficult for us to mentally reconstruct such a scene in another way. And if we now find that the wholesale on-screen slaughter of native peoples in movies like *Zulu* makes them difficult to watch, as if viewing for pleasure makes us complicit in historical acts of genocide, we could see in the abandoned castle at Ballymoon some measure of victory for an indigenous but downtrodden majority. When Harold Leask suggested a date of around 1310 for Ballymoon and pinned it on to the end of his chapters of 'Norman' castles, thereby leaving it as the last building before his long fourteenth-century hiatus, he (inadvertently, I'm certain) made it a powerful metaphor for what we imagine the fate of 'Norman' Ireland to have been at the dawn of the Gaelic resurgence. The absence of a historical record for Ballymoon is part of the same metaphor: for a castle as grand as this to be denied historical representation is a fitting end to an era in which the colonial English seem so comprehensively known to us.

Now, the point about this being a grand castle is important for deconstructing this vision and the politics which breathe life into it. Ballymoon was clearly going to be a castle of considerable merit, complete with a magnificent (by contemporary standards in Ireland, at any rate) great hall for dining and corporate entertainment, and plush *en suite* accommodation for the household and its guests, and set in a landscape especially moulded for effect. We can imagine a prescribed pathway to the castle from the road, maybe leading the visitors around the castle before allowing them to enter, and then some prescribed pathways inside the castle, leading first, perhaps, to a waiting area, and then to the hall for an audience and meal, and then to the lodgings. The spaces to be encountered on this procession were not going to be empty but were to be filled with furnishings. The walls were to be emblazoned with the sort of decorative paraphernalia which we ourselves use in our houses to tell our visitors something about ourselves: when finished, Ballymoon might have on its walls some souvenirs of war, a skull with antlers, and some tapestries, just as some modern houses might have on their walls some souvenirs of holidays, a stuffed fish in a glass case, and some reproduction Impressionists. We all think about display in the same way; all of our houses, whether we are English lords in medieval Carlow or university lecturers in modern Dublin, are in some way autobiographical, and those autobiographies reveal, as Henry Glassie would put it, 'the smallness' of our own experiences.

Like many a big house of a later date, Ballymoon was probably going to be part-empty most of the time, but nobody on the outside was going to know that. The chimneys of its many fireplaces were to be placed on the outer walls, perhaps so that people *on the outside* (both literally and metaphorically) would be able to see smoke billowing from them and would think of the warmth and comfort on the inside. The toilets — all fourteen or more of them — were all provided with chutes emptying within sight (and smell?) of those standing outside the building, and these too may have been intended to communicate something of the household's good diet and therefore also of its control of resources; broken sherds from exotic imported pots might also have ended up at the bottom of the chutes, further firing the imaginations of those not privileged to enter.

So, to think that Ballymoon has to be abandoned because it 'fails' some test of defensibility is surely to misunderstand what its builders were setting out to do. Anyway, who in the Middle Ages told us that 'true' castles had flanking towers for their defence? And who back then told us that castles were essentially military things? Of course defence was important in medieval castles, and when you walk around the outside of Ballymoon and observe just how high those walls are, even in their incomplete state, you can see that this would not have been an easy building to get inside. But we have fetishised defence, and that has reduced our sensitivity to some of the other things which castle-builders had in mind. Perhaps this is the greatest lesson that we can learn from Ballymoon.

Let's return, though, to Ballymoon's abandonment during construction. Yes, the Gaelic-Irish do indeed seem ideal candidates to blame in trying to explain the derailing of this operation. There were almost certainly Gaelic-Irish people in the Ballymoon area, and they would have known very well that Ballymoon was being built. But do we really believe that so sumptuous a place as Ballymoon would have been started by the English in the first instance if these Irish posed such a threat? Surely not. Do we believe that the Irish would have watched in the wings and allowed the construction work to reach this phase before moving in for the kill? Surely not. If a castle like Ballymoon has a hint of medieval polite culture about it, then why not envisage some Gaelic-Irish acquiescence in its construction? Semi-autonomous Gaelic families in the hills of central Carlow might well have seen economic opportunities in the presence of a colonial community at Ballymoon, and indeed at Ballyloughan. I am uneasy about explaining Ballymoon's demise directly in terms of a relationship between medieval 'English' and medieval 'Irish' because such an explanation seems to be informed not by an actual knowledge of how these people interacted but by a perception or assumption that ethnic differences in early fourteenth-century Ireland required a violent resolution. The historical sources may lead us to imagine endless cycles of violence between two well-defined camps, but historical sources do not always give us the full picture. In any case, I think that our imagination is mediated through a whole series of modern understandings of ethnicity and enmity, and that the people of the Ballymoon countryside might not recognise themselves in our visions of them.

There are two more likely explanations, I think, for Ballymoon's abandonment midway through construction. The first one might implicate the Gaelic-Irish indirectly: Ballymoon may have proved too ambitious a project to have survived any sudden or unexpected shortfall in available funds, and a general economic downturn within the region could well have precipitated such a financial crisis. In the second explanation the patron dies and basically brings the Ballymoon project with him to his grave. One candidate for the patron is Roger Bigod, earl of Norfolk and possessor of the Liberty of Carlow, who died in 1306; he was not resident in Ireland, but could Ballymoon have been intended as a country house for him here? Whatever the case, the next time I return to Ballymoon with students I might change the story at a crucial point:

> Suddenly, somebody on the scaffolding spots trouble on the horizon. It's a man on horseback, coming in from the west, carrying the news that the operation is to be closed down. English *and* Irish labourers put down their tools, speculating and gossiping among themselves...

Innocence lost or regained?

There are two reasons why I have discussed Ballymoon in this chapter. First, it is an interesting and exciting castle to visit and to think about, so it deserves to be discussed in a book about archaeology and archaeologists in Ireland. Secondly, it provides an ideal context for discussing the leaps which we, as archaeologists, make between observation and interpretation.

Just as my view of what the discipline of archaeology can be has changed since my student days, so too has my view of what we can say about castles. And what we can say involves opening up, not closing down, the range of possible interpretations. There is no one single, correct, story to be told any more; this is not *The Hitch-hiker's Guide to the Galaxy* and we are not looking for *the* number that answers everything. There is no such number — there is an infinity of numbers, each of which answers a different question. The intellectual journey which some of us make to reach this point is a journey which, in the context of castles, leads away from simple childhood 'readings' and carries on past the 'let's-put-things-in-categories' approach of people like Harold Leask. Embarking on such journeys involves, to quote the late David Clarke (the great Cambridge archaeologist who is lauded/blamed for the so-called New Archaeology), a 'loss of innocence'. When Clarke wrote this in 1973 (in the journal *Antiquity*) he was railing against those archaeologists who, through *innocent* or uncritical assumptions about material culture and the human condition, were able to move blithely from observation to interpretation. Even though we have moved away from the type of scientism which Clarke advocated as a proper methodology, what he and others did was liberating. They began that process of philosophical and methodological introspection which eventually brought post-modernism into archaeology.

There are, of course, many archaeologists who don't like this 'theoretical turn' — they see it as faddish, and they claim that it is irrelevant to the real business of reconstructing the past. Our subject is a broad enough church to accommodate both the hard-line theoreticians who have little engagement with actual archaeological material and the dyed-in-the-wool 'let's get working on the material and finding out what really happened in the past, and stop messing about with this post-structuralism and hermeneutic stuff' brigade. But wherever we position ourselves between these polar opposites, we must accept that reconstructing the past is not an act of common sense. We must accept also that we, as archaeologists, are a part of the stories that we tell about the past, precisely because our visions of the past are constructed out of the smallness of our own experiences. But I wonder, finally, about Clarke's phrase, a 'loss of innocence'. My own journey is, in some ways, a journey back *towards* innocence, if only because from the moment that I read Leask for the first time I have struggled to see any of these buildings — even my beloved Cork castle — through eyes other than his.

20

Light on a saucer

Clare McCutcheon

I love to open presents and I am fascinated by medieval pottery. The study of the material from the Wood Quay waterfront site gave me a wonderful opportunity to open up over 2800 boxes of medieval pottery, all tucked away tidily in stacks of drawers in a basement. When I first went to work on this material, a number of very interesting, unusual or semi-complete pieces were placed in easily accessible drawers. There they could be shown to visitors, particularly ceramic specialists, who might be able to assist with identifications; often short notes, carefully dated and signed, accompany the items. Some of the pieces had been so interesting that they had been put on various displays in the National Museum or other exhibitions since the excavations in the 1970s. Two of these pieces provide the inspiration for this short paper which shows how some special pieces can spur us on in identifying medieval pottery in Ireland. I am grateful to Dr Patrick Wallace, Director of the National Museum of Ireland, for permission to refer to these pieces and to use an illustration in advance of publication.

The first item, at the time on display in the 'Dublinia' exhibition, was a round, grey, unglazed piece that I had seen and passed by several times. It was in a case with other items loosely called 'roof furniture'. This term covers roof tiles, chimney-pots or louvers, and finials or decorative and fun figures put at either end of the roof. When a colleague, Joanna Wren, who specialises in such material came to work on these items from the Wood Quay site, we removed all the roof furniture from Dublinia for accurate measurements and close scrutiny for publication. I still remember the excitement I felt when, walking past Joanna's desk, I idly turned over this particular piece to see the other side. It could only be said that I swiped it off the table, clutched it to my chest and refused to let go — many thanks for your generosity, Joanna!

I was immediately certain that this was the central portion of a tall lamp, of a type made in France in the eleventh and twelfth centuries. The piece itself looks like a saucer and is about the same size, but with straight rather than sloping sides. The top of the lamp is a small cup that holds hot oil and a wick, with the saucer protecting the hand and making it safe to carry around. Convincing other colleagues in the National Museum was somewhat more difficult when I brought it around to 'show and tell' as I couldn't find an illustration of a similar lamp. Several suggested that I had been working too long on my own in the basement and I needed to get out more often (true). Drawings of numerous lamps from excavations at Saint-Denis near Paris were apparently not convincing enough as they were not decorated in the same way as the saucer from Wood Quay. The edges on this saucer were decorated with extra clay, giving a frilled effect, in addition to some fancy rouletting or little indentations around the edges.

Armed with an export licence, I went to London to a Medieval Pottery Research Group conference — yes, over 100 people talking about nothing but pottery for three days and showing each other their odd bits and pieces. The author of the article on the Saint-Denis lamps, Nicole Meyer, was to be present at the conference, so at one of the coffee breaks I pulled the piece from its protective wrapping and handed it to her with no comment but a rather hopeful look on my face. She uttered the immortal words to me, 'This lamp does not come from Saint-Denis', and she was rather taken aback when my face lit up with a huge smile. I explained to her that I was going to simply enjoy the fact that it was a lamp for a while and continue the search for sources later, and I continued smiling throughout the conference.

A year later I took a 2400km trip around France over eighteen days, sponsored by the Royal Irish Academy. I had a silver-coloured metal case strapped onto trolley wheels that I dragged or carried over the cobblestones of numerous medieval city centres. This was carefully packed with interesting but unidentified pieces of French pottery from Wood Quay. My hope was that colleagues in France would recognise some of these and thereby solve some of the mysteries of French pottery around Ireland. For those people whose next question is 'How do you know it is French in the first place?', a very quick explanation. In identifying medieval pottery in Ireland, my very basic rule of thumb is that the clay in French pottery is white except where it's red, Irish is red except where it's grey, and English is grey except where it's white!! In other words, white firing clay is most likely to be French, but in addition there are other indications of shape, design and decoration that mean a piece is most likely to be French rather than English. The English specialists sometimes have a tricky case where French potters came to England with the Normans and made French-shaped pots in English clay. At least here we know that the glazed pots made in medieval Ireland were of English design, primarily for the English in Ireland —

but that's a story for another day.

In Rouen Museum a new temporary exhibition was completely devoted to pottery and a similar lamp was on display. The curator, Natalie Roy, noted my interest and asked me to come into one of the Aladdin's Cave storerooms so characteristic of museums. There on a shelf stood the exact duplicate of my piece, but this time as an almost complete lamp. I offered to bring it back to Ireland, but instead Natalie very generously gave me a photograph of the Rouen lamp with all the relevant information, such as measurements and find-spots and the fact that the lamp was made in Rouen. The differences in size are so small as to be insignificant, and the reconstruction drawing will be relatively simple with so much information available. A generous friend, Cathy Johnson, listened to my story about this lamp so many times that she commissioned the making of a pair of candlesticks, inspired by the lamp, by the potter Anthony O'Brien and presented them to me as a memento of a significant birthday.

My second piece, also from Wood Quay, is still looking for its original home and is of considerable interest. The very fine drawing by John Murray, of the National Museum of Ireland, shows the piece as reconstructed. The spout from this piece had been on display several times as part of an aquamanile or water-jug, again a perfectly reasonable and well-informed description. These aquamaniles were often made in the shape of an animal such as a horse or a sheep, and sometimes had a human figure riding on its back with the spout in a more or less realistic style. Forks were not used in medieval times and so hands could get greasy or sticky during a meal. Between courses hands were washed and dried, and while very wealthy people might afford metal aquamaniles, less wealthy people had handsome pottery pieces made, often resembling the metal shapes. Presumably the poorer people just licked their fingers!

The fine spout, glazed green, with the head of a dragon or dog sat on a shelf near me for the first year, along with a second spout, similar in design but glazed yellow, and both of these had also travelled several times to England to the specialists' meetings. There they simply aroused envy as no one had seen a similar piece and now there were two spouts in Dublin, although it was agreed that they were probably French.

I returned to the methodical search through material in the stacks of drawers to find pieces that were interesting or unusual items for illustration or identification and noticed a couple of odd French pieces with green glaze in one box. Further on there was another sherd, and then another — in all, some twenty small pieces that looked like each other but not like anything else, a truly subjective judgement.

Fortunately all these pieces fitted together but left me with another puzzle, an almost complete rim with no apparent spout but with an odd hole on the 'chest' of the piece and marks to show that something had been attached to it. I would like to be able to say that I immediately saw the potential for my spout, but suffice it to say it slowly dawned on me that I should try the two together as the glaze and clay were so similar. Yes, they fitted as though they were made for each other (which they were), and the whole complexion of the piece changed from an aquamanile to a spouted jug.

'Show and tell' was great fun that afternoon, but next on the list was the search for the handle. Because of the weight of the spout, the handle needed to be fairly solid to balance the jug, but this was a case of making a 3D jigsaw without the picture. It is true that when you are looking for a particular thing you will only find it if you look for something completely different. In the process of quantifying the sorted material and making any changes that were required, I extracted all those pieces thought to come from a large heavy vessel known as a mortar. These particular ones were made in clay rather than stone and had two heavy handles. One handle was complete and now struck me as being too long for the very squat mortars, but it fitted *exactly* into the space in the rim of the 'dragon' jug. Unfortunately I had made this discovery on my own, during lunchtime, and had to wait until civilised people had returned to their desks. Raghnall Ó Floinn of the National Museum appeared to understand the choking sound on the internal phone and came round immediately to Merrion Row, where, for once, I was rendered almost speechless.

I have since located a possible base and so the hatched lines on the drawing show how the complete jug may have looked (Fig. 35). A second rim piece, with the scar from a handle, is evidence that there was a pair of these green-glazed jugs, while the yellow-glazed spout shows a definite third jug. These also travelled with me around France, but the response was polite interest, pursed lips and much shoulder-shrugging as only the French can do. The difficulty with identifying French medieval pottery is partly due to the fact that many of the French prefer to excavate Roman sites and see the medieval stuff as distracting or a nuisance. Even when it is found, the pottery is rarely published so the search can be a bit hit-or-miss.

The mystery remains. It can be suggested that these jugs were made in France as a special commission and were brought to Dublin possibly as a special presentation or gift. While the style of decoration indicates a fourteenth/fifteenth-century date, they were found with other pottery dating from the thirteenth century. Where in France were they made and who brought them to Dublin? To whom were they presented and what was the occasion? Where were they used in Dublin? How long were they used and what was poured from them? How and when were they broken? Were the spouts used as children's toys or were they thrown into the city dump as no one could bear to see them broken in pieces?

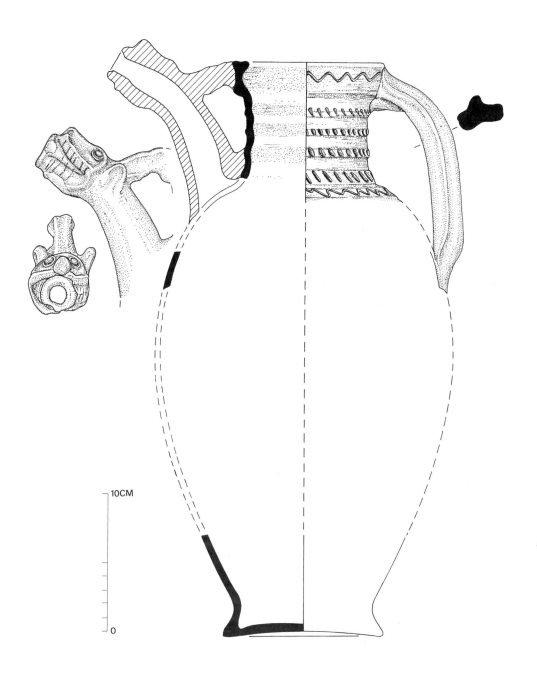

*Fig. 35—Spouted jug (illustration by John Murray, courtesy of the
National Museum of Ireland).*

Lost and found

Many of these questions are asked daily of the sherds of pottery and other artefacts found during excavations. In most cases, we can only attempt to give a reasoned and informed argument as to how they relate to their present context, with all due willingness to be open to a better-informed or more reasoned argument. In the meantime, the spouted jug is now on display in the 'Medieval Ireland 1150–1550' exhibition in the National Museum of Ireland in Kildare Street, and readers can decide for themselves what sort of animal is on the spout. Answers on a postcard, please!

Further reading

Hurley, M.F. 1997 *Excavations at the North Gate, Cork, 1994.* Cork.

Hurley, M.F. and Scully, O.M.B. 1997 *Late Viking-age and medieval Waterford: excavations 1986–1992.* Waterford.

McCarthy, M.R. and Brooks, C.M. *Medieval pottery in Britain AD 500–1500.* Leicester.

Simpson, L. 1995 *Excavations at Essex Street West, Dublin.* Dublin.

Wallace, P.F. 1983 North European pottery imported into Dublin, AD 1200–1500. In P. Davey and R. Hodges (eds), *Ceramics and trade,* 225–30. Sheffield.

21

A day in the life of a medieval fisherman ... and of intertidal archaeologists

Aidan O'Sullivan

A day in the life of a medieval fisherman ...

MacConmara hefted the bundle of rods into his arms and walked down the mudflats to the coracle. Handing the wood to his brother within, he pushed the boat into the water and jumped in. A few dips of their paddles and they were in mid-channel, caught in the current and drifting downstream. As the river slid away beneath them, the ebbing tide slowly exposed the mudflats and reeds along the banks. It was a fine summer's morning, the early sunlight glinting off the muds.

They chatted quietly together, muttering about the coming day's work, while the river carried them up to and past the English settlement at Bunratty. Even at this early hour there were signs of bustle and work outside the houses at the square, and the chatter of people's voices carried across the water. The men and women within the settlement were preparing their stalls and laying out the produce for the coming day's market. MacConmara's daughter was probably there already, with her knives and smoked fish. With luck, they would be back to her in a few hours with a good catch of salmon.

He started as his brother's voice called him back from his musings — 'Mind now!' Yes, they would need to be careful here. Even on a calm morning such as this, the rocks and eddies at Casey's Rock could tip them over. A few deft paddle-strokes and the coracle settled again, peaceably gliding downstream around Lochlainn's Point. They could now see others out before them on the estuary — the O'Deas and O'Briens, all working at their own fish-traps. The two men nodded and grinned at each group in turn as they drifted by, but they took no notice of their ribald taunts. There would be time for talk later …

They could see the old MacConmara weir now. The black, glistening wood protruded out of the muds, its sticks like the bones of a corpse long rotten — it was ghostly in the early morning light. He thought of his father … it was old in his time too, and it marked their place, where their people had fished for generations. And so now, beyond it, they could see the new fish-trap. Its well-built post-and-wattle fence and the wooden framework of its great basket tall and strong, still resisting the wind and tides, though probably not for much longer. The muds around it were getting deeper; since last year they had risen at least a foot, and it would soon be time to abandon it and rebuild.

They steered the hide-covered craft to the side of the channel, climbed out and hauled the boat up onto the mudflats. They would first repair the damage done to the fish-trap by last week's storms. Lifting out the wood, MacConmara walked easily across to the fence, his bare toes squishing in the deep mud. He shoved the top of the post-and-wattle fence back while his brother hammered in stout alder poles beside it, to fix it straight. Taking the thick hazel and willow branches, they tied them up against the poles to brace them up against the force of the ebbing tide. Hazel rods, smooth to their wet, chilled hands, they wove around the remaining posts, up to chest height.

Only then did he walk down the fence towards the basket, now appearing out of the water. Even from here he could hear the fish thrashing within it. Removing the wooden bung at the end, he reached inside the closely woven wicker. The first out was a big salmon, two years old at least, and good and heavy, even for this late in the summer. He placed it wriggling into the bag. 'Ah good'. There were two others, smaller but not bad. A couple of flounder, a sea trout as well, and a few small little fish. He drew these smaller ones out and flung them away across the muds. The gulls, looping and diving around them, shrieked and dived down, fighting for them. MacConmara lobbed the tightened bag into the coracle and returned to help his brother. They had plenty of time to relax now before the tide turned to bring them home…

… and of intertidal archaeologists

Working quickly together in the February morning light, we carried the inflatable boat and its engine down the concrete slipway to the water, before loading it up with our bags, tools, cameras and drawing equipment. As soon as we had manoeuvred ourselves into place, bulky in our raingear and lifejackets, Donal started the engine and reversed the boat out into the channel of the Owenogarney River. Within a few minutes we were motoring swiftly downstream, leaving Bunratty Castle, Durty Nelly's and all the tourist gift-shops behind us.

The storms of the previous night had flooded the fields and carparks around Bunratty, but while the gales and unusually high spring tide had wrought havoc on the land, we were expecting to benefit from the correspondingly low spring tide on the estuary. In a few hours, large areas of previously unseen mudflats would be exposed to view, and we hoped that the archaeological structures surviving there would also be more visible.

It was a cold, windy morning in 1997, and we were a team of archaeologists from the Discovery Programme, working on archaeological excavations of a number of ancient fish-traps on the mudflats. We had discovered them two years previously, in late September 1995, during our archaeological survey of the Shannon estuary and radiocarbon dates had shown that they belonged to the medieval period. Our survey work then had been in the mould of most intertidal archaeology: a 'snatch-and-grab' operation designed to record and sample archaeological sites during the few hours available at low tide. Our discoveries on the Shannon estuary foreshore had included Neolithic submerged forests, a Neolithic occupation or mortuary site, and Bronze Age houses and trackways in former coastal wetlands. However, most of the archaeological evidence could be dated to the historic period. It included early historic and medieval fish-traps as well as an array of post-medieval fisheries, wooden and stone quays, ballast mounds and shipwrecks. All of it testified to the significant role of the estuary in the region's history.

The River Owenogarney broadens out as it nears the north bank of the Shannon estuary. At this point Donal steered the boat out to the west of Little Quay Island and down into a mudflat creek that drained the vast expanse of muds between Quay Island and Clonmoney. Our aim was to get to a site we called Bunratty 6, a medieval fish-trap situated on the muds about 800m from any dryland. In the distance we could see white, wind-tossed waves on the estuary itself, but we would be relatively sheltered within our creek. Nevertheless, as the tide rapidly ebbed away, we were finding ourselves in increasingly shallow water; hardly more than 50–60cm underneath us were the muds. We had some nervous moments when our boat briefly stranded, but with a few chuckles we managed to push ourselves back out into the creek. But we only had minutes to unload the boat when we arrived at the site before Donal steered it down onto the estuary, where he could await the turn of the tides.

And then we simply waited. We huddled together on the mudflats, gazing intently down at the water in the creek in front of us, Eoin and Barry smoking

Fig. 36—Aerial photograph and map (by Shannon Estuary Ports) of the Shannon estuary around Bunratty, Co. Clare. Our archaeological surveys in this locality produced rich archaeological evidence for medieval and post-medieval fish-traps, quays and reclamation banks. While previously archaeologists would have overlooked such spaces, it is now clear that Ireland's coastal zone potentially preserves an enormous cultural heritage.

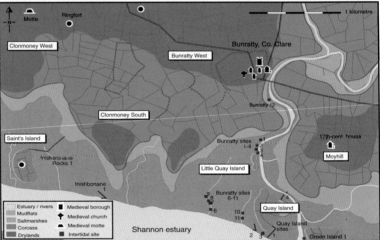

a cigarette, chatting quietly. The minutes ticked by and the water slipped away, bit by bit, the levels dropping ever lower as we watched them. Soon, sure enough, we could see a ghostly shadow in the water, almost a trick of the light — something appearing?

Then there they were at last: black, glistening posts, dripping wet, emerging out of the gloomy water. First we could see the post-and-wattle fence, with its vertical wooden posts, their tops rounded by erosion, and narrower rods woven between them. Then at the end of the fence we could see the rectangular framework of posts within which we knew lay a huge basket, buried deep in the mud. Here and there you could see bark and sapwood, perfectly preserved, as well as toolmarks on a sharpened end, as clear as the day they were cut. Our previous radiocarbon dates for Bunratty 6 had come out between AD 1164 and

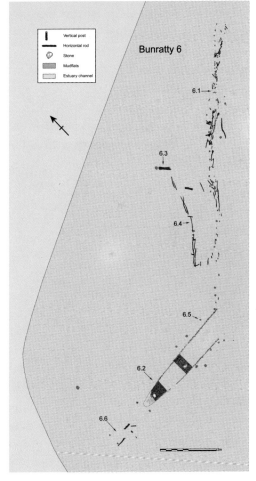

Fig. 37—Photograph and plan of the medieval fish-trap at Bunratty 6 (radiocarbon-dated to 1164–1279). This photograph was taken in summer 1998. The woven basket can be seen in the foreground buried in the clay, while the post-and-wattle fence stretching off into the distance would have guided fish into the trap. It probably caught fish in a creek (now long disappeared) that flowed down from the right-hand side. Perhaps our fictional fisherman, MacConmara, came down this creek from Bunratty, which can be seen in the trees to the north.

1279. Most probably we were looking at a wooden structure that had been built and used in the early thirteenth century AD.

And so we started our work. First, Barry circled around the site with his cameras and video, taking numerous photographs of the structure before our footprints would disturb the muds. In the meantime Eoin and I prepared the drawing-boards, as Sarah gridded out the site with 20m measuring-tapes. Then Eoin, hunched over a planning-frame, began to painstakingly draw at 1:20 scale the wooden posts and wattle on a sheet of waterproof drafting-film mounted on a drawing-board. I wrote a brief description of the site in a muddy notebook, as Sarah called out its key measurements and compass orientations to me. Then, putting our equipment aside, the two of us knelt down over the basket buried in the muds.

We were curious about its construction, form and size, so our intention that morning was to clean out the muds overlying the basket and to plan and photograph its entire length. But we had not reckoned on its spectacular preservation. To assess the task ahead of us, we began by carefully excavating a 20cm-wide trench across its width. As we dug down into the estuarine silts, we were puzzled by the lack of any wood — where were its sides and base? It was not until we had dug down to a depth of 80cm and found its tightly woven sides that the truth slowly dawned on us. The basket at Bunratty 6 was not partially preserved, it was almost entirely preserved! Buried deep in the clays of the Shannon estuary was a remarkable artefact, 4.5m in length, one of the best-preserved medieval baskets known from medieval Europe. There could be no question of exposing it to view in a few hours, as such an excavation would endanger its survival. The flooding tide coming in a few hours would simply destroy it. We would have to be content with the clues offered by our narrow trenches.

As we had been excavating, photographing and planning the basket, Barry had been sampling the entire structure for wood identification and tree-ring studies, placing snapped-off pieces of post and wattle in numbered plastic bags. But now the tide had slackened, stopped and started to turn. Our work over the last couple of hours had been carried out at a smart pace, but now we had to speed up even more. The water-levels in the creek were rising behind us. Working quickly, we completed the last of our tasks and backfilled our trenches, knowing that the flooding tide could wash away any loosened parts of the wooden structure. As we worked, we could see Donal drifting back up the creek with the flooding tide. He stopped beside us and we scurried to load the boat up with sample bags, plans, notebooks, cameras and ourselves. I was the last to step in, just as the rising tide around my ankles lifted the boat off the muds. Off we went, well pleased with ourselves; our morning's work was done.

Thinking and writing about people, place and time on an estuary

But of course our work wasn't finished.

Over the next few years, off and on as I was involved with other projects, I read, wrote and thought about the archaeology of the Shannon estuary. Working with friends and colleagues, I completed a book on our discoveries, recently published by the Discovery Programme (O'Sullivan 2001). And yet ... I'm still struck by a feeling that neither the experience of medieval fishermen nor my own experience of working as an archaeologist on the mudflats can easily be captured in conventional texts or illustrations. In recent years, many archaeologists have experimented with fictional writing to try and convey how people in the past experienced and perceived the landscapes in which they worked. In a sense, these fictional texts also convey a false impression, as it is impossible for us to move outside our own cultural backgrounds into a 'medieval mentality'.

On the other hand, these fictional texts can help us to reflect on the ways in which past communities saw themselves less in terms of their collective social or ethnic origins and more on the basis of their practical engagement with the environment — their daily life and practice. I believe that the Shannon estuary's medieval fish-traps were worked by particular social groups within the broader community who would have had a 'sense of identity' other than that of even the local farmers on the drylands. I also believe that the archaeology of the medieval fish-traps on the Shannon estuary can help us to think in these ways about such local communities, the ordinary people 'outside history' who built no great castles and wielded no political power.

First, we can start thinking about how their daily encounters with the hidden and intimate places of the estuary — the narrow creeks winding their way through the reeds, the windswept islands out on the mudflats — would have influenced how people thought about themselves and others. Local fishermen working every day out on the estuary's creeks and channels would have experienced a sense of isolation and distinctiveness from the broader community. They worked the landscape, while at the same time it worked on them. Furthermore, they would have possessed a unique knowledge of places, an awareness of the dangers of rocks and pools, and an appreciation of how to move through and across treacherous mudbanks (a skill, I can assure you from harsh experience, that takes time to learn!). These were innate bodily skills, learned through daily living. They were also skills that were not available to others. So these same fishermen could have actively used their exclusive and specialist knowledge of place to create and sustain a unique sense of identity within that broader community.

I also believe that people like MacConmara and his brother, living and

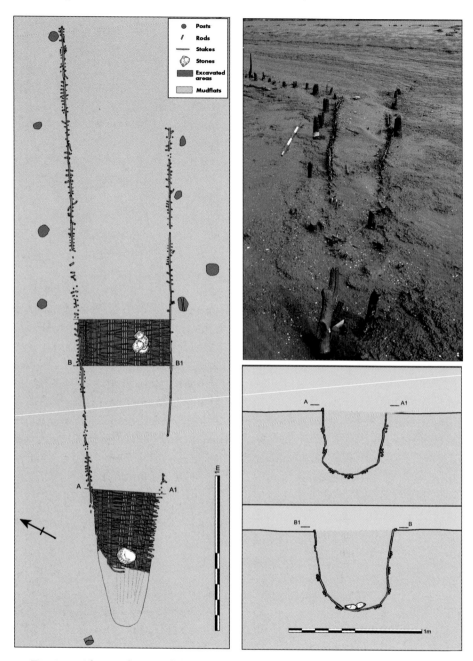

Fig. 38—Plan and view of the medieval basket at Bunratty 6. The basket remains buried in the clay, and is a testament to the basket-maker's craft. It is a remarkable object woven of coppiced hazel rods, each aged between 4 and 5 years. This underwood may have been managed in the famous medieval woodlands at Cratloe, Co. Clare (immediately to the east of Bunratty).

Pl. 63—A view across the medieval fish-trap at Bunratty 6, out towards the main Shannon estuary channel in the background. The post-and-wattle fence in the foreground shows evidence for several phases of repair and reconstruction (especially in the middle). Local fishermen would have repaired these structures for years before finally abandoning them. Its remarkable state of preservation overall might suggest that it was suddenly buried under a mudbank during a storm.

working in this landscape, moved to different temporal rhythms. On an estuary, the passing time is measured by a different clock. There are the unique rhythms of the tides, the daily, monthly and seasonal cycles of low and high tides, of neaps and springs. So, for example, in recent times on the Shannon estuary, the first spring tide in May was known as Rabharta Mór na n-Éan ('the great spring tide of the birds'). It was believed that birds first observed the height of this flood-tide so that they knew where to build their marshland nests out of reach of danger. Indeed, local fishing communities would themselves have marked time by the seasonal migratory movements of those waders, ducks and geese, huge numbers of which overwinter on the Shannon estuary mudflats. They would have watched for the seasonal movements of fish, the summer arrival of salmon, the autumn departure of eels. They would also have watched the seasonal changes in vegetation, cutting reeds for thatch and basketry in early summer. Indeed, if we think about how local fishing communities would have fished every low tide in the month, including those ten night-time tides that are only lit by the moon, then we can get another sense of how they could have seen themselves as a distinctive social group.

We can explore how place, tradition and identity worked on the Shannon estuary through the archaeology of its medieval fish-traps. While the earliest structures date from the sixth century AD, the most intensive period of activity so far seems to have been between the eleventh and fourteenth centuries AD. The medieval fish-traps are all quite similar in location, size and appearance. They are typically constructed of two post-and-wattle fences, each supported by poles and diagonal braces, that converged towards a wooden framework. On this wooden frame was laid a substantial, narrow basket, which acted as the trapping mechanism.

The medieval fish-traps on the Shannon estuary are usually relatively small, being located in narrow mudflat creeks where a single barrier could have literally sieved the water of all fish moving around with the tides. The traps are designed to fish either the flooding or the ebbing tide and could probably in season have taken large catches of salmon, sea trout, lampreys, shad, flounder and eels (the latter in October–November). Medieval fish-traps are of course known from around Britain and Ireland, and many appear to date from this particular period (i.e. *c.* 1100–1300), perhaps indicating an increasingly intensive maritime and estuarine fishing industry. Fish was of course of social, economic and symbolic importance in the Middle Ages, with people's diet influenced by religious rules as well as customary practice. The Shannon estuary fish-traps could have provided food for the domestic table, for the local markets and fairs, and could also have been locally salted, smoked or dried and ultimately exported from the medieval port of Limerick.

Fish-traps, requiring constant maintenance and repair, are usually worked by small-scale operators, typically people who live locally and who may combine this activity with farming or other work. As a valuable source of income and revenue, fish-traps usually attract attention from social élites, and no doubt control of and access to the Shannon estuary fisheries would have been an issue across the period. Traditionally, fishermen and women live in closely knit communities that have little contact with the countryside around them. They have a strong sense of their own traditions and customs and closely guard their own rights and privileges to particular fishing grounds. Knowledge of these is often passed as oral tradition from generation to generation.

So it is interesting, then, that a strong continuity in location and form can be seen in the Shannon estuary fish-traps through the late Middle Ages. We can see this most clearly in the medieval fish-traps beside the Anglo-Norman borough of Bunratty, on the north shore of the upper Shannon estuary. In the twelfth and thirteenth centuries, the broader Shannon estuary region was to witness significant political and ethnic change. After the Anglo-Norman invasion of the late twelfth century, the local native Gaelic Irish lords, such as the O'Briens and the MacNamaras, were displaced by incoming colonisers and settlers, who first gained control of Limerick and then pushed westwards into the district of Tradree. In 1248 an Anglo-Norman manor was established at Bunratty, at a strategic location on the north bank. In 1287 contemporary historical sources indicate that the borough of Bunratty had a castle, a parish church, a weekly market and an annual fair lasting for five days. It had a rabbit warren, a water-mill and a fish-pond. It also had a sizeable population, the presence of 226 burgages implying a potential total of 1000 people resident within the borough. Many of these townspeople would have been 'English' peasant farmers, tenants and merchants, enticed with (as the fourteenth-century Gaelic Irish text *Caithréim Thoirdhealbhaigh* was later to bitterly claim) 'bribes and purchases'. On the other hand, while the Gaelic Irish social élites had been displaced, this by no means suggests that all people of native Gaelic Irish ethnic extraction had departed.

In fact, the archaeology of the medieval fish-traps suggests strong continuities in work and practice on the estuary mudflats below the borough. We can see this in the way that the same fish-trap types, identical in size, layout and construction, were in use between the eleventh and thirteenth centuries. A wooden fish-trap at Bunratty 4 (radiocarbon-dated to AD 1018–1159) was built of a small structure of post-and-wattle, with a horizontal basket supported within a framework measuring 4.6m by 80cm. It was clearly built and used well before the Anglo-Norman colony, indicating Irish settlement somewhere in the vicinity. Intriguingly, precisely the same style of fish-trap can be seen elsewhere on these Bunratty mudflats, at Bunratty 6 (dated to 1164–1269). This structure (the one we so busily recorded in February 1997) has a similar post-and-wattle fence, a wooden framework (4.1m by 70cm) and well-preserved woven basket, now completely buried in the clays. In terms of site plan alone, you could literally pick parts of this structure up and lay it across the earlier, Bunratty 4 site, so similar are the arrangements of the structural components.

This is not unique to the medieval fish-traps at Bunratty. Further to the west, at the mouth of the River Deel, there are also several fish-traps of the same size, form and appearance in use between the eleventh and thirteenth centuries, suggesting repair and reconstruction across time. Interestingly, then, the Bunratty and Deel estuary fish-traps indicate that precisely the same types of structure were in use before and after the Anglo-Norman colony. Similar patterns can be traced amongst a series of wooden fish-traps in Grey Abbey Bay, Strangford Lough, Co. Down, and are common features amongst structures in Wales too.

On the Shannon estuary we could explain this in terms of continuities of practice amongst local Gaelic Irish fishing communities. So, while the Gaelic Irish lordship in the thirteenth century had been diminished, with the upper

Pl. 64—Simon Dick's wonderful reconstruction painting of the medieval fish-trap at Bunratty 6. It is being repaired after a storm, as a woman throws the tide's harvest into the boat. People in the Middle Ages, as today, would have used their practical knowledge and sense of history to build a sense of identity within the broader community in which they lived and worked.

social classes removed, we can imagine that the Gaelic Irish fishermen continued to work the channels in the manner of their fathers. What we may be looking at here is the work of the Gaelic Irish betaghs. These betaghs (from the Irish word *biatach*, meaning 'food provider') are frequently mentioned in twelfth- and thirteenth-century historical documents. They seem to have lived in or near the Anglo-Norman manors, working as unfree tenants and labourers, ploughing land, harvesting crops and herding cattle. At Bunratty they may also have worked as fishermen, accommodating their work to the new social and political order. In the archaeology of medieval Ireland we still tend to think about power struggles of social élites, and their competition for political influence and control of territory. The reality for most ordinary people must have been accommodation to new social orders, while still working within an evolving tradition. On the other hand, we shouldn't be too definitive on the ethnic background of these fishermen. It is a moot point anyway as to what people would have called themselves (Gaelic Irish, English, MacConmaras, etc.) a hundred years into the life of the Anglo-Norman colony. But I would still argue that these were people who were deliberately working within an evolving tradition that deliberately used continuity with the past to recreate and secure their place in society.

In conclusion, in recent years archaeologists have increasingly begun to explore how they personally work and think through the material they uncover. I have no doubt that my own experiences of struggling through wintry mudflats or finding myself alone amongst the reed-beds of a summer saltmarsh have influenced the ways I have written and spoken about this marvellous landscape. It would be a mistake to think that my sense of place and time there gives me a personal insight into the ways people lived and worked in the Middle Ages. But it would also be a mistake to think that these estuarine landscapes, which used to be considered archaeologically empty spaces, weren't places that were rich in human history and experience, named, well known and understood by a knowledgeable people.

Further reading and acknowledgements

The Shannon estuary intertidal survey project was recently published in A. O'Sullivan, *Foragers, farmers and fishers in a coastal landscape: an intertidal archaeological survey of the Shannon estuary*, Discovery Programme Monographs 5 (Dublin, 2001). My debt of gratitude to many people is spelled out there, but I would particularly like to thank Eoin Grogan, Barry Masterson, Sarah Cross and Donal Boland for their cheerful work on that muddy February morning, and James Lyttleton for all his help since.

22

Archaeological survey:
some sobering experiences

David Sweetman

The importance of archaeological survey is often underestimated by archaeologists, especially those of the armchair variety who pontificate and produce marvellous theories without ever having done the necessary fieldwork to establish a database from which to draw their theories. If one has worked in the field, and especially on archaeological survey, it is possible to build up an invaluable source of basic information. From these data you can draw certain conclusions. Unfortunately, many academics go off at half-cock and make wild statements in print, asserting, for instance, that there are few hall-houses and even less ringworks in Ireland without having looked properly at the monuments in the field.

When I was first employed by the Board of Works (Office of Public Works) I was put to excavating at Trim Castle and Ferns Castle and considered this work to be the most important and exciting type of archaeology—everyone's dream, a licence to dig up the goodies. It was therefore with some trepidation that I accepted the post of director of the Archaeological Survey of Ireland in 1984. The Survey was not considered to have much standing and had produced no publication in the twenty-odd years of its existence. Surely nothing exciting could happen in the Survey. After all, if most of the sites to be recorded were ringforts, what a boring prospect awaited me.

My main aim, while director of the Survey, was to publish the data accumulated by the field surveyors. This was intended to have a threefold effect:

1. to raise the profile of the Archaeological Survey;
2. to disseminate the data to as wide an audience as possible;
3. to give the fieldworkers pride in their work by seeing their labours in print.

To be a good field surveyor one has to have stamina, self-reliance, confidence, be

Pl. 65—The hall-house, showing the entrance to the first-floor hall. Steps rise to the doorway and the recess indicates that the door opened outwards. A simple slit-ope provides light for the upper section of the intramural stairs.

good at interpretation and classification of sites and monuments, and have an ability to write with an objective and open mind. I am sure there are other qualities and attributes that go to make a good field archaeologist/surveyor, including long legs!

Field survey, even to the most jaded palate, can be exciting and frequently turns up the most unexpected sites. I am always amazed at how much new material continues to be found — not just unknown megalithic tombs and stone circles in the uplands of the borders of Cork and Kerry, as demonstrated by Connie Murphy, but more controversial types of sites such as hall-houses and ringworks.

On a recent visit to Fethard, under the guidance and protection of Jean Farrelly and Caimin O'Brien, I was taken to view a tower-house that was puzzling them (Pl. 65). The main problem, as far as Caimin and Jean were concerned, was that the building had a first-floor entrance and, as everyone knows, no self-respecting tower-house would admit to anything but a ground-floor entrance. If you are told or it is indicated in a written source that you are dealing with a particular type of site, then you inspect that site with these preconceived ideas. The so-called 'urban tower-house' in Fethard has a typical upper storey, late medieval layout, and architectural details such as large windows and arcading to support the wall-walk (Pl. 66). At the head of the stairs is a very fine piscina, a rare if not unique feature for a tower-house (Pl. 67). The three of us had such a mind-set about this building that we were simply not assessing it objectively. If the building had been identified as a hall-house in the first instance then there would have been no problem. We would have said, 'Great, a late hall-house', and noted all the characteristics it had in common with late tower-houses. As it happened, it took us some time to come to the obvious conclusion. On inspection of two other buildings close by, we pronounced these also to be late medieval hall-houses!

My second, and even more sobering, experience took place before I joined the Archaeological Survey, sometime in the early 1980s. I was requested, or rather told, to inspect a number of medieval moated sites in the south-west of Ireland which we had listed on the advice of Terry Barry, who included them in his PhD thesis. Some of the owners had not responded to our listing notice and I was told to visit them and get them to sign the orders. All began well for it was a beautiful sunny day and I was accompanied by my wife-to-be, a bottle of wine and a picnic. Where better to head to than the sunny south-east, the home counties of my parents?

The morning was uneventful and the owners of two sites signed the listing orders. The third moated site was located on an out-farm and the owner was not about. I enquired at the local village as to where I might find him. At the post office I was given directions, but the local postmistress said that I would not find Mr X at home. Nothing was going to stop me now: I was about to chalk up my third success and then reward myself with a good lunch washed down by a bottle of wine.

It was now after 1pm and clouds were gathering. In fact, by the time we entered Mr X's driveway it was raining. It was a long straight driveway lined with evergreens, which ended at a metal gate. Beyond the gate was a small yard and cottage. I got out of the car and, at the barking of a collie dog, a man emerged from the house and stood at the other side of the gate. I asked him if Mr X was in and he said he did not know, which I thought was a bit strange. However, when I took the official file from the car and said I was from the Board of Works, it had an instantaneous effect. I was told to hold on for a second. The next minute another very enraged man came charging out of the door, shotgun in

Pl. 66— (left) The first-floor hall with later additions, including a fireplace and doorway to its left. The hall shows obvious similarities to sixteenth-century tower-houses.

Pl. 67—(below) The piscina and cross-loop at the head of the stairs in the hall.

Pl. 68—(right) A smaller hall-house, with a blocked first-floor entrance, which is attached to the south gable of the first hall-house.

Pl. 69—(below) The third hall-house, known as 'the bishop's palace', located in the eastern end of the southern town wall.

hand, and took aim at me. I jumped back into the car but was too late to stop the first man from wedging himself between me and the car door. I politely asked him to move, with the intention of closing the door and beating a hasty retreat. While I was attempting to converse, his more enraged brother, Mr X, was now trying to get at me with a slash-hook, having meanwhile decided not to blow my head off with the shotgun. In the ensuing mêlée, I noticed that the arm of brother Y was gashed and was dripping blood on me, washed down by the pouring rain. I seemed to be having a relatively ordinary conversation with brother Y but it was hard to concentrate because of the frequent swishing of the slash-hook and the necessity of having to weave and bob to avoid it. Brother X, deciding I was not yet scared enough, picked up a tree trunk like the Incredible Hulk and proceeded to dance around the front of the car with it over his head while all the time threatening to launch it at me. It must have been at least 30 minutes later that the antics stopped and brother Y said to me that he would not mind our pestering them so much were it not for the fact that he had a sister inside the house who was suffering from 'the nerves'. I was very glad not to have met the sister. It was a very subdued picnic and a not so pleasurable bottle of wine that Rosanne and I consumed.

I subsequently learned that another member of staff on official business went to visit the moated site. While he was walking up the laneway Mr X leaped across the hedge with a slash-hook, caught hold of his tie and chopped it off. Some months later a local newspaper reported that the father of Mr X was found floating in the moat in suspicious circumstances. There are two morals to this story: firstly, don't visit moated sites in the south-east of Ireland without first talking to Terry Barry and, secondly, never say you are from the Board of Works!

Further reading

McNeill, T. 1997 *Castles in Ireland: feudal power in a Gaelic world.* London.
Murphy, C. 1992 Recorded hills? *Archaeology Ireland* **6** (4), 13–14.
Sweetman, D. 1999 *The medieval castles of Ireland.* Cork.
Sweetman, D. 2000 *The origin and development of the tower-house.* Kinsale.

23

Ambrose and archaeology

Kenneth Wiggins

Ambrose Jones was a man who made a significant contribution to the archaeological excavations carried out at King John's Castle, Limerick, beginning in February 1990. Dr Jones was not employed with the rest of the personnel who made up the working team, but was in fact a seventeenth-century cleric who died over 300 years before the excavations took place!

Ambrose's connection with King John's Castle, or Limerick Castle, as it was known in his day, was restricted to a tumultuous five-week period during the months of May and June 1642. It was at the start of this year that the impact of the Catholic rebellion in Ulster began to be felt in Munster. Disturbances in rural areas led many Protestants to move to Limerick City for protection, but when this too started to become unsettled and dangerous many sought admittance to the king's castle, which occupied a prominent position within the urban defences of Limerick. Among those availing of the apparent security offered by the castle were Ambrose Jones, precentor (chantor) of Limerick, and his superior, Dr George Webb, bishop of Limerick. Ambrose had been made treasurer of the diocese of Limerick in 1639, before resigning in 1641 to become precentor; at the same time he was prebendary of Emily, an office which would have provided him with a substantial income. He was joined in the castle by his father, Dr Lewis Jones, bishop of Killaloe, a sprightly, tough Welshman well into his nineties. Old Lewis was proud of his five high-achieving sons, at least three of whom, Henry, Theophilus and Michael, were to make a lasting mark on the pages of seventeenth-century Irish history. Ambrose himself went on to become bishop of Kildare in 1667, but he was far from certain what the future held when Limerick City was occupied by an Irish army commanded by General Garrett Barry, and the castle closely besieged from 18 May 1642. His unique contribution to our knowledge of the siege stems from the fact that he

Pl. 70—View of the excavated area along the eastern side of the castle, in the spring of 1990, seen from the north-eastern corner tower, facing south-east. The foundations of the eastern curtain wall are visible in the bottom half of the picture, and remains of the seventeenth-century bastion towards the top. (Photo: C. O Rahilly/ Limerick Corporation.)

commenced a diary of the unfolding events, which he continued until the castle was surrendered 37 days later on 23 June. A copy of the diary is in Trinity College Dublin, part of MSS 866 (formerly F.4.16). The existing document does not in fact bear his name, and when M. J. McEnery published a full transcript in 1904 he was unable to solve the mystery surrounding the identity of the diary's author, an enigmatic 'person of importance' who was allowed to keep two of his own horses, despite all others in the castle being turned out at the watergate six days into the siege. From careful analysis of the text, together with clues provided by other sources for the siege, it is clear beyond any doubt that the diary could have been written by nobody other than Ambrose Jones.

The siege presented a considerable challenge to the Irish from the outset as they did not possess any heavy artillery and therefore were unable to batter the castle into submission. General Barry decided at the end of the first week that a breach in the walls could only be achieved by the digging of tunnels, or mines, under the foundations of the castle. The timber props which shored these mines would be set on fire ('sprung') once they were securely positioned below the castle walls, and the resulting subsidence would in theory shatter the above-ground masonry. According to Ambrose's diary, mining directed at the eastern curtain wall of the castle commenced on 25 May from a house situated along High Street to the east of the castle. The defence forces, commanded by Captain George Courtenay, were fully aware of the absolute importance of ensuring that their walls were not undermined. They were compelled to respond by digging tunnels of their own, countermines, with the specific aim of detecting and spoiling incoming mines before any damage was done to the castle's foundations. Ambrose tells us that in fact two countermines were commenced on the eastern side of the castle on 30 May.

Before the end of the second week, mining and countermining were in progress on the eastern side of the castle and, by the start of the third week, also under way along the southern side. Siege warfare by tunnelling continued to form the predominant strategy until 21 June, when mining works wrecked a substantial part of the bastion at the south-eastern corner of the castle. The conclusion of articles of surrender the following day led to the departure of George Courtenay and the garrison, along with the other survivors, on 23 June.

From the point of view of the castle as an archaeological site, the 'underground' nature of the siege was noteworthy, as the construction of timber-shored tunnels underneath the courtyard and outside the curtain walls could in theory result in the *in situ* preservation of a considerable amount of evidence dating from May and June 1642. This potential came to be fully realised when large-scale archaeological excavations commenced at the castle in February 1990.

The brief storm that was the siege of 1642 was eventually forgotten, as life in Limerick returned to normality. Ambrose Jones died in Dublin, following a lengthy illness, on 15 December 1678. The castle continued to endure as a military barracks and an imposing feature of Limerick's urban environment. In the year 1793 the castle underwent extensive renovations. The whole of the eastern curtain wall and the south-eastern corner bastion, scene of so much of the action during the siege, were levelled, greatly expanding the infantry parade ground hitherto confined by the enclosing walls of the castle. After the last British garrison departed in 1922, much of the old barracks was levelled, and in 1933 many terraced dwellings were built in the courtyard by the local authority. The castle was poorly appreciated as a monument and its history commanded little attention. All this was to change at the end of the 1980s when decisive steps were taken jointly by the Office of Public Works, Limerick Corporation and Shannon Development to have one of the most important Anglo-Norman

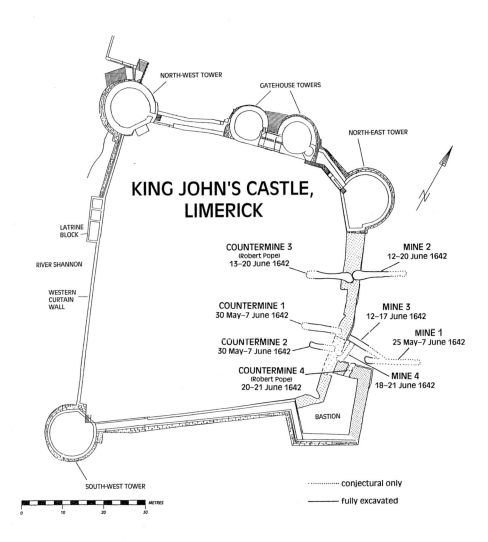

NORTH-WEST TOWER

GATEHOUSE TOWERS

NORTH-EAST TOWER

KING JOHN'S CASTLE, LIMERICK

LATRINE
BLOCK

RIVER SHANNON

WESTERN
CURTAIN
WALL

COUNTERMINE 3
(Robert Pope)
13–20 June 1642

MINE 2
12–20 June 1642

COUNTERMINE 1
30 May–7 June 1642

MINE 3
12–17 June 1642

MINE 1
25 May–7 June 1642

COUNTERMINE 2
30 May–7 June 1642

COUNTERMINE 4
(Robert Pope)
20–21 June 1642

MINE 4
18–21 June 1642

BASTION

SOUTH-WEST TOWER

METRES

0   10   20   30

············· conjectural only

———— fully excavated

Fig. 39—Plan of the castle, showing the location of the siege features excavated in 1990–1. (Based on a survey made in 1988 by Peter Murphy, Consultant Surveyor.)

*Pl. 71—View of Countermine 3, extending beneath the foundations of the eastern curtain wall, facing north-east. This was built by Robert Pope between 13 and 20 June 1642. The visible timber props were inserted during the excavation for safety reasons. The original timberwork was removed by Pope himself before he commenced work on Countermine 4 at some point late on 20 June 1642.
(Photo: K. Wiggins/Limerick Corporation.)*

military buildings in Ireland finally restored and made accessible to visitors. To help achieve this objective, excavations had to take place to expose the long-demolished foundations of the eastern curtain wall and the bastion (Pl. 70). It was expected that significant archaeological material relating to the origins of the castle in the twelfth and thirteenth centuries would come to light, and this was very much the case. But the discovery of tunnels, trenches and timbers from the siege of 1642 made it clear that this was a site with an extraordinary tale to tell, and allowed the spirit of Ambrose Jones, the long-deceased chantor of Limerick, to play a vital role in the careful work of understanding this exceptional body of evidence.

Altogether the Irish built a total of eleven mines during the course of the siege, five on the eastern side of the castle, where the excavations in 1990 were located, and six on the southern side. Courtenay's warders responded with eight countermines, five on the eastern side and three along the southern side of the courtyard. Archaeological evidence was uncovered in 1990–1 for four of the eastern mines and four of the eastern countermines (Fig. 39). Ambrose Jones's diary is crucial in placing these excavated features into the chronology of the siege with absolute precision. He provides little detail on what the structures looked like, or how they were made and so on, but these questions could be answered by analysis of the physical remains, thanks to the excellent preservation of many of the timber elements.

Mine 1 was constructed between 25 May and 7 June, a two-week period which was longer by several days than the time spent on any other mine or countermine. Ambrose tells us that the besieged were alerted to the start of the work by the sound of 'some digging ham[m]ering and sawing' in one of the houses along High Street close to the eastern side of the castle. The mine was directed towards the angle formed by the southern limit of the eastern curtain wall and the northern flank of the bastion. The archaeological excavators, coming upon the western terminal of the mine, found well-preserved timbers *in situ* but no obvious clue as to why it came to such an abrupt halt well short of its target, the base of the eastern curtain wall. The answer to this puzzle is supplied in the lines of Ambrose's diary. By 7 June the minehead had only just cleared the northern salient of the bastion when the ground overhead broke, exposing the inside of the tunnel to the gaze of the warders peering down from behind the bastion parapet. They pumped as much water into the mine as possible, increasing the breach to such an extent that work in it was abandoned.

The successful flooding of Mine 1 on 7 June meant that work on the two countermines commenced adjacent to the eastern curtain wall could be discontinued, as in Ambrose's words 'we were in small feare of yt [that] part'. According to Ambrose, these two structures, Countermine 1 and Countermine 2, were built in different ways, one described as 'slope', the other as 'downe right'. The meaning behind this distinction is clear from the excavated evidence. The gallery of Countermine 1 'sloped' towards the foundations of the eastern curtain wall, i.e. becoming progressively deeper as it advanced eastwards. The Countermine 2 entrance shaft was sunk to a greater depth ('downe right') to begin with, from which the gallery was driven horizontally towards the east. The timber preservation in Countermine 1 was particularly good, with 115 individual timbers recovered from the excavated part of the structure.

For several days after the setback in Mine 1, the Irish mining effort was focused on the southern side of the castle. However, following reverses there on 11 June, a tactical switch back to the eastern front occurred, resulting in the digging of another three mines from the convenient shelter and security of the High Street houses. Only one countermine, Countermine 3, was commenced by the besieged, on 13 June, as they had now run very low on timbers for making the props (Pl. 71). After more than three weeks spent labouring in the mines the Irish finally scored their first tangible success when, as reported by Ambrose, the warders noticed 'a great cracke in the bulwarke [bastion] of our castle from the top to ye bottome'. Two days later another crack appeared in the 'bullwarke', and it started to look as if the garrison might soon be overwhelmed.

Although there was clearly a lot of action taking place under the bastion, perhaps the most dramatic evidence for the subterranean operations of this siege emerged when an enormous intact tunnel was revealed under the eastern curtain wall close to the north-eastern corner tower. This tunnel was produced when Mine 2 and Countermine 3 met head to head below the wall. No timber material was found to survive in either structure, but Ambrose's diary is particularly helpful on what exactly took place when the two galleries converged. The breakthrough occurred on the morning of 20 June, near the end of the fifth week of the siege. Ambrose tells us that the countermine was constructed by an individual named Robert Pope. With the help of a few who came to his assistance Pope 'made in to ye enemyes myne' and 'pull[e]d downe all the[i]r timber and brought it into the castle'. Because the hand-to-hand combat was a total success for the besieged side, Pope was able to dismantle all the timber props, hauling them back up into the courtyard to replenish the garrison's depleted supply (but leaving no timber material behind for the archaeologists!). Thanks to the pen of Ambrose Jones, the surviving remains could be interpreted with complete certainty. He goes on to relate that Robert Pope proceeded to use the reclaimed timber to begin 'a new drift to meete with an other myne w[hi]ch we conceived to run southward towards our bullwarke'. The remains of Pope's 'new drift', Countermine 4, were excavated directly under the sallyport in the northern flank of the bastion. The mine he was hoping to intercept, Mine 4, aligned north–south, was actually a branch of Mine 3, aligned east–west, which reached the base of the eastern curtain wall but was not deep enough to continue underneath it (Pl. 72).

Robert Pope seems to have discontinued digging in Countermine 4 soon after it was started, for the structure's gallery barely extended beyond the edge of the bastion. Why was the countermine abandoned so quickly? Again, Ambrose is on hand to supply the explanation. At one in the morning on 21 June, only a matter of hours after Pope sank his shaft in the sallyport of the bastion, 'the upper part of ye wall of ye bullwarke fell downe almost as low as ye sally port dore'. The dramatic breaching of the northern salient of the bastion, the climactic moment of the siege, was caused by a mine for which no archaeological evidence was uncovered in the course of the excavation. However, ample evidence for destruction survived in the form of a dense spread of mortared limestone rubble adjacent to the bastion flank. These cut blocks had clearly tumbled from the

Pl. 72—View of the western limit of Mine 3, along the base of the eastern curtain wall, seen from the north. This would have reached the base of the wall (to the right) by around 17 June 1642, but was not deep enough to continue beneath the masonry. The Irish miners opened a branch to the south, Mine 4, which eventually undermined the angle between the eastern curtain wall and the bastion on 21 June 1642. The charring of several of the props resulted from the firing of Mines 3 and 4 on the afternoon of 21 June 1642. (Photo: R. Ó Baoill/Limerick Corporation.)

corner of the bastion, and many of them were in fact used to reconstruct its eastern face after the excavation was completed. The ruin of the bastion corner was the event which precipitated the surrender of the castle two days later, and when it toppled Robert Pope had little choice but to reluctantly give up Countermine 4 as a lost cause.

King John's Castle, Limerick, an important urban fortress in a strategic port town, is a very well-documented building for all periods of its history. This wealth of written material is a great boost to the archaeologist excavating the site. However, the contribution made by available sources to the interpretation of excavated evidence is given an entirely new dimension when applied to the turbulent episode that unfolded in the early summer of 1642. The archaeological evidence for the siege is remarkable, but nonetheless would be of limited value if it were little more than a jumble of contemporaneous features. In order to fully understand how the excavated mines and countermines related to each other they must be organised into a chronology, which means refining the dating in each case to particular weeks and days of the siege's overall duration. That it is possible for the underground works to be identified and sequenced is due entirely to the writings of Ambrose Jones.

In the midst of a frightful crisis, buoyed up by genuine religious faith and seemingly impervious to despair, Ambrose Jones compiled his journal of the siege. He did so out of a strong sense of duty, feeling that it was incumbent on him to report what happened at the king's castle in Limerick when it was besieged by Irish rebels. He would have been certain that sooner or later those principally responsible for the outrage, many of whom are named in his journal, would be brought to justice for their misdeeds, and his record of the actions of the siege would help to prosecute and convict them. The idea of retribution being visited in the fullness of time on those daring to attack and expel the king's Protestant subjects in Limerick would have sustained Ambrose as he sat at a table in a chamber somewhere in the castle and carefully logged the events of the day. As it turned out, those Irish who participated in the rebellion were ultimately deprived of their possessions in the Cromwellian settlement of Ireland in 1654–6. Ambrose himself was granted land in the barony of Coshlea, Co. Limerick, formerly in the hands of Sir Edward Fitzharris, one of those he identifies in the diary amongst the besiegers of Limerick Castle.

Ambrose Jones would not have imagined that his experience of Limerick Castle would be valued long after his death by individuals, calling themselves 'archaeologists', driven by a desire to understand the castle's origins and development by the scientific excavation of clay deposits and artefacts. With the castle under attack, and lives being lost on a daily basis, we can be sure that he would have spent little time wondering about the men who first built the old fortress that was now a haven for the British settlers in Limerick, or about what other events had happened there in the past. His mind naturally enough was focused on much more immediate concerns. He must have feared that he would not live to complete the diary, as at any moment he could be slain by a musket ball, or fall sick and perish from want of food and medicine. What, then, would he have made of the inquiring discipline we know as archaeology? As an educated and highly intelligent man, he would have quickly grasped the thinking behind such academic endeavour, and would have found the subject a fascinating one. A seventeenth-century clergyman he may have been, but with his detailed knowledge of what lay under the ground at King John's Castle, there can be no doubt that in our own era Ambrose Jones would have made a fine archaeologist!

Further reading

McEnery, M.J. 1904 A diary of the siege of Limerick Castle, 1642. *Journal of the Royal Society of Antiquaries of Ireland* **34**, 163–87.

Wiggins, K. 2000 *Anatomy of a siege: King John's Castle, Limerick, 1642*. Bray.

Wiggins, K. and Whyte, E. 2000 Something worth crowing about. *Archaeology Ireland* **53**, 30–3.

24

Lost and found — one glasshouse

Jean Farrelly

Finding a new archaeological monument is an exciting event. However, rarely is such a find a truly new discovery; it is more likely to be something which has been found by someone else and lost again. But what exactly is a discovery? Often by discovery we mean recognition of a monument for what it is and recording that monument in such a way that it enters into the public domain. For those living near the monument it is usually already a known entity, a familiar landmark, something that has been part of the scenery for generations. Monuments become lost when they are not recorded and brought to the attention of a wider audience. It can also happen that the description of such monuments was published in obscure places in the dim and distant past and their rediscovery can take place either physically in the landscape or on paper. The glasshouse at Shinrone, Co. Offaly, is one such monument.

Imagine being shown a sandstone-vaulted structure, slightly taller than the average person and as wide as the span of an adult with outstretched arms (Pl. 73). Inside, the walls and roof are covered with a beautiful smooth blue and green glaze. What is it? It is on the lands of a former 'big house' and 'garden folly' flickers through your mind. The connection with glass-making should have been immediately obvious, especially given the name of the townland, Glasshouse. However, the word glasshouse is more likely to conjure up images of a glass building for housing plants, also known as a greenhouse. Certainly the structure was known locally as being associated with glass-manufacturing, and after some research by my colleague, Caimin O'Brien, we discovered that we had in fact come across a glass-making furnace. This was unusual enough, but we further discovered that upstanding wood-fired furnaces of this type are extremely rare and were in use throughout the medieval period up until the early seventeenth century.

As the history of glass-making in Ireland was entirely new to me, I went in

Pl. 73—Glasshouse furnace.

search of someone who could throw some light on the subject and was directed towards a well-known figure in the glass scene in Ireland, Mary Boydell. This proved to be a most fortuitous meeting and was in itself a marvellous discovery. It transpired that Mary had in fact visited the glasshouse in Shinrone twenty years before. Her interest in the archaeological/historical side of glass-making had been aroused when editing a reprint of Dudley Westropp's definitive work on the subject. Mary had acquired some of Westropp's papers and there among them was a letter written in 1928 to Mr Stelfox, staff member of the Natural History Museum, containing a sketch-plan and description of the glasshouse (Fig. 40). Unfortunately the author's name is unclear, though it looks like Henry Puie. He had cycled from Shehills, near Roscrea in north Tipperary, to visit the glasshouse and was obviously well versed in glass-making technology as he had readily identified the structure as a furnace and had described it in some detail. No one appears to have taken much interest in the furnace until Mary appeared on the scene. In an attempt to ascertain the date and historical background of the furnace she engaged in a vigorous information-gathering campaign which also led to the organising of a magnetometer survey of the vicinity of the glass furnace conducted by Dr Strange, University of Nottingham, with the aid of the Offaly Historical Society, the Office of Public Works and the Royal Irish Academy. Mary's research was not just confined to the glasshouse at Shinrone but also extended to other locations in Offaly where there were historical references to glasshouses. Though no other upstanding structures were found, fieldwalking at Glaster, near Banagher, produced a number of glass finds associated with the glass-making process, and built into a stone wall there was a large furnace fragment, almost identical to the furnace at Shinrone.

Westropp's research had established that very little glass-making had taken place in Ireland before the sixteenth century. Indeed, it was really only towards the end of that century that glass-making took a hold in Ireland. Certainly in Offaly the chief instigators of this industry were the Huguenots. Many Huguenots had fled religious persecution in France in the sixteenth century, finding refuge in England. As economic situations changed, many of these Huguenots subsequently crossed the Irish Sea to ply their trade here. Two such families in particular are associated with glass-making in Offaly, the Bigos (de Bigot) and the Henseys (de Hennezel). These glass-makers were members of the gentry in France and were granted land in Offaly during the plantation period. Their wealth is evidenced in a historical account of the 1641 rebellion when Philip Bigo, owner of the glasshouse at Glaster, was robbed of his goods by Irish rebels and forced to flee to his castle in Galway.

The story of these two families is fascinating in itself. The original Bigo arrived in Ireland in 1623, having illegally imported glass goods into the London

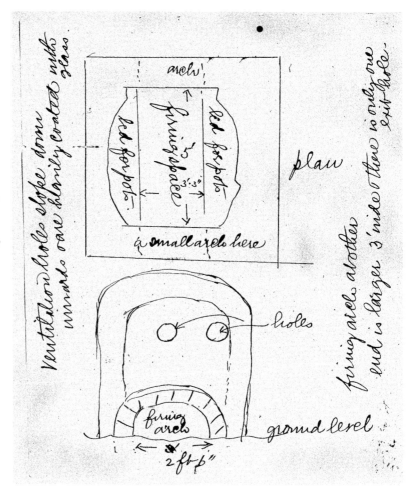

Fig. 40—
Sketch-plan and
side elevation
from the letter to
Stelfox, 1928
(courtesy of
Mary Boydell).

market from a glasshouse in Kimmeridge Bay, Dorset. The glasshouse was destroyed by orders of the government and Abraham appears to have left for Ireland almost immediately afterwards, possibly fearful of arrest. He came to Birr, Co. Offaly, and set up a glasshouse on lands leased from Lawrence Parsons of Birr Castle. Surviving records indicate that he manufactured both vessel and window glass at this glasshouse. In 1627 Abraham surrendered his lease to his son, Philip, who obtained permission from Charles I (1625–49) to set up a glasshouse in Birr. According to Gerald Boate's *Ireland's naturall history*, published in 1652, Birr provided Dublin with 'all sorts of window and drinking glasses and such other as are in common use'. Huguenot families, especially glass-makers, tended to marry within their own closely knit circle, keeping any secrets of the trade 'in the family'. We know that Philip's son, Ananias, married Katherine Hensey, a daughter of another glass-making family who had acquired land in Offaly. It would appear that the Henseys owned much of the land around the Shinrone glasshouse and therefore it is probable that they operated it. If this hypothesis were correct it would imply that the glasshouse was in operation in the first half of the seventeenth century, coinciding with the arrival of the Huguenots and ending with a bill prohibiting the exportation and manufacture of glass in Ireland in 1638/9. Fortunately the next stage in the story established just that.

In order to gain more knowledge about this important site a research excavation was undertaken. One of the aims of the excavation was to obtain a date for the manufacturing of the glass. This was done by archaeomagnetic dating. Basically, when there has been intense burning, as would have resulted from the high temperatures needed to melt raw materials into glass, the iron oxides in the fire-reddened clay acquire a remnant magnetism with a direction paralleling the earth's magnetic field; once the clay cools the fired clay holds that magnetism until reheated. This 'frozen' magnetism can be measured and compared with a calibration curve which displays the fluctuations in the magnetic field over past centuries. It is thus possible to date the last firing that took place at the furnace. At Shinrone this was found to have occurred between AD 1620 and 1650.

The bill of 1638/9 does not seem to have been immediately effective as in 1641 it was necessary to enact another bill prohibiting the felling of trees as a fuel supply for glass furnaces. Interestingly, one of the reasons why glass-makers had been attracted to Ireland in the first place had been the abundant supply of timber, which by the middle of the seventeenth century appears to have been severely reduced by fuel-hungry industries.

The research excavation at Shinrone has revealed that the site is quite complex. The deep stratigraphy has shown a build-up of over 1m of industrial debris, implying that the site was utilised over a longer period than first suspected. It is likely that the present upstanding furnace was the last of a series of furnaces.

One of the most satisfying things about the rediscovery of the glass furnace at Shinrone is the great adventure that it sparked. It opened up the world of sixteenth- and seventeenth-century glass-makers, the story of the Huguenots, and the economic and political factors at work which brought about the downfall of wood-fired furnaces. It also revealed a story of a monument which had excited interest over the last hundred years and which hopefully will now take its rightful place as one of the great survivors of a pioneering seventeenth-century industry.

Acknowledgements

Many thanks to the following: the landowner Éamon Cleary for all his cooperation; Noel McMahon for introducing us to the furnace; Caimin O'Brien, my colleague and partner in the research project; Mary Boydell for her enthusiasm and generous sharing of information; and the National Committee for Archaeology of the Royal Irish Academy for recommending the research excavation project, assisted by funding from Dúchas The Heritage Service, Department of Environment and Local Government.

Further reading

Farrelly, J. 1998 Seventeenth-century forest glass furnaces in County Offaly. *The Glass Society of Ireland Newsletter* **19**, 12–16.

Farrelly, J. 2001 Excavations of an early seventeenth-century glasshouse in Shinrone, Co. Offaly. *The Glass Society of Ireland Newsletter* **26**, 6–7.

Farrelly, J. and O'Brien, C. 2000 Seventeenth-century glasshouse. In I. Bennett (ed.), *Excavations 1999: summary accounts of archaeological excavations in Ireland*, 260–61. Bray.

Fenlon, J. 1998 Some brief notes on Abraham and Philip Bigo and glassmaking in seventeenth century Ireland. *The Glass Society of Ireland Newsletter* **19**, 16–18.

Lee, G.L. 1936 *The Huguenot settlements in Ireland*. London and New York.

Vose, R.H. 1980 *Glass*. London.

Westropp, D. 1978 *Irish glass*. Dublin.

25

In a harbour long ago

Connie Kelleher

Introduction

Through a friend I discovered a map — a simple but detailed sketch of a town and its people in the early 1600s (Fig. 41). The map forms part of the collected papers of Thomas Wentworth, earl of Strafford. He was lord deputy of Ireland from 1635 until 1641, when he was impeached and executed in the Tower of London during the Confederate Wars. His correspondence provides a valuable contemporary insight into the socio-economic and political situation in Ireland at that time. Now housed in the Sheffield Archives in Yorkshire, the Strafford Papers open with this map. E.J. Priestly had previously published a copy of the map in 1984, but when the chance to finally view the original came the anticipation welled up in me, producing an almost adolescent sense of excitement. The map, delicately attached to the first page, provides an immediate visual connection to the 1630s in southern Ireland. On parchment, it appears as a mid-brown line-drawing of the town of Baltimore and its nearby islands. Somewhat faded and smudged in places and with obvious inaccuracies, both topographical and geographical, the essence of the town and harbour is nevertheless clearly displayed.

The map of Baltimore — a description

Illustrated is a vibrant maritime harbour with vessels of various types utilising its waters and surrounding islands. Settlement and associated sites are also clearly shown and industrial activity in the form of fishing is depicted. The map represents a view of what was one of the most important ports in the south-west of Ireland at that time. Indeed, the village of Baltimore has changed little in layout over the past 400 years. The illustrator is unknown but it is obvious that the emphasis was on the maritime use of the port and the various settlements utilising its resources. These settlements are shown in two main areas — an organised layout of buildings centred on the early Anglo-Norman castle of Dunasead (lower centre of map), and more isolated structures in what may have been the earlier medieval settlement in the Cove area (shown as *The Coe* on the map). The Cove, with a single line of houses between it and the main settlement, is quite similar to today's cluster of fishermen's cottages and individual coastal abodes.

The coastline and islands, though obliquely drawn, are shown to have an undulating topography of scrub and cliffs, having been deforested during earlier centuries for the shipbuilding industry. The various tower-houses that speckle this landscape are shown, with a representative enclosed area around a number of the sites. Habitations appear to be differentiated from industrial buildings by the inclusion of a smoking chimney, a feature lacked by the probable fish palace depicted in the Cove. Sherkin Island friary is clearly drawn as *The Abbie,* with two substantial buildings making up the monastic complex, again surrounded by an enclosure wall. Tullagh Church, referred to on the map as *The Church of Baltimore,* to the south-east of the main village settlement (lower right of map), is a dominant feature and obviously central to the social and religious life of the community. It is drawn as a substantial stone building with central spire and large enclosure wall, though probably by then under English religious control. The houses in the Cove could also be described as sizeable as they compare closely to those illustrated in the main settlement group. There are three types of structures shown — single-, double- and three-storey buildings, all with chimneys.

From a maritime perspective, the variation of ship typology depicted on the map is valuable in that it not only illustrates three types of vessels but also shows them utilising the harbour in different ways. Though representative, the vessels are shown fishing or at anchorage, while others may be on patrol along the harbour mouth or involved in the import and export trade. One ship appears to be leaving the harbour and is firing its transom gun, a customary parting gesture. The larger vessels are of two types, all with three masts. Three have seven gun-ports shown aside and one has four ports shown. A fifth fully rigged ship is shown anchored at *The Keye* off Ringaroige Island but is drawn too small to reveal further detail. The smaller single-mast fishing-vessels are illustrated with sails both furled and unfurled. Three have fishermen aboard and one is being tended from the shore. The scene clearly illustrates what is known as seine fishing, whereby two boats (the 'heuer' or 'main seine' and the 'follower') cast out the seine net to encircle the shoal of fish. The follower closes the net around the

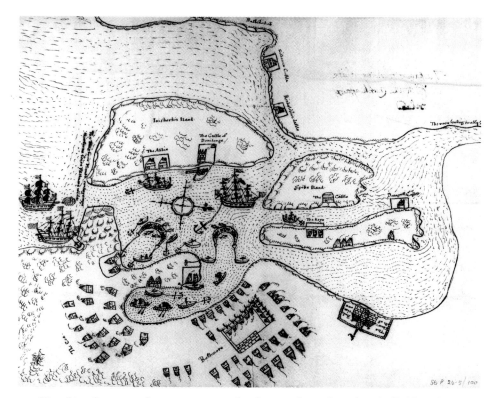

Fig. 41—Seventeenth-century map of Baltimore housed in the Sheffield Archives (photo: ©Sheffield Archives).

shoal and ties it off to the main seine boat. This is known as open seining, where the fish are caught in the open water. The second method depicted is that of 'fixed engine' seine fishing, when one boat casts out the seine net and the other end is fixed to an onshore mooring. Pilchard would have been the primary catch and a valuable commodity to the local economy, as well as for export as salted fish.

At the harbour's mouth is written *The Harbour Mouth contayninge thirteene Score Fathums wide* — being 500m, this is in keeping with the actual width of the entrance. Also illustrated is a small circle denoting a rock in the lower part of the harbour entrance. Later, in the year 1697, this was to become known as the Looe Rock when the English man-of-war HMS *Looe* was wrecked on it. The narrowing of the inner harbour is shown where it joins the Ilen Estuary at the extreme eastern edge of the map. The map appears unfinished here as the words run off the page. Written is *The insore trading to ably throw (go?)...*, presumably referring to the shallower-draft vessels called lighters that could carry cargo upriver to places like Skibbereen (loosely translated as 'the town of the small boats'). To the extreme north of the map Ballydehob is indicated as *Ballidahab*, and the tower-houses of Kilcoe and Rincolisky are depicted.

275

Historical background

The years after 1601 in Baltimore, following the Battle of Kinsale, were a time of prosperity and change. This economic boom continued until the famous Algerine raid on the town in 1631, which decimated the community and led in no small way to the decline in settlement there, as well as locally affecting the fishing industry. However, at the start of the 1600s large numbers of English settlers arrived to avail of the rich fishing reserves that the south-west coast could offer, with the Calendar of State Papers recording at the time that 'the richest fishing grounds in European waters lay upon Baltimore's doorstep'. Merchants focused on the growing trade in exported fish and meat products and imported exotic goods such as wine and spices. In 1613 Baltimore received its Charter of Incorporation as a town from James I. The English settlement grew around the main castle of Dunasead, and Thomas Crooke, who had received a royal grant of the lands in Baltimore, began to expand the settlement from 1608 onwards.

Up until the late sixteenth century Baltimore was the main seat of the powerful Gaelic O'Driscoll lords, who ruled the coastal area of what is now known as West Carbery but was then called *Corca Laidhe*. The O'Driscolls made their wealth from the sea, essentially exploiting those who availed themselves of the marine reserves and utilised the sea as a means of transport. In 1261 the O'Driscolls supported their overlords, the McCarthys, in fighting the Anglo-Normans at Callan outside Kenmare, Co. Kerry. It was quite probably this victory that allowed the O'Driscolls to take over the Anglo-Norman castles in their territory. It also essentially halted the advance of Anglo-Norman domination into the south-western region and ensured the continuation of Gaelic rule there until the end of the sixteenth century. The O'Driscolls are known to have possessed a large fleet of ships and wielded power and authority through both official trade and illicit undertakings, primarily a combination of piracy and privateering. With allegiances and loyalties being as fickle as they were, there was an even greater need to fortify the coastline and control the use of the sea. All the fortified structures depicted on the map, apart from Kilcoe, which was an O'Mahony tower-house, were O'Driscoll fortifications. The map appears to show a well-fortified harbour with the headlands defended. The period to which the map belongs —the 1630s — was also one in which piracy had been curbed to a degree through the issuing of pardons, but clandestine activity was still a traditional part of local life at all levels of society. It is important to bear in mind that Baltimore at that time and before the Algerine raid of 1631 was economically wealthy and socially diverse through its import, export and fishing trade.

Archaeological survey

Dunasead Castle (*Dún na Séad* or 'Fort of the Jewels') (Fig. 74) stands like a sentinel overlooking the harbour of Baltimore and is shown on the map as a substantial rectilinear structure with attached bawn walls. This agrees with the remains existing today, which are located on the seaward side of its rocky prominence. However, the map shows the castle as being at a distance from the shore, with houses inside the enclosing bawn and between it and the harbour. The castle is depicted as a large stone-built structure with a possible turret in the top northern corner, shown in black. It could be argued that this too agrees with the surviving remains. The southern wall of the castle today on the seaward side is mostly blank but has four rectangular opes at the top course and a box machicolation on the south-western corner. This could mean that the illustrator was looking at the site obliquely and drew the castle from a different angle. On the first floor the four large rectangular lights on the west wall are matched on the eastern side by three smaller rectangular windows and a doorway entrance at the south-eastern limit. On this level too are three large fireplaces. The present castle may represent a later construction than that of the Anglo-Norman Sliney castle of 1215, if we are to take the map literally. The present bawn wall is immediately adjacent to the castle but originally extended much farther to the east, on a lower level. This was not included as part of the registered site and modern buildings have been built in its interior.

It is possible that we are looking at a later hall-house, similar to the late medieval hall-house in Ballycarbery, Co. Kerry, referred to by Sweetman, though with no vault evident and with sixteenth- or seventeenth-century additions such as the machicolation. During excavations undertaken in 1998 Cotter found evidence of earlier wall structures at the south end of the present bawn wall. The entrance on the first floor, which Cotter felt formed part of a garderobe tower, could alternatively be interpreted as the primary entrance for a hall on the first floor. It would have been more practical to build a garderobe chute on the cliff side of the castle, where waste would be washed into the sea (prior to nineteenth- and twentieth-century reclamation there) rather than emptying inside the bawn area. Indeed, the castle has all the attributes of a later hall-house, with the 2:1 dimensions, clearly residential, large fireplaces, large rectangular openings, lack of obvious vaulting and no internal divisions. To add weight to this interpretation, the Carew Manuscripts record that the castle was used as 'the great hall ... of Dunasead ... where O'Driscoll and his kinsmen and friends were sitting at boards making ready to sup'. This, along with the archaeological remains on the ground, suggests that, rather than being built as a military structure, it was used as a grand hall to entertain and to demonstrate status and

Pl. 74—(left) Aerial view of Dunasead Castle, which consists of a main hall with attached bawn. Extended bawn walls are evident behind the houses situated to the right of the castle.

Pl. 75—(below) Aerial view of Ilen estuary. In the top left-hand corner is the site of Dunagall Castle, on Ringaroige Island, at the water's edge, with the remains of the castle pier lying below. Inisbeg Castle may have stood on the raised, subrectangular platform on the opposite shore. Also visible are the possible double fish-traps joining Ringaroige Island and Oilean Saor (the island to the left of the shot), and the single fish-trap on its southern side extending into the channel.

Pl. 76—Inane tower-house in foreground, with attached later corn store.

Pl. 77— Aerial view of Inane corn store following the destruction of the tower-house, the quay structure (which ran in front of the tower-house and into the water) and the substantial sea wall that encircled the site.

279

control through social intercourse and political debate.

Illustrated to the east of Dunasead is *The Church of Baltimore*. This refers to the present-day site of Tullagh Church, which was the main church for Baltimore and the remains of which can be seen on the outskirts of the present village. It is obvious that the illustrator has gone to great lengths to portray the importance of the church, with the inclusion of wall, spire and roof structure as well as the addition of a flag on the top of the spire. On Ringaroige Island, opposite Tullagh Church, four possible houses and Dunagall Castle are depicted. The castle is recorded again in the Annals of Inisfallen as having been built in 1215 by the same Anglo-Norman, Sliney. Dunagall would have commanded the upper reaches of the Ilen estuary. The name Dunagall or 'Fort of the Foreigners' may indicate the location of an earlier ringfort or point directly to its Anglo-Norman origins. The castle, drawn on the map to the north-west of Ringaroige Island within an enclosure that extends into the water, is shown complete with chimney, similar to a house, suggesting that it had a residential function. The O'Driscolls were in residence in the castle until the 1640s through the surrender and regrant system.

The rectangular raised platform on which Dunagall (Pl. 75) once stood is now overgrown and retains only scant evidence of the stone foundations within an area of collapsed masonry. The location of the castle is directly parallel to the island of Inisbeg. Aerial survey revealed undulations on the ground which suggest that there may have been some structure facing Dunagall on the opposite island. This would be in keeping with the local place-name evidence of *Poul na Caisleáin* or 'hole of the castles'. This probably refers to the depth of water next to the castle site, which is quite deep but shallows sharply to the north-east. The remains of the pier attached to Dunagall Castle were located during fieldwork. Now very eroded by tidal action, linear stone uprights extend in a north–south direction into the water from the base of the castle platform. These may have formed part of a much more substantial structure that would have been used at high water by small to medium-sized vessels. Also discovered during the aerial and intertidal surveys were the degraded remains of two possible fish-traps adjacent to the castle. These are clearly seen in the aerial shot: a double-stone feature is evident between Ringaroige Island and the smaller island of Oilean Saor to its north-east, with a second at the north-eastern extent of Oilean Saor extending into the channel (Pl. 75). The double stone feature appears to have exploited both the ebbing and flooding tide, whilst the second possible fish-trap availed of the flooding tide only.

The *Keye,* as indicated also on Ringaroige Island, is shown with three associated buildings inside an enclosed area, almost denoting a little community in itself. Though no fortified structure is shown, this was the site of Inane Castle and Quay. The site is shown with an associated quay on a Petty map of 1652 and, as suggested by the drawing on the map of Baltimore, the quay must have been a safe anchorage for vessels as well as servicing the tower-house itself.

Field and intertidal survey of this site located the quay and the remains of the tower-house, which had been reused and extended as a later corn store (Pl. 76). At the north-eastern gable end of the corn store, through collapse into a possible subsurface chamber, the remains of the tower-house were clearly evident, consisting of a three-storey tower with its internal divisions having either collapsed or been removed in the process of conversion into the corn store. However, some features were still evident, including the remains of a first-storey vaulted arch, a slit opening which splayed inward on the first floor, and higher up a larger rectangular window with chamfered mullions. The stone quay attached to the tower-house was intact and extended due north for 16m. It was of drystone construction, 7m wide, and continued out from a stone platform southward around the castle and later store. It continued northwards as a well-constructed sea wall, measuring 24m along the intertidal zone. The quay itself was innovative in that it facilitated two types of vessel. The western side sloped gently to become level with the seabed at low water, allowing small boats to pull up and land on the shore. The eastern side, however, stood proud of the water at high tide to allow larger vessels to pull alongside. The stone construction of the quay tied in with the foundations of the tower-house. This contemporaneity was significant, especially given the intact condition of the quay. However, shortly after survey by the author in 1994, the site was purchased as a private residence. As the quay structure or sea wall was not included as part of the recorded site, it was destroyed in the course of renovation. Ironically, as can be seen from the aerial photograph (Pl. 77), the main body of the structure that was retained is the later corn store, while the earlier tower-house and quay are now gone.

On *Spike* Island opposite *The Keye* another 'castle' is drawn. This is somewhat different from most of the others depicted. It is shown almost as a subcircular structure with possibly three storeys, located on a rocky prominence. McNeill mentions that there are a number of round tower-houses to be found in the south-west and that those of Munster tended to be more elaborate than in the east or north of the country. It may be that this was a round tower-house, perhaps explaining its subcircular depiction. No remains of this structure were located.

Dunalong tower-house on Sherkin Island ('Fort of the Ships') provided an important secondary command post at the main harbour entrance (Pl. 78). As its name suggests, this was the main safe anchorage for the harbour — the map shows large, three-masted vessels moored there — but with military intent, indicated by the inclusion of the cannon on the battery. The tower-house itself appears to have been altered at a later period, when a double layer of internal walling was added with beam slots. These are not unlike the beam holes of the

Pl. 78—Aerial view of Dunalong tower-house on Sherkin Island.

Pl. 79—Aerial view of Sherkin fish palace (lower left), which was attached to the east range of the friary (out of shot). The walls that retained the press beams are seen running parallel to the friary, attached to the enclosure wall.

fish palace that was a later addition to the external eastern range of Sherkin Friary, and may indicate the reuse of Dunalong tower-house as another fish palace. Sherkin Friary is located at the top of the shore of a natural harbour inlet and this would probably have been the preferred landing area. It is shown on the map as *The Abbie,* and General de Zubiaur recorded it as being in a ruinous state when the Spanish arrived in 1601.

Richard Boyle, earl of Cork, was heavily involved in the fishing industry in west Cork, and fish palaces in Baltimore would therefore have been of economic importance to him. Only the sockets for the press beams remain as evidence for both these sites. The Sherkin fish palace (Pl. 79) is evidenced by beam holes in the wall attached to the east range of the friary and an associated wall to the west. In the Cove, cut into a rock outcrop, are another series of beam holes. Though cruder that those on Sherkin, here a single line of fourteen holes is visible. Two sets of unenclosed buildings are illustrated without chimneys, possibly indicating an industrial usage, and they are situated in the approximate location of the present fish palace site.

Discussion

The map can be utilised on a number of levels. Purely as a historical source, it provides an illustrated view of Baltimore harbour in the early 1600s. It can also be used as a guide to trace potential archaeological remains on the ground, leading to the discovery of previously unrecorded sites, and can suggest the location of sites with no above-ground trace, such as those in the Cove area. The buildings there appear to be quite substantial, ranging from single-storey structures to a three-storey building. This would suggest that the community was well organised, with sturdy houses and a structured settlement. In his account (published in the *Journal of the Cork Historical and Archaeological Society*) General de Zubiaur mentions 'straw huts' in the Cove area, but these may have been too inconsequential to illustrate. However, a possible interpretation is that those illustrated were timber-framed buildings with thatched roofs. What is distinctly noticeable is that both groups of buildings are typologically similar, suggesting that there was no community divide in Baltimore at that time, and it may well be that most of the residences were English, including those in the Cove area. This may explain why the majority of people taken captive during the Algerine raid of 1631 were in fact English. Barnby, in his account, records that the Turkish raiders suddenly 'surprised all the houses on that parte of the towne called the Cove, to the number of 26'. This account is even more valuable when compared with the map, as the number of houses referred to exactly matches the number illustrated within the Cove grouping, including the line of three. Could the map, then, be accurate? The archaeological remains on the ground suggest that the map is comparatively accurate in that most of the sites represented produced physical archaeological remains as well as associated sites.

From a social perspective the map is interesting in that all the illustrated fortified sites, except Kilcoe tower-house, were O'Driscoll fortifications. This was a clan-run harbour up until the middle of the sixteenth century. This powerful Gaelic sept may have dominated the seas along the south-west coast for centuries, and would have been in close contact with visiting merchants, sailors and fishermen. The wide-brimmed hats that the fishermen appear to be wearing are an interesting detail. Pine engravings of Armada shipping (housed in the Ulster Museum) dating from the latter part of the sixteenth century — as seen in a detail from Appleby's book — show sailors wearing very similar headgear (Fig. 42). Could the Baltimore fishermen have adopted Spanish attire following their encounters with them during the 1601 Battle of Kinsale? More plausibly, it is indicative of communication through trade and exploration between southern Ireland and the Continent, when social interaction through exchange of goods resulted in an equivalent exchange of ideas. Lynch's excavations at Sherkin Friary in 1987 and 1991, for example, produced a wide range of exotic pottery sherds, providing positive evidence for international maritime trade and exchange of

Fig. 42—Detail from engraving of Armada shipping showing headgear similar to that worn by Baltimore fishermen (courtesy of the Ulster Museum).

goods. Many of these ports in their heyday could be described as cosmopolitan.

The history of the map itself may be traceable to the earl of Cork, Richard Boyle. It is obvious that the map post-dates the 1601 Battle of Kinsale as the English settlement is well established, but it also pre-dates the 1631 Algerine raid as the settlement in the Cove area is still a vibrant community. A letter forming part of the earl's Letter Book and found in the Devonshire Collection in London was written on 14 February 1631, only four months before the raid took place. In it the earl refers to enclosing '... a Mapp of the Harbour and Towne of Baltimore, which I have cause to be drawn to present you withall, and that your Lordship may observe how the Town and Harbour lyeth and how narrow the entry of the Harbour mouth is and how easily and fitt it is to bee fortified and secured ... I have receaved new intelligence that the Turkes are preparing to land [and] infest those Maritime parts of Munster'. There is a high probability that the map that Boyle had drawn up is the same map discussed here. The reference to the narrowness of the harbour mouth is striking in detail to that on the map. It is also interesting to note that Boyle apparently did not consider the harbour to be well fortified. Once more, it appears that it is the economic value of the harbour that is being highlighted. Much of Boyle's wealth would have come from maritime trade and the fishing industry, and it was in his interest to seek support from England as much as it was his duty as earl of Cork to protect the vested interests of the Crown in the province.

It cannot be said with certainty that the map in the Strafford Collection is that commissioned by Boyle. Indeed, it may be that a second map has yet to be discovered. What is certain is that the study of such early maps can lead both to further discoveries of physical archaeological remains and to the reinterpretation of sites. It can also provide a better understanding of such 'maritime' landscapes, preventing the unnecessary loss of associated archaeological sites through the expansion of archaeological perspectives. Such maps are not a definitive source for archaeologists but should be seen as a fundamental aid to fieldwork and as thought-provoking parchments that stir the imagination and motivate the mind.

Acknowledgements

I am grateful to the Head of Leisure Services, Sheffield City Council, for access to the Wentworth Woodhouse Muniments, which have been accepted in lieu of tax by HM Government and temporarily allocated to Sheffield City Council. I am also grateful to the Ulster Museum for permission to reproduce the detail of Armada shipping. Further thanks are due to Rob Marson for his comments and suggestions, and to Fionnbarr Moore and Karl Brady for their input and advice.

Further reading

Brewer, J.S. and Bullen, W. (eds) 1871 *Calendar of the Carew Manuscripts*, vol. VI. London.

Calendar of State Papers (Ireland), 1625–32.

Carew MSS (ref. MS 103) N.L.I. microfilm n.5491 p. 5658.

Cotter, E. 1998 Test excavations at Dunasead Castle, Baltimore, Co. Cork. Unpublished excavation report, Dúchas, Dublin.

Journal of the Cork Historical and Archaeological Society, particularly 1946 (Went), 51; 1958 (Coombes), 63; 1963 (Coombes), 60; 1969 (Barnby), 74; 1978 (Coombes), 60; 1984 (Priestly), 89.

Kelleher, C. 1995 The maritime archaeological landscape of Baltimore, Co. Cork. Unpublished MA thesis, National University of Ireland, Cork.

Lynch, A. 1988 Sherkin Island Friary, Farranacoush. In I. Bennett (ed.), *Excavations 1987. Summary accounts of archaeological excavations in Ireland*, 11. Dublin.

Lynch, A. 1992 Sherkin Island Friary, Farranacoush. In I. Bennett (ed.), *Excavations 1991. Summary accounts of archaeological excavations in Ireland*, 11. Bray.

MacAirt, S. (ed.) 1951 *The Annals of Inisfallen*. Dublin.

McNeill, T. 1997 *Castles in Ireland: feudal power in a Gaelic world*. London and New York.

Sweetman, D. 1999 *The medieval castles of Ireland*. Dublin.

Wentworth, T. (ed.) 1896 *Pacata Hibernia — A history of the wars in Ireland* (ed. Standish O'Grady). London.

WWM (Wentworth Woodhouse Muniments) Str P20(b)/100. Strafford Folio Map, Sheffield Archives, England.

26

Dublin's Smock Alley theatre:
lost and found

Linzi Simpson

The question most often and consistently levelled at archaeologists throughout their careers must be 'What is the most valuable thing you have ever found?' (while comments like 'Let me know if you find my granny' must run a close second!). In defensive response, as the majority of archaeologists tend not to have found the gold, jewels and Ark of the Covenant of Indiana Jones fame, stock answers are often provided, usually tired and usually modelled as closely as possible on Indy's trinkets. Thus, in an attempt to live up to the romantic reputation of archaeology, we often try to satisfy the thirst for valuables and precious objects, almost as if to justify our careers. The reality is usually different, as most students eventually figure out on their first dig up a mountain or in a bog. While it is true, without question, that most archaeologists like very much to find valuable objects, the truth of the matter is that we need far less than that to keep us going, and our successes are often very low-key and personal to ourselves.

The innovative idea behind this book certainly set me thinking, as the stock answer usually wheeled out clearly wouldn't do. When I had separated out the 'most valuable' from 'the most exciting' I was suddenly overwhelmed by the many exciting discoveries that I have been party to over the years. Trying to decide on my best experience was certainly a challenge, and I hope that I have made the right choice — I know building surveys aren't everyone's cup of tea!

As with all good adventures (*à la* Enid Blyton), mine happened unexpectedly in 1994. At the time I was excavating in Essex Street West, Dublin, as part of the Temple Bar project. Our site lay directly east of the Catholic church of SS Michael and John, which was first built between 1811 and 1815, and with which we formed an intimate relationship, as we stored our many samples inside (Pl. 80). The church, with its sumptuous stone façades, was historically important,

Pl. 80—The northern stone façade of the church of SS Michael and John, looking towards the Liffey.

famous for the fact that it was the first Catholic church to ring a bell in Dublin in nearly 300 years. This act, in defiance of the penal law (which prevented Catholics from openly practising their religion), prompted the aldermen of the city to attempt to prosecute the priest, Fr Michael Blake. These charges, so the story goes, were famously and hurriedly dropped when it was learned that the young Daniel O'Connell had been engaged to defend him. In 1989 the church was deconsecrated and the building was redeveloped by Temple Bar Properties for Dublin Tourism as 'Dublin's Viking Adventure'.

The church was also important historically because it was known to be located on the site of the famous — or, more accurately, infamous — Smock Alley theatre, first built in 1662 by John Ogilby. This theatre was probably one of the most colourful institutions of post-Restoration Dublin, and even the most casual glance into its history will captivate the reader. It was established in 1662 but was substantially rebuilt in 1735 after several serious collapses (caused by the fact that it was built on land that was reclaimed in the medieval period). Smock Alley quickly began to dominate the theatre scene, enjoying the enthusiastic patronage of both the upper and lower classes. It was invariably crammed on most nights, the patrons actively participating in the plays, which were chosen for their political undercurrents as well as their entertainment value. The theatre-goers not only occupied the stage (literally sitting on the stage) but roamed freely around the dressing rooms, an act that often provoked full-scale riots which could go on for days throughout the city. Thus the Dubliners clearly felt that Smock Alley was their theatre and that they owned it lock, stock and barrel. The players who did not please them were pelted with eggs and rotten oranges, while their heroes were so well loved that it was also the custom '…when the principal character was about to die, for two men to walk on with a carpet and spread it on the stage for the hero to fall on'.

Many famous players from the London stage passed through Smock Alley's doors, and the quality of the plays enacted was certainly equal to the best theatres in London. The young Thomas Sheridan took Smock Alley by storm and the Dublin public is said to have gone 'wild about its discovery'. Sheridan became manager and quickly filled the theatre with fresh new players, including the famous Peg Woffington. Peg had started out as part of Madame Violante's famous acrobatic 'tumbling troupe', all of whom were under the age of ten. She quickly became a Smock Alley favourite with both players and patrons alike, and had the distinction of being the only woman admitted into the exclusive 'beef-steak club', a type of after-hours drinking house established by Sheridan.

Many other famous theatrical performers and characters graced the stage of Smock Alley. The description of player/manager Richard Daly, however, remains my favourite:

'As a preparation for the course he intended to run through this life, he had fought sixteen duels in two years, three with small-sword and thirteen with pistols ... he had gone through the said sixteen trials of his nerve without a single wound or scratch of much consequence. He therefore used to provoke such meeting on any usual or even uncertain grounds ... Daly in person was remarkably handsome and his features would have been agreeable but for an inveterate and most distressing squint, the consciousness of which might keep his courage eternally on the look-out for some provocation ... he must have been a very unwelcome adversary to meet with a sword because his eye told the opponent nothing of his intentions ...'

Competition from other theatres in Dublin, mainly Crow Street (the entrance was through Cecilia House, at Cecilia Street), was eventually to lead to the demise of Smock Alley, although it struggled on until 1790. The theatre was then closed and converted into a warehouse, which had 'three great timber lofts'. In 1811 Father Blake leased the plot to build his church, an action that probably would have caused a great deal of ironic amusement amongst the more colourful of the Smock Alley characters. According to the diarist Austin Cooper, writing in 1811, 'the old playhouse in Smock Alley was nearly pulled down … and a large popish church is erecting'. So that was that. The famous theatre, which had been substantially rebuilt in 1735, had been demolished to make way for the church, perhaps in some sort of divine retribution for its many past sins.

The first indication that all was not as it seemed came in 1995 when, on moving archaeological samples, we first noticed faint impressions in the east wall, beneath the plaster. Although it was barely visible, an unmistakable arch-like feature could be seen from a distance, but only in a certain light. This immediately struck us as curious as we knew the arch probably related to a window or door at ground-floor level (there were no windows in the church at this level) which was now obsolete. Thus the east wall of the building, as it stood, had at least two phases of construction. Neil O'Flanagan had carried out an archaeological investigation previously inside the crypts of the church in which a series of walls had been identified, which were presumed to relate to the

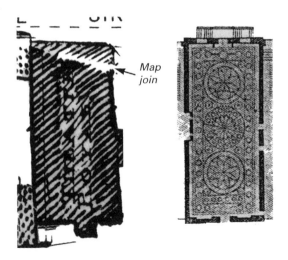

Fig. 43—The theatre on the left (as depicted on Rocque's map, dated 1756) and the church on the right (1847).

demolished theatre. However, crucially, these were internal dividing walls rather than the main walls of the building.

Temple Bar Properties engaged Margaret Gowen and Co. Ltd to survey the building and, aided by Tim Coughlan, Ed O'Donovan and Conor McHale, our investigations began in earnest in advance of the redevelopment. The most cursory glance at the Smock Alley theatre building revealed a startlingly simple fact: the theatre building depicted on Rocque's map of Dublin, dated 1756 (which has been found by the writer to be very accurate), was identical in size to the church building depicted on the Ordnance Survey (Fig. 43). Although the plot size (which was specified in the lease) may have dictated this, it was still a remarkable coincidence, all the more so since it was now coupled with the fact that the east wall had at least two phases. A second glaring fact immediately noticeable was that the church was orientated north–south rather than east–west. In addition, it also had this curious north-east/south-west orientation which was at variance with the buildings on either side. It was certainly of note that the theatre was similarly orientated.

Also extremely significant was one sentence in J.T. Gilbert's *History of Dublin* (1854–9), where he recorded:

'the only vestige now existing of the Smock-alley theatre is a portion of an arched passageway on the south-east side of this church'.

Thus the brick passageway which led into the underground crypts of the church on the eastern side was originally the passageway into the pit of the theatre. This structure, at least, had evidently not been demolished in 1811, an indication that some of the theatre buildings were left standing. This, we concluded, explained the two phases noted in the east wall of the theatre, which had evidently been left standing as part of the passageway.

However, a second discovery, which was not as easily explained, followed hard on the first. On exploration of the crypts of the church we noticed that the north main wall had a plain doorway which went nowhere as it was blocked by a flight of external stone steps leading into the church. This doorway, therefore, belonged to an earlier phase, presumably the same early phase identified in the east wall. The stone threshold of the curious doorway had a well-defined worn shallow depression, the result, we realised, of the constant tread of feet. Were these theatre-goers, perhaps on their way into the pit? To date, this was the closest we had come to the Smock Alley theatre, and our excitement began to mount as we realised the church building had a lot more to offer.

Our third observation was something of a puzzle and one that hinted, even at this early stage, at the full extent of the survival of the theatre. The external face of the west wall had been partially stripped of concrete render, revealing that it was made of Dublin stock brick. At the southern end a distinctive vertical line or feature was visible, which extended up through the brickwork of what we presumed was the church wall. It was evident that this staggered line was the result of a change in the mortar, which is usually caused by the heat from the flue of a chimney and can be seen in many buildings in Dublin. It extended almost the full height of the building but its position within the church wall was something of a puzzle for two reasons. Firstly, a fireplace is a relatively unusual feature in a church, and secondly, there was no visible fireplace inside the church.

The stripping also revealed that the western wall had been heightened on at least two occasions as two distinctive bands of different brick were identified at the upper levels. As this upper portion of the heightened wall contains the ornate plaster ceiling, this can be dated to the early nineteenth century. Most importantly, it was noted that the vertical feature did not extend through the rebuilt sections.

Our investigations, however, were stalled until redevelopment of the building began in earnest. The new design, by Colman O'Donoghue and Derry Solon, then of Gilroy and McMahon Architects, included the removal of the underground crypts and plaster on the walls, apart from the northern end where a section of the church was left intact and restored for public presentation. This work, we knew, would accelerate our findings and the challenge began of trying to survey and record the building as this was being carried out.

We considered our position in the lull before work started. We knew that the lower section of the east wall was probably the theatre wall, rebuilt in 1735, and we suspected that the lower section of the northern wall could also be dated to this phase. What we didn't know was how far up the building the theatre remains extended, although we were puzzled by the flue feature, which unified the entire western wall.

All we had to go on was a line-drawing of the theatre dated to 1789, which depicted the southern elevation of the building, fronting onto Smock Alley (Essex Street West) (Fig. 44). This showed an attractive building with a central doorway, flanked by segmented arched windows. The central door led to the boxes, while two external gates on either side led to the upper gallery (west) and the lower gallery and pit (east). The front façade was shaded, probably to denote brick, but the basement level was not visible. Also of note was the distinctive parapet on either side of the roof.

The work, carried out by Rohcon, was necessarily slow and steady and began with the removal of the crypts. Discovery number one solved the problem of the enigmatic feature in the west wall, which did turn out to be a chimney flue. The remains of a large kitchen fireplace, complete with oven and warming hob, were located at the southern end of the church, marking the location of what must have been a basement kitchen (Pl. 81). While expecting to find some sort of fireplace to explain the flue, this was a very defining moment in our investigations because we suddenly realised that the fireplace could not have functioned in the church phase, as the crypts comprehensively blocked it.

The question then arose: were the crypts original to the church building and, if so, did the fireplace and flue, which extended the full height of the west wall, therefore, by default, have to relate to the theatre phase? If the answer to this question was yes it effectively meant that the entire west wall was in fact the

Fig. 44—The imposing Smock Alley theatre, dated 1789.

Smock Alley theatre. While very excited by this possibility we managed to stay relatively calm as there was still a slight possibility that the fireplace and flue might have belonged to an earlier church phase.

Realising that where there's a fireplace there must be a chimney, we were very keen to get out onto the roof (a fairly tricky and hair-raising manoeuvre, which involved climbing unending scaffolding and crawling out a dormer window). As we crawled on all fours along the western parapet we could see clearly, in all its glory, a rectangular hole cut through the stone in the exact location of our flue. Looking into the flue it was clear that the rebuilt upper sections of the building comprehensively blocked it. This is the moment that I remember as being the most exciting, fuelled by the fantastic if dizzy view all around us. We finally had the one clue that opened the door to all the others. The flue was blocked in the church phase when the roof was heightened to accommodate the plaster ceiling. This fact, coupled with the fact that the church crypts blocked the fireplace,

Pl. 81—The kitchen fireplace in the west wall.

effectively meant that almost the entire building was the Smock Alley theatre, from basement to just below roof level.

Not only that, but the parapet we were gingerly balancing on was evidently the original stone parapet of the theatre, which had been removed when the building was heightened but replaced in the same location, as demonstrated by the defunct flue. This parapet was evidently the very parapet depicted in the drawing of the theatre, dating from 1789 (Fig. 44).

Once we accepted that the theatre survived to almost the full height of the building, the early date of the roof arrangement was also easier to explain. The roof trusses had been identified previously as queen-post trusses, dating from the eighteenth century but presumed to have been reused in the church and not necessarily originally from the theatre. However, a study by Derry Solon established that each truss was marked with a Roman numeral (for assembly purposes) and therefore that they all formed part of the same group. Moreover, the numbers were out of sequence, clearly suggesting that they had been removed and reinstated at some later date. The balance of probability suggests, therefore, that these also represent the original Smock Alley roof timbers, which were removed when the building was heightened and then replaced, albeit out of order.

The suggestion that almost the entire building was the Smock Alley theatre was quickly confirmed when work began on stripping the walls. The lower 6.5m of the building was found to be of limestone and, more importantly, punctured by a series of segmented-arched windows. These windows were also found in the south (Pl. 82) and west walls (Fig. 45), thus establishing that the entire building at basement level pre-dated the church phase. The windows indicated that the basement was divided into a series of underground rooms, which were probably the dressing rooms and apartments of the manager and players referred to in the documentary sources.

The remainder of the building was built of brick and, at ground-floor level, the arched opening in the east wall first seen as an impression in the plaster was found to be one of two pretty round-headed doorways. These doorways, neatly bricked up, marked the two entrances depicted in Rocque's map of Dublin and were probably accessed along a passageway. The walls continued to give up their secrets with a myriad of windows and relieving arches, which extended almost the full height of the building. A second fireplace, which tapped into the flue of the kitchen fireplace in the basement, was found at ground-floor level, and this may have been the very fireplace which was attacked in a riot of 1754 during which the grate was pulled out in an attempt to burn down the building.

The Smock Alley had one further surprise for us, however, and this was first noticed in the external face of the east wall, which was also stripped (after the

Pl. 82—The windows in the south wall.

brick passageway was removed). The segmented windows in this wall also had external brick surrounds but several windows, blocked up, were very irregular in size. In addition, the surrounds were of hand-made brick, usually dated to the late seventeenth century. Their location in the east wall may suggest that, incredibly, portions of this wall could date from 1662, the primary phase of the theatre. Several enigmatic joints and rebuilt sections in the west wall (at the northern end) and a large curving wall found during the excavations also relate to this phase (Pl. 83). Thus it was established that the original theatre of 1662 measured internally at least 19.4m north/south by 12m wide. It was partially demolished in 1735 and the present building was constructed along the same lines and incorporating parts of the original theatre.

The construction of this surprisingly large building at such an early date is supported in the historical sources, which record that the Smock Alley theatre was the first purpose-built theatre in the British Isles after the Restoration and was not the result of a gradual accumulation of several buildings. It caused great excitement when it was first built as it cost the enormous sum of £2000. The money was reputedly well spent as the theatre had the distinction of marvellous acoustics, and was considered superior to the many theatres in London at this date.

So what now for the Smock Alley theatre? Well, the mystery of how the

Pl. 83—The northern foundations.

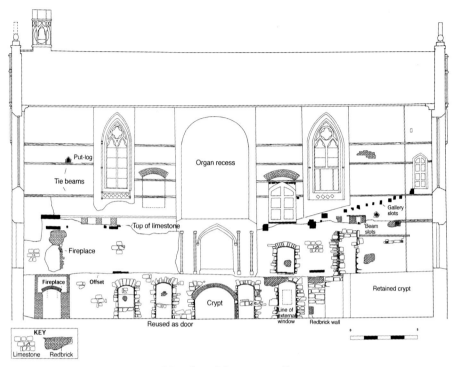

Fig. 45—The west wall.

parishioners of SS Michael and John managed to build this church in seven months and in their spare time has finally been solved. As with an increasing number of buildings in Dublin, it was evidently easier to adapt than to demolish, in the absence of large mechanical diggers. Their actions, thankfully, have left us the main walls and roof of the theatre intact, although successfully disguised for many years. The new development was sensitively designed to be totally reversible and, as a result, there was very little physical intervention into the theatre walls, which were superbly photographed in advance by Bill Hastings. Is it possible, therefore, that some day the present building will be converted back into a theatre, and the acoustics, first designed by Ogilby in 1662, will be tested in a modern setting?

For now, the east wall of the theatre, where it all began, is on permanent public display and can be viewed through the glass doors which front onto Lower Exchange Street (to the east of the Viking boat sculpture on Essex Quay). From this vantage point the two arched entrances can be seen, where once the populace of Dublin trooped, rich and poor. For me, Smock Alley will always be special as it triggered a passionate interest in building investigations which has not yet abated. More importantly, it alerted me to the ingenuity of builders operating in a time when it was not easier to simply flatten everything and start again.

Smock Alley Theatre (Anon., composed in 1747)

High on a hill their gothic structure rose,
Tall as an *Alpine* mountain crown'd with snows;
A lusty fabric whose stupendous height,
O'ertop'd the bounded reach of human sight.
Three various gates three various quarters fac'd,
With Golden valves and portal grac'd:
This at the north, a spacious entrance gave,
Where the smooth *Liffey* rolls her silent wave;
And seeks with tardy steps her silent main,
Well stor'd with cats and dogs untimely slain.
This to the east, beholds the eastern skies,
That to the south sees *Wicklow* mountains rise.

In four divisions, form'd by art within,
The various quarters of the world are seen:
And first the STAGE, like *Africs* desert land
Where gold abounds, and APES and MONKEYS stand
And next, like *Europe* fame'd for Arts, the Pit,
Where artful pimps, and artful parsons sit:
The Boxes then, *America* display,
With naked charms, and painted feathers gay;
Where ev'ry fair one deck'd in paint appears,
While gaudy Gewgaws gravitate their ears:
And then the GALL'RY *Asia's* medium hits,
Between the *Lybian* APES, and Europe's WITS;
While overhead, no less than GODS I trow,
Survey the world, in every act below;
And pleas'd or vexed, their smiles or vengeance deal,
Their smiles a clap, their vengeance orange peel,
Such was their structure, such Smock Alley stage ...

Further reading

Fitzsimon, C. 1983 *The Irish theatre*. London.

Gilbert, J.T. 1854–9 *A history of the city of Dublin* (3 vols). Dublin.

Simpson, L. 1996 *Smock Alley Theatre: the evolution of a building*. Temple Bar Archaeological Report no. 2. Dublin.

27

It's funny how one thing leads to another ...
Discovering antiquarian drawings by Beranger

Peter Harbison

Archaeological discoveries are usually associated in the public mind with the unearthing of spectacular items wrested from the earth where they have lain unseen and untouched for thousands of years. But other more mundane-seeming and less newsworthy discoveries resulting from patient research or felicitous happenstance are, nonetheless, also of significance in the world of archaeological exploration, and can give an equal amount of pleasure and satisfaction to both the researcher and his or her public.

This latter category certainly applies to my own interest in eighteenth-century Irish topographical drawings that permitted me the privilege of chancing upon some fascinating material that sheds new light on the beginnings of antiquarian studies in this country. How this came about is something of a personal odyssey and a tale that will hopefully be found worth telling in the congenial company of this imaginatively-conceived volume.

It all started just over a decade ago when Joan Jennings, then Secretary of the Royal Irish Academy, asked me to do a book on Gabriel Beranger, many of whose attractive watercolours were preserved in one large and two small albums in the Academy's library. She set up a small committee which included Aidan Clarke (the Academy's President at the time), Joan Jennings and myself, to make a selection of 47 pictures from the large album that were to form the basis of the book. I had previously dipped into it and its companion volume in the National Library but, with few exceptions, had never studied Beranger's works in great depth. What we know of the artist comes largely from the pen of Sir William Wilde, who championed his cause in a series of articles published during the 1870s in the *Journal of the Royal Historical and Archaeological Association of Ireland* under the grandiose title *Memoir of Gabriel Beranger and his labours in the cause of Irish art, literature and antiquities from 1760 to 1780.* With some justification, the word 'literature' was dropped from the title when Wilde's widow, otherwise known as the poetess 'Speranza', gathered the articles into a book published in 1880, in which she added details of the drawings in the two small Academy albums (and a third now sadly lost), together with an appendix containing two valuable lists of further drawings then in the private collections of Austin Cooper and the antiquarian Huband Smith respectively. These Wilde had obviously seen but had never published.

Beranger had been born to Huguenot parents in Amsterdam around 1729/30 and, some twenty years later, came to Dublin, where he lived until his death in 1817. He worked at various times as a civil servant and print-seller, but it is as a painter of antiquarian watercolours that he is best known. These illustrated many ancient monuments, some still surviving, others not, and were executed as part of a scheme devised around 1779 by William Burton (later Conyngham) of Slane Castle and his Hibernian Antiquarian Society to produce volumes of engravings showing off the beauties of Ireland's ancient monuments — a project which never came to fruition in its intended form.

Soon after the original meeting at the Royal Irish Academy in May of 1991, I set to work with a will, researching the background to the 47 monuments chosen for illustration and, within three months, had produced a book under the title *Beranger's views of Ireland*, which was launched by Nicholas Robinson on 31 July. A project to reproduce the remaining drawings from the Academy's Beranger albums is already well under way.

In the following month, I had a telephone call from a Mrs Mossop of Terenure, who asked me if I were the man who had written the volume on Beranger that had recently appeared. When I told her that I was, indeed, the author, she revealed to me that her family had had a large collection of unbound Beranger watercolours, of which I had known nothing. It had been owned by her mother-in-law, who had successfully offered the single sheets for sale individually in 1965 after a selection had been illustrated in *The Irish Times* of 15 October of that year. They were sold separately to a considerable variety of individuals, as well as to University College, Dublin, and Mrs Mossop has given me invaluable help in sleuthing out the present whereabouts of almost all of them. I am very grateful to her also for having given me access to an invaluable and comprehensive list of all the items formerly in the collection that her mother-in-law had written out in longhand at the time of the sale.

There is only one drawing on that list that I have not been able to trace, and that is, sadly, one of Newgrange. Mrs Mossop had given it to Miss Jago, the then headmistress of Diocesan School, in memory of Miss Dora Casserly, an inspiring teacher of history, whose special interest was the prehistory and early history of Ireland. What has happened to the drawing in the meantime I do not know, but

I would be delighted to hear from anyone who could enlighten me as to where it is now.

Mrs Mossop recalls that her mother-in-law inherited the collection from her father, a Mr MacAlpine, but we do not know who owned the drawings before he purchased them sometime in the early decades of the last century. Mrs Mossop further recalls that Mr MacAlpine frequently pored over the watercolours, and he may well have been the person who made additions in pencil to some of them, without it being clear how he arrived at the dates they give. This Mossop collection does not appear to be the same as that listed by Wilde as having been owned by Huband Smith, which I have not yet been able to trace.

The other private collection which Wilde's appendix records as having contained Beranger material was that formed by the antiquary Austin Cooper (1759–1830), who had purchased a part of it from the estate of William Burton Conyngham (1733–96), which is presumably how the Beranger drawings came into his possession in the first place. My quest for this Beranger material led me to Nottinghamshire, where the collection was carefully kept by Austin Cooper's direct descendant, who bears the same name. It is remarkable how the family had managed to keep so much of the material intact for virtually two centuries, though it should be mentioned that it did not contain drawings of two mysterious Fermanagh castles, Crannerlo and Ischaoman, listed in the Wilde appendix, and which are probably misreadings of the original titles. I needed two days to photograph the collection of drawings, and I would like to take this opportunity of thanking Austin Cooper and his wife Peg for their kind hospitality during my stay, during which we discussed not just the collection, but wine and Austin's poetry as well!

My inspection made clear to me that, in addition to drawings by Beranger, the collection also contained sketches by Austin Cooper and various members of his family. A selection of these had been published in Liam Price's excellent monograph entitled *An eighteenth century antiquary. The sketches, notes and diaries of Austin Cooper (1759–1830)*, printed by John Falconer of Dublin in 1942. Two years ago I published virtually all of the drawings by Cooper himself from his own collection in a book entitled *Cooper's Ireland. Drawings and notes from an eighteenth century gentleman*, issued by the O'Brien Press in Dublin in association with the National Library of Ireland — a volume which would never have appeared had it not been for the vision and encouragement of the Library's Director, Brendan O Donoghue.

I had not been the first person by any means to show an interest in the collection, but my examination of all the drawings made me realise that here was an archive of tremendous national significance for the study of early archaeological enquiry in Ireland, and one which should be returned to its

Kilgobbin Caftle.

Murphys-town Caftle.

Fig. 46—Typical of the Berangers in the former Mossop collection is the spectacle-like juxtaposition of the two images, as exemplified by these two tower-houses in south County Dublin (private collection). (Photo: Brian Lynch.)

homeland. So, when Austin Cooper was driving me to the railway station at the end of my stay, I asked him if he would be interested in repatriating the collection. He expressed considerable enthusiasm for the idea, saying that he had long felt that its proper home should be in Ireland.

On my return, I contacted Dr Pat Donlon, Brendan O Donoghue's equally energetic predecessor as Director of the National Library, who warmly embraced the suggestion. After consultation with Dónal Ó Luanaigh, the Keeper of Manuscripts, discussions with the owner were initiated and, on behalf of the National Library, Elizabeth Kirwan paid a visit to the Cooper household to make a preliminary catalogue of the material. Through the commitment of Dr Donlon and the warm-hearted cooperation of Austin Cooper, the National Library was able to acquire the Cooper Collection in 1994. This was to become a very significant addition to the Prints and Drawings Department, where it has since been lovingly curated by two successive Keepers, Colette O'Daly and Joanna Finegan. To commemorate the event, I illustrated a colourful selection of artistic plums from the collection in an article which appeared in *The Irish Arts Review Yearbook* for 2001, where I also stressed the importance of the collection in our understanding of the monumental heritage of Ireland.

The Berangers in the Cooper collection, however, belonged neither to the watercolour series in the National Library and Academy nor to those in the Mossop collection. They are black and white sketches and plans which, together with the even more important pen-and-ink sketches by Beranger's Italian stage-designer friend, Angelo Maria Bigari, emanated from what may be described as the first detailed provincial survey of Ireland's archaeological monuments — a tour of Connacht undertaken by the two artists in the summer of 1779 at the behest of William Burton Conyngham. These drawings from the Cooper collection opened up a whole new vista of this significant sketching expedition and, together with Wilde's excerpts from Beranger's lost diary of the journey and some manuscripts in the National Library, provided much of the material for my most recent book, *'Our treasure of antiquities'. Beranger and Bigari's antiquarian sketching tour of Connacht in 1779*, published last year by Wordwell in association with the National Library of Ireland. It should also be mentioned that, with the help and enthusiasm of both Dr Pat Donlon and Brendan O Donoghue, the National Library published my second book on Beranger in

Fig. 47—This watercolour of St Patrick's Cathedral in Dublin was one of the single, unbound sheets of the Mossop collection bearing an image that is repeated in the large Beranger album in the National Library (private collection). (Photo: Brian Lynch.)

Fig. 48—This drawing of 'The Druid's Temple in the island of Ennishowen, Co. of Mayo', twice initialled GB delt. *('drawn by Gabriel Beranger') and dated 1784, turned up in a German private collection, having been looted from a Belgian castle at the end of the First World War (author's collection). (Photo: author.)*

1998, *Beranger's antique buildings of Ireland*, which reproduced in full the National Library's album of the artist's watercolours. I may add, in parenthesis, that Dr Donlon was also instrumental in acquiring for the National Library a number of drawings that had gone out to Australia with Mrs Mossop's sister-in-law in 1955 — and which were brought back home in the diplomatic bag!

My interest in Beranger and other antiquarian sketches of the period led me to illustrate the 1992 version of my *National Monuments Guide* with eighteenth- and nineteenth-century drawings and engravings in place of the photographs used in earlier editions. This was to have one unexpected knock-on effect in my search for Beranger material. In the early summer of 2000, I received a phone call from the publishers of my *Guidebook*, Gill and Macmillan, to ask if they could give my name to a lady in Germany who wanted to contact me, as they do not normally give out such information without the author's permission. I had no idea what this was all about, but imagine my surprise when, some weeks later, I received a letter from a Frau Dr Middendorf, an art historian in northern Germany, to say that she had a drawing signed by GB, which showed an unusual monument called Ennishowen in County Mayo (Fig. 48). Her researches into the monument had obviously led her to my *Guidebook,* which did not, however, list it, and the reason why she wrote was to ask if I knew whether the monument still existed. At my request she sent a copy of the drawing, which portrayed what looks like a passage grave on the shores of Lough Mask. I did not know of the monument, and tried to visit it during the autumn, but could not because the island on which it lies is cut off by the rising waters of the lake from about mid-autumn to early spring. I had to wait, therefore, until the early summer of 2001 before visiting the monument, and confirming for Frau Dr Middendorf that it really did still exist. Beranger's drawing is valuable in showing the somewhat flattened top of the mound studded with a number of upright stones that can no longer be seen—some having been removed many years ago, while a few others, I was told, are still concealed in the undergrowth.

But how had the drawing got to Germany? Dr Middendorf explained that she and an art dealer had bought it from a local dentist as part of a collection of drawings that contained no other Irish material but which is known to have been looted from some Belgian castle at the end of the First World War. This unusual circumstance, together with the date of 1784, which is not found on any other Beranger drawings known to me, provides hope that other drawings of a hitherto unknown Beranger series may yet come to light — in Belgium or elsewhere —

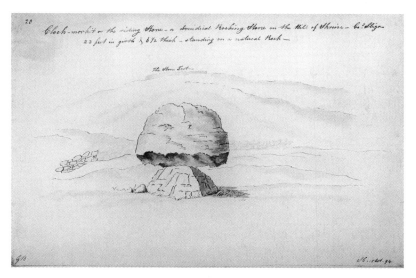

Fig. 49—Drawing of a 'Druidical Rocking Stone' at the foot of a hill bearing a stone fort at Skrine, Co. Sligo, drawn by S.C. (probably Samuel Cooper) on 15 October 1794, after a lost original by Beranger — the GB on the bottom left — and formerly in the Department of Archaeology in University College, Dublin. It is now in the Royal Irish Academy, and reproduced here by kind permission of the Royal Irish Academy © RIA. (Photo: The Green Studio.)

but how this lone specimen came to Belgium in the first place will probably never be known. Lest it disappear on the international art market, I decided to save the drawing for Ireland and bought it myself — at considerable expense, I might add!

We know from Beranger's diary that he visited this monument on Inishowen during the Mayo section of his journey, and the 'Belgian' drawing is clearly a copy of one of his own originals made during his tour of Connacht in 1779. A plan and cross-section of the same mound were present among a collection of drawings that had languished for years in a drawer in the Department of Archaeology in University College, Dublin. Some, at least, of these drawings belonged to the Academy, as one of its early stamps was clearly visible on some of the sheets. They may have been borrowed from the Academy, possibly by Petrie or Margaret Stokes, and, for whatever reason, never returned. At some period unknown, they appear to have come into the possession of Françoise Henry, who would seem to have left them to the Department. I was kindly reminded of the existence of these drawings by Professor Barry Raftery, whose Department has now graciously returned them to their proper place in the Royal Irish Academy's Library.

This small collection formerly in the University included plans and views of megaliths and other items in the Sligo area that were clearly further fruits of the 1779 tour of Connacht (Fig. 49). They are important in filling a major gap and have enabled me to assemble originals or copied drawings or plans of all but a few of the monuments visited on that tour, which is of such significance in the history of early antiquarian studies in Ireland.

We know from Beranger's own manuscript catalogue that there were other drawings and plans, since lost, and it would be wonderful to think that the publication of the surviving drawings of the tour — derived as they are from a variety of sources — might help to reveal the present whereabouts of some more.

In the same year as the tour of Connacht, 1779, Beranger undertook a rather shorter journey to Glendalough, and some of the material from it is preserved in the Royal Irish Academy. Through the kindness of Siobhán Ó Rafferty, the Academy's Chief Librarian, and Patricia MacCarthy, I have been able to examine the little-known drawings and plans, which will be published in the Leo Swan memorial volume.

That meeting in the Academy just over ten years ago helped to change the direction of much of my research during the last decade. This has borne far more fruit than I could ever have envisaged at the time and — if the good Lord spares me — there is plenty more to come.

It's funny how one thing has led to another...

28

The beads of Ballykilcline

Charles E. Orser Jr

Archaeologists have learned through experience that beads have been common ornaments throughout the entire course of human existence, and they truly have an ancient history. Excavators working in the former USSR discovered over 1000 ivory beads in the burial of a 55-year-old man interred during Upper Palaeolithic times, and beads made of lapis lazuli were common articles of adornment during Central Asia's Bronze Age. People living in northern Africa used ostrich shell beads as ornaments by 10,000 BC, and ancient Phoenicians, Egyptians, Romans and the cultures of the Indian continent all made, traded and wore beads of many different kinds.

Beads also have an ancient history in Ireland, and excavators often find beads made of amber, stone, jet, bone, gold and even faience at prehistoric sites throughout the countryside. Excavations have also taught medieval archaeologists that Irish artisans maintained an interest in beads and produced glass specimens of many colours, with the height of their manufacture probably being reached during the seventh and eighth centuries.

When they think about the past social and cultural meanings of beads, archaeologists realise that ancient beads must have had different meanings depending upon the contexts of their use. In some places they were ornaments used simply for their beauty, but elsewhere they may have been seen as powerful objects important in sacred ceremonies. Some people used beads to protect themselves from harmful spells, whereas in other places young admirers gave beads and beadwork to members of the opposite sex to indicate their intentions. In other situations, the presence of beads in graves may suggest that some beads were intended as objects useful in the afterlife, if only perhaps for personal ornamentation.

The archaeologists' interest in beads and their possible meanings are not topics intended strictly for ancient history. In fact, archaeologists investigating sites inhabited during the past 500 years have studied beads extensively. In North America, for instance, archaeologists have learned that glass beads found at Native American villages often reflect cultural interaction and exchange. They often view beads in these cases as commodities, objects that were created in Europe with the specific intention of being traded outside the continent. Europeans setting up shop in North America's fur-rich regions and along Africa's far-reaching coastlines exchanged handfuls of glass beads for furs and human cargo. As a result, glass beads — though tiny and seemingly insignificant — can be powerful interpretive tools for archaeologists working to unravel the complexities of multicultural, colonial encounters. These archaeologists often find beads in the hundreds and even in the thousands.

But what about places outside the colonised world? What do tiny glass beads mean in contexts where cross-cultural trade is not a major element of daily life? What interpretations might archaeologists offer in these cases? What about sites in Ireland dating from the early nineteenth century?

During our excavations at Ballykilcline in north County Roscommon from 1998 to 2001, we discovered 9087 artefacts from two early nineteenth-century house sites. These artefacts represent a cross-section of the objects the houses' residents used every day: pieces of Irish-made coarse earthenware bowls and jugs, fragments of English-made fine earthenware plates and cups, bottles made using many colours of glass, bone-handled forks and spoons, white clay smoking pipes, and brass buttons. Within this collection are five tiny glass beads. These beads comprise only 0.055 per cent of the total collection, yet we believe they have a significance that far outweighs their number.

Glass beads have a long historical pedigree to be sure, but they became extremely important as part of the European merchants' stock-in-trade almost as soon as their countrymen and women began to travel to faraway places. Traders began to use beads in an often elaborate process of exchange that involved indigenous participants from around the globe. Centred in Venice and later also in Amsterdam, the European glass bead industry expanded and flourished during the seventeenth to nineteenth centuries. Seeking to meet the demand while at the same time attempting to keep their products fresh and interesting to the world's consumers, bead manufacturers produced hundreds of varieties of beads and experimented with new designs and colours. On the low end of their product line were single-coloured varieties made in simple ways. They used more colours in their exotic beads and decorated them with many-coloured stripes and intricate inlays, including half-moons and stars. They made their famous 'chevron' beads, for example, with a star-shaped decoration centred around both perforations. Thus, while the outer surface of the bead might be blue with thin, white stripes, when looked at from the perforation end, different layers of the star pattern would be visible, possibly as alternating star-shaped colours of blue, green, white and red. In addition to varying their products' colours, Europe's bead-makers produced beads with many different shapes. The simpler beads were tubular, round, doughnut-shaped and flat, while the more intricate ones were faceted and star-shaped. Some even resembled raspberries.

The glass beads from Ballykilcline date from the first half of the nineteenth century, or from around 1800 to 1847–8. The terminal date is well established because in the years 1847–8 the residents of the townland were evicted and sent first to England and then on to the United States. The 1800–48 period represents the mature phase of European bead manufacture and marketing, and was a time during which the industry enjoyed unparalleled international success. Manufacturers had many highly successful varieties of beads on the market and they were constantly experimenting with new styles.

Within the huge range of styles that existed in the early nineteenth century, the five Ballykilcline beads appear rather unremarkable. All of them are of a single colour and are small in size (Fig. 50). The beads, however, are not identical, as each one is a distinct colour and has a unique shape. Bead 1 has a 'segmented' form, meaning that it looks like several small beads stuck together, with their individual perforations creating one long hole. This bead is over three times as long as any of the others. Bead 2 is round or oblate in shape, and bead 3 is cylindrical. Bead 4 has six facets, but is still of simple design, and bead 5 is doughnut-shaped.

One of the problems archaeologists face when interpreting glass beads is that they can never really know how their owners once used them, unless they happen to discover them in a straightforward context: in a burial attached to a garment or as part of a rosary. In cases with such obvious associations, archaeologists are

Bead	Colour	Munsell Colour	Shape	Length (mm)	Diameter (mm)
1	Bluish green	2.5BG 6/2	Segmented	17.71	4.44–5.29
2	Cobalt blue	7.5B 2/6	Round	5.88	8.10
3	White	N 9.25	Cylindrical	4.42	5.39
4	Clear grey	N 7.25	Faceted	5.86	10.11
5	Amber	10YR 7/8	Doughnut	5.46	11.90

Fig. 50— The beads of Ballykilcline

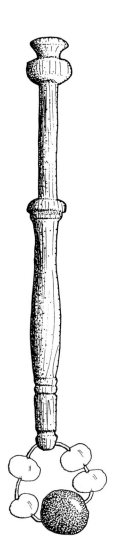

Fig. 51—Wooden lace bobbin showing the location of the spangle made of glass beads — adapted from Seymour by Jack Scott (drawing not to scale).

perfectly justified in making firm interpretations about the past functions of the beads. It is reasonable to conclude that glass beads were largely ornamental when they are discovered on a cloak wrapped around a skeleton in a grave. (Even in these cases, however, archaeologists can never be completely certain of the accuracy of their interpretations because it is possible that beaded cloaks were used in some past cultures specifically to guide the deceased to the afterlife. In these cases, the beads' functions would be decidedly spiritual.)

Archaeologists are understandably less certain of their interpretations in the more typical instances where they find individual beads with no clear functional associations. In these cases they must use other sources of information to help provide plausible interpretations for the past use of beads. Archaeologists working in the modern era have access to historical and ethnographic materials that can help them to develop valuable insights about the past functions of such mundane materials as glass beads.

We will never know with certainty how the residents of Ballykilcline used the beads we found during our excavations. Bead 1, for example, may have had a purely decorative function because it is the most ornamental of the five, but we will never really know if this interpretation is correct. We can suggest, however, a unique interpretation for three of the other beads. Based on their context of discovery and our reading of the historical literature, it is possible that beads 3, 4 and 5 were associated with the tatting of lace in the townland.

Historical accounts indicate that women involved in lace-making during the nineteenth century used a series of hardwood or bone bobbins to keep the strands of their threads separate as they constructed the lace. To increase the weight of the often unruly bobbins they frequently strung a series of different-coloured glass beads on a wire extending from the end of the bobbin, sometimes placing a larger bead in the middle of the strand (Fig. 51). They called this arrangement of beads the 'spangle' or 'jingle.'

Beads 3, 4 and 5 appear to fit the description of a spangle in that they are of different sizes and colours, with beads 4 and 5 being the largest. Given the appearance of the beads — coupled with what is known about spangles — it is plausible to interpret the beads as having been related to the production of lace.

This interpretation, though tentative, is strengthened by the discovery of two other items that can also be associated with sewing: a small pair of scissors and a brass or copper-alloy thimble embossed with the words 'FORGET ME NOT'. Although the beads, the scissors and the thimble were not found in the same excavation unit, they and beads 3, 4 and 5 were found within the remains of one early nineteenth-century house site within a 35m^2 area. (The segmented bead (bead 1) was also found in this area, but bead 2 was found in isolation, at least 30m from the others.)

Given the post-occupation history of Ballykilcline, it is not surprising that the beads, the thimble and the scissors were found in proximity but not in absolute, direct association. After the evictions of 1847–8, agents of the landlord demolished the tenants' houses, carted away the large stones, and — as our excavations indicate — then dispersed the buildings' remains to flatten the ground surface in preparation for grazing. Their efforts to spread the house remains across a wide area are substantiated by the cross-mending of several ceramic sherds from different parts of the site.

The idea that the Ballykilcline beads were part of a lace-tatting bobbin provides a new interpretation of life in the townland. Historical records make no reference to this cottage industry there, and although we cannot say for certain that the women of the household did in fact make lace, just the possibility puts a new face on their daily activity. This interpretation could not even have been suggested before the discovery of the beads of Ballykilcline. At the very least, the beads open up a new line of investigation into the lives and industries of one part of rural County Roscommon.

Further reading

Beck, H. C. 1928 Classification and nomenclature of beads and pendants. *Archaeologia* 77, 1–76.

Kidd, K. E. and Kidd, M. A. 1970 A classification system for glass beads for the use of field archaeologists. *Canadian Historic Sites: Occasional Papers in Archaeology and History* 1, 45–89.

Sciama, L. D. and Eicher, J. B. 1998 *Beads and bead makers: gender, material culture, and meaning*. Oxford.

Seymour, J. 1987 *The National Trust book of forgotten household crafts*. London.

van der Sleen, W. G. N. 1973 *A handbook on beads*. York, Pennsylvania.

29

The elephant and the tunnel

Conor Newman

It is common knowledge that every ringfort and castle in Ireland is connected to some other one by a tunnel. Inaccessible contradictions to the practical difficulties of burrowing across vast landscapes, belief in tunnels is perpetuated by the occasional intrusion of a tractor wheel into a subterranean chamber, accidental openings to the cavernous vaults of the Irish underworld. Faced with such universal certitudes, it is inevitable that the credibility of archaeology sometimes rests on confirming what is already known, on finding these tunnels. A no-win situation, someone is going to taste the bitter pill of failure.

And so it was, after three weeks of very public failure to find the tunnel known to connect Castlederg Castle with the ruins on Garvetagh Hill, a couple of miles to the south, I resolved to put an end to it, to declare that it was our considered opinion that it was unlikely to exist at all. Apart from the great distance, there was the question of the river and the hill, and the more academic point that tunnels like that were not, *sensu stricto*, a common feature of Plantation period Ireland. The receiver of our prognosis happened to be a coalman visiting the site mid-delivery, covered from head to toe in coal dust, wider than he was tall.

'Have you found the tunnel yet?'

They have a way in that part of the world of addressing such questions away to the middle distance as though out there lies the true substance of the matter, hovering in some hazy, parallel space. Deprived of the necessary supersensory perception, the outsider is wrong-footed from the outset, doomed to come up with an inadequate answer and to be cast, thereafter, as a little slow on the uptake.

'Well, you know something? There is no tunnel.'

'Och. You'll not have seen the old map then?'

See what I mean? That sinking, sinking feeling that accompanies the realisation that whatever shred of credibility you consoled yourself with is lost, lost in a mythical tunnel in west Ulster, lost with the piper sent down there many years ago to play out a map for those listening at the surface, never to return.

It was cold comfort to discover that the map in question turned out not to be the ancient parchment described but instead a poor photocopy of the six-inch Ordnance Survey sheet for the area, glued on to a schoolchild's project hanging in the local library. And no, it did not show a tunnel.

The word spread and questions about the tunnel abated for a few days. Not, I suspect, on account of our pronouncement to the contrary but more out of silent pity for our lack of faith and manifest incompetence. Qualifications have a way of making people stupid. We were obviously, maybe even stubbornly, digging in the wrong places. Moreover, surely our negativity towards the idea of the tunnel might also somehow be an obstacle to our finding it. After all, whether you believed in them or not, unseen and often temperamental forces are at play at the moment of discovery: the object, the treasure, has to condescend to reveal itself too and is unlikely to do so if the karma is bad. The local diviner was meanwhile called in and his rod duly rose and dipped a couple of times above some undulating ground where the entrance to the tunnel was expected to be. And then there was the testimony of a local man, now dead, who could hold his breath for about five minutes and had dived down to the bottom of the river behind the castle, found the roof lintels of the tunnel and was able to make out on one of them an inscribed date that no one could quite remember. Such long-held beliefs are not easily shaken.

Week six and a new cutting was opened to investigate the undulating ground. The scrutiny and expectation reached near fever pitch. The local schools were now on holidays, there were kids everywhere. Three boys and an older woman set up a daily vigil and had requests played for us on the local radio station. And though they did not say, I suspect prayers too were offered up. Alas, all for nought. The divining rod, it transpired, had bucked about not above a tunnel but over the foundations of an earlier building, possibly a tower-house, dismantled and reconfigured by the Planters.

A tower-house. Not a tunnel, mind you, but food for thought just the same. A few morsels to feed a deeper hunger among the nationalists working on the site who were daily grappling with the irony of the care and reconstructive attention they were now lavishing on a Planter's castle. For them it was the confirmation they needed: we were here first.

Then came the skeletons. Three of them. An elderly man, a young teenager and an eight-year-old child, buried in shallow, unmarked and long-forgotten graves now under the cobblestones in front of the gates to the castle. So shallowly were they buried that the brown dome of the man's head had eased itself upwards through the soil and taken its place, anonymously, among the cobbles. He had a hard head. It had not cracked in spite of years of traffic heavy enough to wear grooves across the great stone step. And his jaw had dropped into a raucous laugh while his head was being tickled by countless feet and wheels and the cool splatter of raindrops and gentle breezes. A strong, tall man, he appeared most comfortably reposed in his shallow grave, feet crossed, as though he had been taking a break from saving hay and slipped away at the end of a good joke (Pls 84 and 85a & b).

The young child's bones told a different story. Eight short years, twisted by

Pl. 84—A man emerges feet first from the ground; his head, a little distance away, was on the same level as the cobbled surface.

319

Pl. 85 (a & b)—Fully unearthed, legs crossed, hands clutching his sides and head thrown back in a post-mortem roar.

Pl. 86—Heir to that most 'Celtic' of ailments, this young child's back is contorted by spina bifida.

unclosed vertebrae. This little boy or girl had just begun to stretch out, with gangly legs and arms and a beautiful oval-shaped face, almond eyes and a gapped, gummy smile. The remaining teeth were strong and white, and told of a child carefully nurtured. And looking at this child I could not get out of my head the story of the two children lost on the way home from the market in the hills above Castlederg about a hundred years ago, only to be found the next morning, frozen like Andean mummies, the little boy wrapped in his older sister's clothes.

The young teenager's mouth was a fright of contorted teeth, extra ones growing down from the roof of his mouth like a shark. A surrogate but nonetheless anxious parent, I sat with this boy in the dentist's waiting room in the late afternoon sunshine wondering what would be made of all these supernumeraries, and relieved but also saddened that for this boy there would be no injections or squealing drills. Sober mothers with their mute children nodded to me sympathetically across the room, no doubt wondering what I was in for and what I had bought for tea in that shopping bag. And probably thinking it was a strange thing to bring your shopping to the dentist.

As with all interesting archaeological discoveries, these bodies appeared late on a fantastically sunny bank-holiday Friday evening — though not on the last day of the dig, which is more common; and yes, one of them was poking out of the baulk in accordance with Leo Swan's adaptation of Murphy's Law to archaeological excavations, which says that the best finds are always found in the baulks and on the last day — and of course had to be dealt with there and then. A great crowd gathered round jostling for a view. Children kept tumbling into the cutting and were immediately grabbed back out by the grown-ups, dusted down and told off a bit. People went away for tea and then came back. The questions were ceaseless. Who were these people? How did they die? Who buried them here, and when? The RUC officer observed that the child's skeleton was 'wild wee' and then told everyone to stand back from the edge. Suddenly, a baldy jogger, all in white and wearing plimsoles, not real runners, burst through the crowd, bounding straight into the middle of the cutting where he began jogging on the spot, inches away from the skeletons and clearly oblivious to them and to the protocol that had established itself around this square hole. Everyone froze.

'What's going on here then? Have you boys found the elephant?'

Oh, for that supersensory vision now.

'The elephant?'

'Aye. The elephant.'

'No.'

'Tuh.'

And with that he turned on his heel and ran off through the castle gate.

The elephant. They were coy about that one.

I suppose you want to hear about the elephant? Sometime in the late 1960s or '70s, so the story goes, a circus came to Castlederg, one of those slightly ad hoc family affairs with the usual motley and half-banjaxed menagerie of performing animals. Anyway, the elephant fell ill and died, despite the best efforts of the local vet, who, though possibly slightly out of his depth, was at least game enough to try something. I suspect the novelty was too much to resist. The elephant was duly buried on the waste ground behind the town near the castle and there was an unspoken expectation that we might find it again, chance unexpectedly upon its great, cavernous ribcage.

Acknowledgements

This essay is dedicated with affection to the irrepressible people of Castlederg, to those who worked on the excavation, and to Franc Myles, Roddy Moynihan and his horse, Pappadoc, who helped break the ice.

<h1 style="text-align:center">30</h1>

Great expectations — archaeology

Michael Ryan

Archaeology is a funny old business, because we applaud discovery a great deal more than doing something about it — the urgency of excavations is not matched by an equivalent urgency in publication. It's one of the constant moans of archaeological conferences that much of what has been found fails to make it into the scholarly prints. As a result, we tell ourselves that there is a great deal 'out there' that would make what we write much better if only we knew about it. This is of course true, but it is as true of archaeology as it is of almost anything else and we can only use what we know.

It is possible to be extremely po-faced about the virtue of hard graft but it is completely misleading to overlook the sheer glamour of discovery. The cry of the finders of Tutankhamun's tomb of 'wonderful things' rings a bell for every archaeologist, whether working in the hot sunshine of the Nile Valley or flogging through bogs of the Irish midlands in the hope of a few scraps of data. The trouble with most discoveries is that they don't come neatly packaged. It is easy to imagine the thrill of the immediate discovery when you open a tomb that has lain untouched for thousands of years or when chance spills a valuable hoard into your lap.

The significance of what has been found may strike home at once, or it may not be until long afterwards while working through notes and plans that the importance suggests itself.

Making the slow, hard-won discoveries requires a prepared mind — at least so we are told. I suspect that the process is more internalised, more random and mysterious than that. In my own experience I am unable to decide whether finding something in the field or simply reading something in a library and having it click with something else that I have learned is the best form of discovery. For many years, working with the National Museum, every spring ploughing brought with it its harvest of Bronze Age burials. There are few thrills in Irish archaeology to compare with that of lifting the capstone of a cist grave and seeing within it the human remains and accompanying Food Vessel which have lain undisturbed for almost 4000 years. Sometimes the sense of discovery can be diluted by the fact that the finders — farmers, mechanical digger driver and so on — have been there before you.

One substantial cist grave, which contained a crouched inhumation accompanied by a particularly fine Food Vessel, was found at Sliguff, Co. Carlow. The stone was in place when we arrived on the scene but it had previously been disturbed and replaced. So had the skeleton. Out of consideration, the long bones had been neatly tidied up and stacked for our inspection at one end of the cist. A few limb bones and the spine were still *in situ* and indicated the original crouched position of the skeleton.

Another even more exciting Bronze Age burial was an urn burial which I investigated at Ballintubbrid, Co. Wexford, on the site of a family's summer caravan home — this time in the autumn. They had been in the habit of digging pits regularly to empty the contents of their chemical lavatory. While digging one of these, the spade sliced through the top of a Cordoned Urn which contained a substantial amount of cremated bone and the burnt fragments of a stone battleaxe. All the fragments of the axehead were found so that it could be completely reconstructed. The cremated remains were those of two individuals — all kinds of explanations suggest themselves for such a paired interment, including, but not necessarily, suttee. It was a deeply interesting and even exciting discovery, and one which I will long remember — but the sheer glamour of the circumstances of discovery were muted in the report.

Not the least part of its interest for me was the difficulty of lifting the urn out of the pit. With a large part of its inverted base removed by the spade it had become structurally weak, and the fabric of the pot was wet through and soft and friable. Nevertheless it proved possible to lift it out intact — a ticklish and long-drawn-out task, improvised with masking tape, wads of tissue and newspaper — and convey it safely to the National Museum.

In most cases, working with the National Museum involved examining the sites of other people's discoveries. This usually took the form of fire brigade action, where you responded as quickly as possible to reports of burials or some perceived oddities. (Romantic images of Spitfire pilots during the Battle of Britain spring to mind — forget them: it wasn't quite like that.) I seem in retrospect to have visited more disturbed sites than intact ones.

One such case was the discovery of the Derrynaflan hoard, which had been located by means of metal-detecting on the site of an early medieval monastery in County Tipperary. Nevertheless, excavation of the pit in which the hoard was buried revealed some important components of the paten, which was the principal object in the hoard (Pl. 87). From these some valuable information about the structure of the piece was recovered. Here the efforts were designed to gain an element of context for something that had been hastily removed from the ground. The find provided other excitements. Archaeologists profess to find valuables a little dull and distracting, and even misleading. Coal-face grafters have often implied to me that they are probably a bit immoral, but I still remember vividly my first sight of the chalice and paten in their cardboard boxes on the day they were brought to the Museum, 20 February 1980. (My first reaction to the Derrynaflan Chalice was that we already had one of those!) The find has proved to be revolutionary in early medieval Irish studies in many ways and I have derived enormous satisfaction and not a flicker of guilt from studying and writing about it.

Perhaps the most interesting discovery that I investigated during my career with the Museum was in Broughal townland, Lough Boora, Co. Offaly. There, on the bed of a lake that had been drained in the 1940s, turf-cutting began to reveal what looked uncannily like a sinuous stone trackway across the floor of the bog. It seemed on the face of it to be a particularly long and ambitious example of the shorter but well-known causeways which connected many crannogs to lakeshores. There was a hummock on the lakebed near the alleged footpath,

Pl. 87—Detail of the filigree panels that form part of the rim of the Derrynaflan paten prior to its conservation (photo: National Museum of Ireland).

which had been very severely abraded by the passage of Bord na Móna machinery. It looked superficially like the core of a crannog. So we set out to investigate what we took to be an early medieval phenomenon. In laying out the site — almost from the moment we began to put pegs into the ground — artefacts of ground stone and flaked chert began to appear. We found a number of axeheads, blades and cores — not in itself surprising, I suppose, as stone axeheads crop up in many different contexts and are by no means necessarily an exclusively Neolithic phenomenon. We found numerous small flakes, the typical product of chert tool-making. It became clear at once that we had found a prehistoric habitation site of some sort, especially when spreads of charcoal with burnt bone began to turn up.

Finds of microliths were few initially, but it soon became apparent that we were dealing with an early Mesolithic site. Our 'crannog' proved to be a natural rise. The pathway was likewise natural: it seemed to be an eroded moraine core against which a lake had formed in early postglacial times.

On the shore of that ancient lake, later inundated by bog, was the early Mesolithic habitation. Most interesting of all, stratified under the archaeological deposits were the bones of giant Irish deer. This remarkable site provided interesting insights into the growth of midland raised bogs. It shed light on the succession of deposits in a typical lake basin and pegged some of those data to archaeological and other environmental remains. It seems to show the presence of giant Irish deer at a late Holocene date — although the jury is still out on that issue. For archaeologists, the evidence of the exploitation of the resources of lake and wood by the Mesolithic settlers between about 7000 and 6000 BC is very important. Not least is the location of the site in the heart of the midlands, which at a stroke changed the perception of the earliest Mesolithic settlement of Ireland, the discussion of which had prior to that naturally concentrated on the well-documented finds from Antrim, Down and Derry.

At long last, in an advanced stage of preparation for publication, the true value of the site is beginning to reveal itself. Going through the old site notebooks and plans is itself a voyage of discovery as well as one of memory.

It would, however, be completely dishonest of me to claim that the significance of the site was blindingly obvious from the first day of excavation. Such was the mind-set of archaeologists going into excavation in the Irish midlands that the notion of an early Mesolithic site there (possibly the notion of an early Mesolithic at all) was fairly alien in the 1970s. The discovery gradually revealed itself over the first weeks of the excavation and its significance began to impose itself on our minds. We were glad of this accident of discovery — we got lucky.

31

To *Look* and to *See* and to *Take Note*

Etienne Rynne

As a student many years ago I was gratuitously and *inter alia* informed that there were two kinds of archaeology: 'desk archaeology' and 'dirt archaeology', the former dealing largely with artefacts and practised by those working at home or in museums, the latter dealing with monuments in the field. It was also made quite clear that many important discoveries remained to be made in both types of archaeology: for the desk archaeologist by looking carefully at artifacts to be seen in museum exhibition cases or stored in museums and other collections, and for the dirt archaeologist by visiting and carefully examining field monuments and also — in that manner mistakenly believed by many amateur and non-professional archaeologists to be the main or only method — by excavation.

In both classes of archaeological discovery, what is important is not just to *look* but also to *see*. I was further instructed by my professor, Seán P. Ó Ríordáin, that every archaeologist — and indeed every amateur in the subject likewise — should carry a notebook when visiting museums or field monuments, so that important and interesting objects and site features could be recorded, even roughly, and consequently more easily recalled.

Believing that I had little of worthwhile significance to fulfil the editor's aims, namely to 'share with the reader the thrill and novelty of a "discovery", however big or small, which has shed some light on the understanding of past societies', I researched quickly through my thirty-plus notebooks, racked my memory, and even considered my as yet unpublished master's thesis and some of my own publications, which may well lack 'the sense of excitement and enthusiasm that is so much a part of archaeological work but [which] tends to evaporate in the dry format required of academic publication' (both quotes from the editor's initial letter to me regarding the present book).

The result? I found numerous 'discoveries' which excited me at the time, of several of which I am foolishly rather proud, including a few which I will briefly comment on here in the hope that they might fulfil the editor's request.

To start with my 'discoveries' in dirt archaeology. I received an extraordinary surge of excitement when I first visited the Aran Islands — on the weekend of 24–26 May 1969 with Professor Michael Duignan and the University College Galway Archaeological Society — as we entered through the imposing and impressive cyclopean gateway into the innermost citadel of Dún Aengus. I was immediately struck as if by a revelation from above as there, before me, I saw what clearly was a stone stage or platform, centrally placed on the almost 300ft (90m) high cliff edge. Nobody had ever mentioned it to me before, and I had never seen or noticed mention of it in print. I had gone to the famous site convinced that the well-known monument was truly a fort, happily thinking of defending Firbolgs and attacking Formorians or Tuatha Dé Danánn, or whatever, but within a split second, on seeing that 'stage-like' natural rock platform (Pl. 88) and the terraced wall around it on the three landward sides (Pl. 89), I realised (with a flash of inspiration?) that I was in a sort of amphitheatre and not a military fortification. I should perhaps point out here that I found out later that I was not the first to suggest this. In 1887 Margaret Stokes wrote in one short statement that 'these forts are amphitheatres, encircled by outer walls rather than towers' (*Early Christian art in Ireland*, Part II, p. 27), but her inspired comment was apparently ignored by all. I later researched the idea more fully and proudly lectured on it several times, even in French at the Celtic Congress held in Paris in 1991, after which I was further bucked when an elderly lady came up to tell me that she had been to Dún Aengus before the war and she had been wondering about it ever since — and to thank me for at last explaining the monument to her! It also gave me great pleasure to give a fuller and more complete account of my ideas on Dún Aengus as my Presidential Address to the Royal Society of Antiquaries of Ireland on 17 November 1988, and to publish it as 'Dún Aengus and some similar Celtic ceremonial centres' in Agnes Bernelle (ed.), *Decantations — a tribute to Maurice Craig* (Dublin, 1992), 196–207.

I could recount other 'discoveries' arising from dirt archaeology in Ireland, such as driving up a lonely boreen and being amazed to see three Early Iron Age stone heads in the garden wall (Pl. 90) and gate-pillar (Pl. 91) of a rather ruinous thatched house at Woodlands, near Raphoe, Co. Donegal, in January 1962. On 14 February I obtained them for the National Museum and later published them in the *Journal of the Royal Society of Antiquaries of Ireland* 94 (1964), 105–9, and discussed the hole-in-the-mouth feature of the head from the gate-pillar in 'Some Irish affinities with the Mšecké Žehrovice stone head', published in *Sborník Národního Muzea v Praze* 20 (1966), 151–4, in a Festschrift for Jiří Neustupny. Such holes are more widely occurring than had been previously

Pl. 88—Natural stage-like rock platform in the centre of Dún Aengus.

Pl. 89—Aerial view of Dún Aengus showing the rock platform centrally placed at the cliff's edge.

Pl. 90—(above) Two
Early Iron Age stone
heads in the garden wall
of an old farmhouse,
Woodlands, near Raphoe
— the larger head is
three-faced.

Pl. 91—(right) Stone
head with hole-in-the-
mouth feature that had
been built onto the gate-
pillar at Woodlands, near
Raphoe.

noticed and have since been accepted as a useful identifying feature of Celtic stone heads.

More interesting still was a totally unexpected 'discovery' I was fortunate enough to make during a visit in January 1988 to Tournus, a small, charming, medieval town somewhat south of Dijon in central France. In the centre of the village is the fairly famous and reasonably well-known Abbaye Saint-Philibert, which has many fine medieval carvings in the church, cloisters and adjoining buildings. Ardain, who was abbot there between the years 1028 and 1056, apparently constructed the northern gallery of the cloisters after a major fire in 1006, and this subsequently became known as the cloister of Saint Ardain. On his death his remains were buried there until his canonisation, at which time his relics were transferred into the adjoining church in 1140. Part of the northern side of the cloister was rebuilt in 1237 and yet again between 1471 and 1497. Finally, in 1950, thanks to my mother's cousin Madeleine Chavanon, founder in 1952 of the *Centre International d'Etudes Romanes*, the cloisters were properly restored and the arches unblocked. I was being shown the various capitals supporting the arches, and more particularly the seventh one, which has often been pointed out as being decorated not with vegetal motifs like the others but in the manner of the '*décors préférés de l'époque carolingienne, l'entrelacs de tradition celtique*' (Fig. 52). A discussion followed during which I pointed out, somewhat to the disappointment of my elderly cousin and that of her friend (Marguerite) Magy Thibert, Secrétaire Générale of the Centre, who were so proudly trying to show me something 'Celtic' even if not Irish, that whatever about the simple twisted ribbons being of Carolingian ancestry they certainly owed nothing to the Celts. However, well trained as I was by my first mentor in archaeology, I not only *looked* at the cloister arcade but *saw* something no one had apparently ever noticed before: there, one pace distant on the northern face of one of the stones of the base of the rectangular pillar (against which column no. 7 was backed), was carved, in false relief, an interlaced 'Celtic' knot of typically Irish type (Fig. 53). Honour — mine and my cousin's — was saved!

I have since published this important 'discovery' in 'Un tacheron irlandais à Tournus au 15e siècle', *Société des Amis des Arts et des Sciences* 92 (1993), 78–82, arguing that it is a mason's mark of the same type as found, for instance, in the fifteenth-century churches of County Tipperary, including the Franciscan friary at Fethard (see D. Maher, *North Munster Antiquarian Journal* 31 (1990), 35–40), and in the Cistercian abbeys at Hore, Holycross and Kilcooly (see R. Stalley, *The Cistercian monasteries of Ireland*, London, 1987), and no doubt elsewhere too. I put forward the undoubtably attractive idea that the carving is secondary on the diagonally axe-dressed (i.e. Romanesque) stone, and was probably put there during the restoration in the late fifteenth century, most likely by an Irish

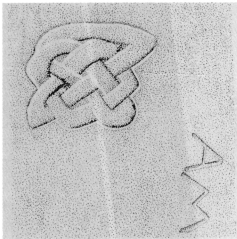

Fig. 52—(above) Column in cloister arcade, Abbaye Saint-Philibert, Tournus, France; note position of Irish-type mason's mark carved in one of the lower supporting stones.

Fig. 53—(left) Mason's mark in the form of an interlaced Celtic knot, Abbaye Saint-Philibert, Tournus, France.

Cistercian monk. He may have stayed a while at this French monastery, itself famous as a place of pilgrimage at the time, having already visited the tombs of saints Malachy and Bernard at nearby Clairvaux. Perhaps this passing pilgrim gave a hand at the reconstruction work and was allowed to leave his own special mason's mark on the cloister before continuing on to visit Bobbio, Lucca and maybe even Rome — it's quite on the cards!

Returning to Ireland and the prehistoric period, I recall another exciting 'discovery', made this time with a group of undergraduate and graduate Galway students during a St Patrick's Day weekend bus-tour visiting primarily the earlier stone high crosses of counties Tipperary and Kilkenny. On the national saint's feast-day, 1984, we visited several of the high crosses, starting with the two at Ahenny and following with the four at not-so-distant Kilkieran. Both sites are positioned considerably downhill from the roads leading to them, particularly the latter site. These slopes were clearly regarded as an invitation to the students to start racing down to the ancient monastic sites, and off they tore. Such a rush was uneventful at Ahenny but resulted in a lot of noise from the students leading the way at Kilkieran. Why? Well, the way down to the site had been recently laid with gravel, allowing for a helter-skelter approach, and the prominent and imposing high crosses apparently did excite them — or so I, following down at a more sedate pace with some of the more senior/serious students, thought. However, when I entered the ancient graveyard I was surprised to meet up with the group of first arrivals rushing over to me and exclaiming 'You were quite right Prof., come and see this stone — it proves what you've always said!'

I wondered what I was quite right about until I saw the 2.5ft (75cm) high, light brownish, sandstone pillar they were all crowded around — it was undoubtedly the most phallic-shaped standing-stone I had ever seen (Pl. 92; Fig. 54). It certainly bore out, emphasised in fact, everything I had ever suggested about many Early Iron Age standing-stones being erected probably as part of

Pl. 92—Phallic pillar-stone at Kilkieran, Co. Kilkenny.

inauguration ceremonies at which the newly elected *rí* would ritually 'marry' the mother earth/fertility goddess of the *tuath*, e.g. Tara's reasonably phallic Lia Fáil (*Bod Fheargusa* as it has been recorded from an Irish-speaker over a century ago).

I met the man, William Dalton, who had found the pillar-stone when the graveyard was being 'cleaned up' in 1983 [not 'following excavation there in 1985' as briefly mentioned by the Hon. Editor of the Royal Society of Antiquaries of Ireland, in its *Journal* 121 (1991), 172], and he informed me that it now stands about 6in. (15cm) deep in concrete, giving it a total length of about 90cm. It measures 1.2m in circumference at base, where it is about 35cm by 32cm across — almost round yet almost four-sided, rising 45cm from the ground before becoming dome-shaped to represent the glans. This deliberately carved stone must surely be of Early Iron Age date and, like the pillar-stone and adjacent holed-stone at Killadeas, Co. Fermanagh, clearly help to show that the ancient monastic site must have formerly been a pagan Celtic sanctuary. Supporting such a conclusion is a nearby holy well (30m to the east of the cemetery wall) and part of the graveyard boundary being slightly curved, in addition to the fact that the high crosses in the graveyard are among the earliest in Ireland (see my article on 'Ireland's earliest "Celtic" high crosses: the Ossory and related crosses' in M. A. Monk and J. Sheehan, *Early medieval Munster* (Cork, 1998), 125–37, where a date approaching about AD 700 is suggested for them). But wasn't it grand to have 'discovered' yet another piece of useful evidence for continuity in the transitional phase between paganism and early Christianity, having elsewhere argued for such continuity *vis-à-vis* the possibly even more ancient monastic sites of Armagh and Inismurray, Co. Sligo? I felt particularly pleased!

Dirt archaeology has provided me with many other surprising 'discoveries', but so has desk archaeology — an aspect of the subject that was always my favourite, blest as I was when younger with a near-photographic memory. While 'mitching' from school, particularly during the 1947 period of severe snow and frost, to keep warm before the cinemas opened I used to visit the National Museum and Art Galleries and learned a lot about ancient artefacts — and about art ... but I was found out and corporal punishment was liberally administered! Later, while researching my M.A. thesis and, later still, spending more than a decade employed in the Irish Antiquities Division of the National Museum of Ireland, I was well qualified to make a number of at least personally interesting 'discoveries'.

My first real 'discovery' was as a postgraduate student in 1954 while undertaking research for my thesis. It arose when working on the iron weapons, including axeheads, from Lagore crannog, Co. Meath. A nineteenth-century find from the crannog included a heavy iron axehead of bearded type, which Hencken understood as being from the site (*Proceedings of the Royal Irish*

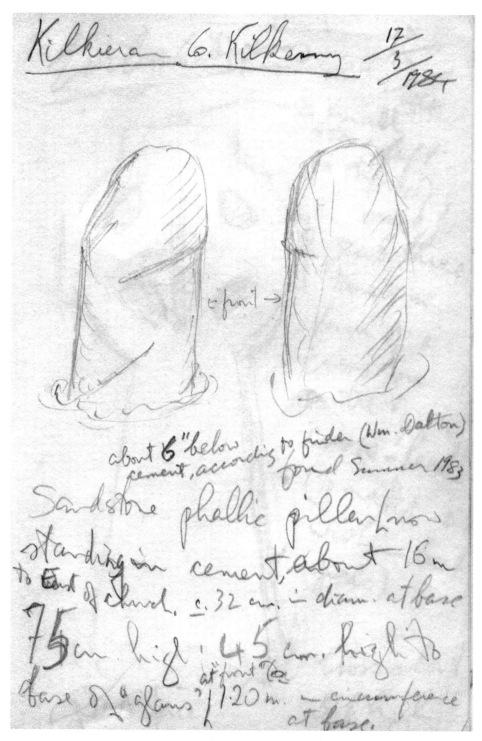

Fig. 54—Notebook sketch of phallic stone, Kilkerrin, Co. Kilkenny.

Academy **53**C (1950), 107–9, fig. 40,D) (Fig. 55). The most recent and significant label adhering to the axehead is a small circular white one, which gave its registration number as Wk.36 and the letter L. This indicated not only that it was from Lagore crannog but that Wakeman himself had found it there. Hencken described the axehead as 'a derivative of a Roman bearded axe with a long socket' and compared it with his fig. 41,B, an axehead published by L. Jacobi in *Das Römerkastell Saalburg* (1897), 206, fig. 27,9 (Fig. 56). Although telling us that the type is rare in Anglo-Saxon England, that it was known from Frankish cemeteries of between about 450 and 650 AD before becoming the standard Norwegian form of the eighth and ninth centuries, he boldly states that 'the example from Lagore is connected directly with the Roman bearded axes by the long socket, a feature which does not occur in the Germanic ones' — fascinating stuff for a young student who tended to take the printed word as gospel, but ... but ...

Another registration label, a formerly white rectangular one adhering to the axehead gave the number 240 printed in heavy black ink. This refers to a catalogue of iron objects apparently started by Sir William Wilde with the intention of completing his other famous museum catalogues dealing with stone, bronze, pottery, etc., but which was never finished and has long since been lost — so that registration number is of no apparent use as such now. There is also another circular label adhering to the axehead, formerly greenish in colour and with a number written on it, but which was then so grimy that it was almost illegible. Next to this is yet another larger, handwritten, rectangular label adhering to the axehead's shaft-hole, even more grime-covered and to all appearances completely illegible. My legitimate and justifiable curiosity aroused, I endeavoured with a magnifying glass to try to decipher something on these two corroded labels, without success. So I tried a little harmless(?) trick I had seen the Keeper of Irish Antiquities, Dr Joseph Raftery, employ now and again in similar situations: I licked my finger and with my wet fingertip wiped the labels and — hey presto! — I thus managed to pick out enough of the writing on the small circular label to read the letter 'A' below a line and the number 148 above, and to vaguely decipher (partly guess) the place-name 'Bannagher' on the larger label. The earlier registration A.148 describes it as a 'Grubbing axe' and includes it among the objects dredged from various Irish rivers in the mid-nineteenth century. It therefore is probably from the site of the Old Bridge at Bannagher, Co. Offaly, later getting confused with an axehead from Lagore crannog and being registered by Wakeman as such. The axehead, with its bearded blade and wide, long and flat shaft-hole, finds many parallels in late medieval Ireland and Britain, both as an artifact type and in depictions on several medieval graveslabs, and a date for it of about 1400, or even later, might more adequately fit. But

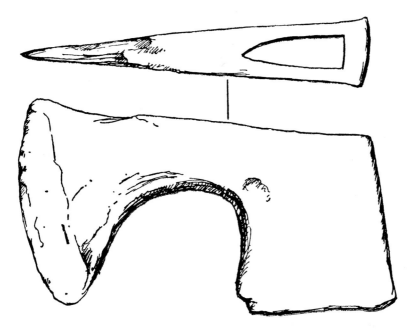

Fig. 55—Bearded iron axehead, allegedly from Lagore crannog but from the River Shannon at Bannagher.

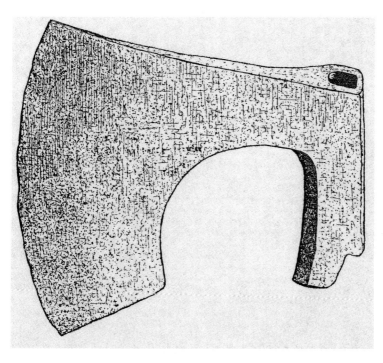

Fig. 56—Roman bearded iron axehead from Saalburg, Germany (from Jacobi via Hencken — see text).

339

wasn't I pleased with my discovery! I was — and am! At the time it was even more important as it removed a very late artefact from the Lagore repertoire where it didn't belong, although more recent research seems to indicate that the crannog may have had a late medieval period of use. In January 1956 I 'discovered' a late medieval, perhaps even post-medieval, large harp-peg of bronze (Reg. no. 68,7–9,49) in the British Museum which allegedly is also from Lagore, though there's a lot more material to suggest a late medieval phase of activity at Lagore than that.

And I can enumerate several other personally exciting and original 'discoveries' as a desk archaeologist, not only in Ireland but also abroad.

While in Wales in 1976 I spotted a small iron sword from Llyn Cerrig Bach, Anglesey — incorrectly exhibited as a dagger in the National Museum of Wales, Cardiff — with its bell-shaped bronze hilt-guard placed upside down just as in its illustration in the museum catalogue (see H.N. Savory, *Guide catalogue of the Early Iron Age collections,* National Museum of Wales (Cardiff, 1976), p. 61, no. 20; fig. 30:b2). Its small size, bronze hilt-guard, general appearance and proportions show it to be of Irish type and clearly an import, one which could be placed alongside the bronze trumpet fragment and other imports from across the Irish Sea ritually deposited at the site.

At least three other interesting 'discoveries' made in Continental museums excited me. The first was made in 1957 when on a Travelling Studentship Prize I noticed a gilt-bronze fragment in the Musée Cinquantennaire in Brussels, Belgium. To all appearances it came from an eighth-century Irish reliquary but was not exhibited as such, so I made a note and a rough sketch of it. Feeling very proud of myself I mentioned it to my late friend Liam de Paor, who was also on a National University of Ireland Travelling Studentship at the time, when we met up on Bersue's excavation at Konstanz, Germany, in April of that year. I admit to being a little deflated when he told me that he also had spotted the object and, with that, produced a beautiful drawing he had made of it — clearly much more accurate than mine, and of publishable standard too! However, we both lost out — the object was fully published by Michael Ryan in 1986 as 'A gilt-bronze object in the MRAH', *Musea* **56** (1986), 57–60.

The second of what I would consider an important 'discovery' made in a Continental museum was during my first visit to Florence (Firenze), north Italy, again when on the Travelling Studentship. I visited the Museo Nazionale, known as the Bargello, on 10 May 1957. My eyes nearly popped out of my head when I saw a small, flat, rectangular bronze plaque, the upper surface of which is decorated with two clearly Celtic spiral designs in coloured champlevé enamel of red, yellow and turquoise on a blue background. It measures 6.6cm by 4cm and is only 3.5mm thick — I know because I not only sketched it carefully through

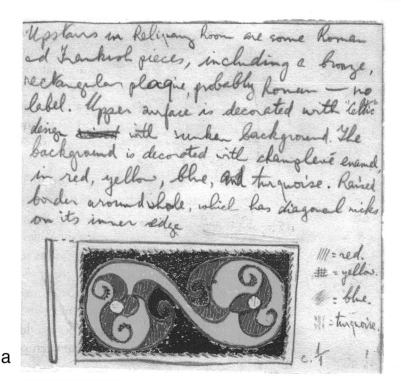

Upstairs in Reliquary Room are some Roman and Frankish pieces, including a bronze, rectangular plaque, probably Roman — no label. Upper surface is decorated with "Celtic" design ~~~~~ with sunken background. The background is decorated with champlevé enamel in red, yellow, blue, and turquoise. Raised border around whole, which has diagonal nicks on its inner edge

//// = red.
= yellow.
    = blue.
    = turquoise.

c.½

a

½/₁

    = enamel gone entirely

b

Red enamel cracked, but still all there.
Yellow enamel all there.
Blue and Turquoise enamels gone in places.

Background does not appear to have been hatched or otherwise prepared to hold the enamel: just cut away.

Fig. 57 (a and b) — Enamelled Celtic bronze plaque, probably British but from France or Italy, in the Museo Nazionale (the Bargello), Florence, Italy —see text.

341

the glass of the exhibition case (Fig. 57a) but was so excited about it that I later looked for and found a curator, and I was privileged to be allowed to take the object out to draw and measure it more accurately (Fig. 57b). The object had no accompanying label, but the helpful curator informed me that it was registered as No:930^c and that as it was acquired in the Coll. Carrand it was most probably from France or Italy. Maybe, but the style of art is neither Celtic French nor Italian but unmistakably Insular, probably British and of first-century date. I was also informed that it could be found on page 168 in the *Catalogo del R. Museo Nazionale di Firenze,* published in Rome in 1898, though whether merely listed or more fully described I have now forgotten. But if from France or Italy and not a recent import from England, is it not especially interesting? Could it perhaps be a souvenir of adventures abroad carried home by a Roman soldier in one of Caesar's raids on Britain in 55 and 54 BC, or more likely in the conquering army of Claudius in AD 43; or perhaps, even more romantically, a trophy from Suetonius' defeat of Boudicca's (Boadicea's) revolt in AD 60?

Also in Florence, Italy, but a month short of forty years later, on April Fool's Day 1997, I made what I consider another 'discovery' in the Museo Archeologico there. Exhibited without a proper label in an old case with several lots of other miscellaneous corroded iron objects I noticed what I recognised as an Early/Middle La Tène iron sword still in its very own corroded iron scabbard — with distinctive chape — resting (for the last several decades?) on a wooden tray. Unfortunately I had no time or occasion to do more than roughly sketch it in my notebook (Fig. 58) but was, as I had always been, keen to recognise archaeological evidence of Celtic incursions into non-Celtic Italy. Although I had seen other such evidence in the past I was thrilled to think that I had recognised another major piece of evidence which seemed not yet to have been realised by the museum authorities — the explanatory information sheet available in the relevant room described it as 'of uncertain date' — would *c.* 390 BC be perhaps acceptable? If so, then perhaps it could have come with the Celtic invasion of Italy, to the very gates of Rome, by the Senones under the leadership of Brennos.

I could continue recounting several other perhaps not so impressive or exciting 'discoveries' but will end with a brief, tantalising (I hope!) mention of one of my more satisfactory ones: my discovery of what the four missing panels on the upper foot-girdle and the two missing panels, those under each handle, on the bowl-girdle of the Ardagh Chalice must have looked like. When Edward Johnson made a copy of the chalice for the Victoria and Albert Museum in 1868 he included panels in the missing spaces, and the panels he produced, although different from any others, in fact were clearly versions of the silver pressblech panels on the lower foot-girdle. They made sense, however, including the fact that they were of gold, not silver, and, of course, that those under the handles

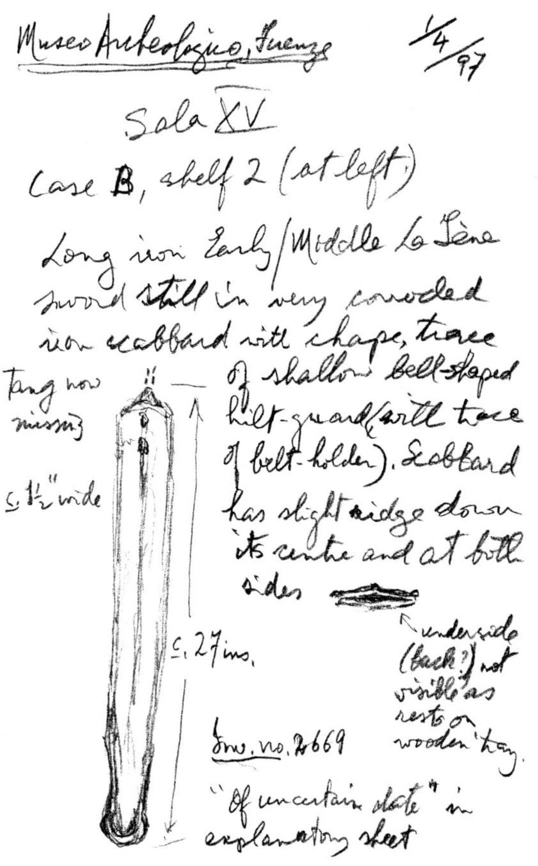

Fig. 58— Notebook sketch of very corroded Early/Middle La Tène sword in the Museo Archeologico, Florence, Italy.

would be relatively plain and not decorated with filigree like the other panels on the bowl-girdle; were they so decorated they would have scratched the holder's fingers and thus damaged the panels — the same differences are to be seen in the bowl-girdle of the later but similar Derrynaflan Chalice. But this last 'discovery' needs more explanation than is available here, and anyway deserves a proper, detailed account elsewhere — sorry! However, anyone who follows up the information above should be able to discover the answer for himself or herself.

* * * * *

Ergo: 'Those who use their eyes obtain the most enjoyment and knowledge. Those who look but do not see go away no wiser than than when they came'—to quote Frederick Horniman (1835–1906), Founder of the Horniman Museum, London, in 1901.

Biographical notes

Dr Patrick F. Wallace has been the Director of the National Museum of Ireland since 1988. Before that he directed the archaeological excavations at Wood Quay, Dublin. Well known for his lectures, his work on radio and TV, he is a Member of the Royal Irish Academy, a Fellow of the Society of Antiquaries (of London) and a (Danish) Knight of the Danebrog. He recently received the Civic Honour of his native County Limerick from Limerick County Council.

Ms Margaret Gowen began a career in development-led archaeology on completion of her MA at University College Cork. She cut her 'archaeological teeth' on the National Museum of Ireland's Wood Quay excavations on Fishamble Street, and since then has accumulated twenty years of experience in excavation and survey projects around Ireland. Margaret heads a large, integrated consultancy company, which has managed several gas pipeline projects, the Temple Bar excavations, and the Limerick Main Drainage and Kilkenny City Flood Alleviation Schemes. In 2001 she was appointed a member of the Directorate of the Discovery Programme and also a member of the Heritage Council Standing Committee on Archaeology.

Dr Gabriel Cooney is a professor in the Department of Archaeology, University College Dublin. He was the founding editor of *Archaeology Ireland*. Among his recent publications is *Landscapes of Neolithic Ireland* (Routledge, 2000). He was co-author of *Irish prehistory: a social perspective* (Wordwell, 1994; 1999). Major current research interests include the Irish Stone Axe Project and archaeological and historic landscapes. Excavation and survey work on Lambay Island complement both of these areas of research.

Dr Muiris O'Sullivan is a lecturer in the Department of Archaeology, University College Dublin, and Director of the UCD International Summer School. He specialises in the areas of megalithic art, Neolithic ritual and archaeological resource management. He has directed excavations at Knockroe passage tomb, Co. Kilkenny (1990–5), at a complex of Iron Age and medieval activity at Haynestown, Co. Louth (1993), and at Ballyvanran ringfort, Co. Tipperary (1990–1). He is the author of *Megalithic art in Ireland* (Dublin, 1993) and has published widely on his areas of special interest.

Dr Stefan Bergh is a lecturer in the Department of Archaeology, National University of Ireland, Galway. His research focuses primarily on the landscape archaeology of Neolithic Ireland, with special emphasis on how landscapes have been used, created and transformed. Other research interests include megalithic monuments and the archaeology of mountains. He is the author of *Landscape of the monuments* and has written extensively on various aspects of ritual monuments and the landscape.

Professor George Eogan's research embraces various aspects of archaeology. One of his specialist concerns is Bronze Age studies, with particular emphasis on Ireland and the comparative archaeology of that period, upon which he has published a number of books and papers. His other main field of study is the Knowth passage tomb complex and the archaeology of Brú na

Bóinne in general. There he has undertaken extensive investigations over many years and has also published widely on the results of those researches.

Dr Edel Bhreathnach, specialising in early Irish history, received her PhD for her study of an anthology of Leinster poems at University College Dublin under Professor F.J. Byrne. She held the Tara Research Fellowship from 1992 to 2000 and is now a Research Fellow at the Mícheal Ó Cléirigh Institute for the Study of Irish History and Civilisation, University College Dublin.

Mr Joe Fenwick received his primary degree from University College Dublin in 1991 and completed his Master's degree in Archaeology at the National University of Ireland, Galway, in 1997. He specialises in the area of archaeological survey and is currently employed as Field Officer in the Department of Archaeology, NUI, Galway. Prior to this appointment he worked in the commercial sector as an archaeological consultant trading under the name *ArchaeoLogical* and before that lectured at NUI, Galway. He has participated in a number of major research projects, including the ArchaeoGeophysical Imaging Project (NUI, Galway), the Tara Survey (the Discovery Programme) and Knowth excavations (UCD).

Ms Mairead Carew is an archaeologist. She graduated from UCD with an M.Phil. in Irish Studies (Archaeology and Early Irish Language and Literature) in 1993. She was short-listed for a Hennessy Award for short story-writing in 1994. *Tara and the Ark of the Covenant* (Discovery Programme/Royal Irish Academy) was published in 2003.

Ms Aideen Ireland is an archivist with the National Archives of Ireland. She holds an MA in Archaeology from UCD, the subject of her thesis being 'The Royal Society of Antiquaries of Ireland, 1849–1900'. She has published in many national and local journals. She is currently a Council member of the Royal Society of Antiquaries of Ireland and Chairman of the Society of Archivists.

The Irish Archaeological Wetland Unit (IAWU) was established in UCD in 1990 and is currently contracted to Dúchas The Heritage Service to conduct archaeological surveys of Bord na Móna-owned bog in the Irish midlands. To date, some 3000 previously unidentified sites and artefacts have been recorded and a small number of excavations have been carried out. The project consists of four archaeologists, Mr Conor McDermott (Director), Ms Cathy Moore, Ms Cara Murray and Mr Michael Stanley, and an archaeological administrator, Ms Nathalie Rynne. Each archaeologist has accumulated extensive experience working in Irish archaeology and in peatland archaeology in particular. Since 1990 the IAWU has become a leading body in the study of peatland archaeology.

Barry Raftery is Professor of Celtic Archaeology in University College Dublin. He specialises in the study of the Celtic Iron Age and, among his other publications, he has written *Pagan Celtic Ireland* (Thames and Hudson, 1994), which is the standard text on the subject. He has also excavated extensively and carried out research on the archaeology of Irish wetlands. He is a Member of the Royal Irish Academy, a Fellow of the Society of Antiquaries of London and a member of the German Archaeological Institute.

Mr Richard Warner has worked in the Ulster Museum for over 35 years and is presently Keeper of Archaeology and Ethnography. Having been originally trained, at college, in both the Natural Sciences and Archaeology, he is particularly interested in the use of the one in the pursuit of the other. He is optimistic that the Irish/British team now working on the characterising and sourcing of ancient Irish gold will produce interesting results in the near future, and promises that as these results become available they will be published.

Dr Elizabeth FitzPatrick lectures in Medieval Archaeology at the Department of Archaeology,

National University of Ireland, Galway. Her research interests include Gaelic royal assembly places, the archaeology of the medieval Irish Church, and the cultural landscape history of the later medieval professional classes in Gaelic Ireland. She is co-author with Caimin O'Brien of *The medieval churches of County Offaly* (Dublin, 1998), and co-editor of *Gaelic Ireland, c.1250–c.1650: land, lordship and settlement* (Dublin, 2001).

Mr Michael Monk has been a lecturer in the Department of Archaeology in University College Cork since 1978. While much of his research has centred on environmental archaeology, in particular archaeobotany, he has other research interests, which include early medieval settlement studies, the beginnings and development of agriculture, site formation history and excavation recording methodology. His archaeological career began in his early teens while working on excavations in Britain. In addition to Ireland and Britain he has worked in France, the Lebanon and, most recently, Russia.

Dr William O'Brien is a graduate of University College Cork, where he completed doctoral research in 1987 on the subject of ancient copper-mining in south-west Ireland. He now lectures in the Department of Archaeology, National University of Ireland, Galway. His research interests lie in the area of Bronze Age studies, early European metallurgy and all aspects of prehistoric settlement in south-west Ireland. He has recently completed a study of megalithic monuments in coastal west Cork and is currently completing a study of Copper Age metallurgy in Ireland based on the Beaker copper mine at Ross Island, Co. Kerry. He is also working on the analysis of ancient field systems and settlement landscapes in the Beara Peninsula, west Cork.

Mr Raghnall Ó Floinn is Assistant Keeper in the Irish Antiquities Division of the National Museum of Ireland with particular responsibility for the early medieval collections. He has published widely on the subject of medieval Insular metalwork, the archaeology of the early Irish Church and bog bodies. He is the author of *Irish shrines and reliquaries of the Middle Ages* (Dublin, 1994) and co-editor of *Ireland and Scandinavia in the early Viking Age* (Dublin, 1998), and is a Fellow of the Society of Antiquaries of London.

Dr Brian Lacey studied Archaeology and Early Irish History at UCD, obtaining his D.Phil. from the University of Ulster. He lectured at Magee College, Derry (1974–86), and later headed Derry City Council's Heritage and Museum Service, setting up four museums and a municipal archive service. In the mid-1970s he directed a series of salvage excavations at bomb sites in the centre of Derry, and in 1980–3 directed the archaeological survey of County Donegal. Since May 1998 he has been Chief Executive at the Discovery Programme. He is currently editor of the *Journal of the Royal Society of Antiquaries of Ireland*.

Dr Tadhg O'Keeffe is senior lecturer in the Department of Archaeology, University College Dublin. He has written several books and many articles on a range of topics in medieval archaeology. His research interests are in settlement history, architectural history and theory in historical archaeology. His passions include castles and Romanesque art, and everything recorded on the Blue Note label in the 1960s.

Ms Clare McCutcheon, MA, HdipE, MIAI, is a freelance ceramic researcher specialising in the study of excavated pottery in Ireland dating from the medieval period onwards. She completed her Master's thesis at the National University of Ireland, Cork, on the subject of the locally made pottery of Cork. She has a particular interest in the Continental pottery imported into Ireland, primarily from France, between the eleventh and fifteenth centuries. She is currently working on pottery assemblages from excavations at urban and rural sites around the Republic of Ireland.

Lost and found

Mr Aidan O'Sullivan is a lecturer in the Department of Archaeology, University College Dublin. He was formerly (1992–2000) a research archaeologist and project director in the Discovery Programme. He is mainly interested in exploring the ways in which past peoples organised their homes and dwellings and how they lived in, worked and thought about their landscapes. Having spent most of his archaeological career damply squelching around in Ireland's rain-soaked bogs, lakes and estuary marshes, he most definitely does not regret that he didn't choose instead Mediterranean archaeology or underwater archaeology in the Caribbean.

Mr David Sweetman, MA, FSA, MRIA, was Chief Archaeologist in Dúchas The Heritage Service, Department of the Environment and Local Government, and General Editor of the County Archaeological Inventory Series until April 2003. He specialises in castle studies and has excavated several Anglo-Norman fortresses, including Trim, Co. Meath. Publications include *The medieval castles of Ireland* and *The origin and development of the tower-house in Ireland.*

Mr Kenneth Wiggins is a consultant archaeologist based in County Limerick. He graduated in 1981 from Queen's University, Belfast, with an honours degree in Ancient History and Archaeology, and holds an M.Phil. in Archaeology from University College Cork. He directed excavations at King John's Castle in Limerick City between 1990 and 1998, and in 2000 commenced the publication of the results of this work with his first book, *Anatomy of a siege.*

Ms Jean Farrelly is an archaeologist with Dúchas The Heritage Service, Department of the Environment and Local Government. She is an MA graduate from University College Dublin and wrote her thesis on ringforts in County Leitrim. Specialist interests include research into prehistoric barrow monuments. She has directed the Urban Archaeological Survey of County Kilkenny and County Tipperary and recently published the Archaeological Inventory of North Tipperary with co-author Caimin O'Brien. She is currently conducting an archaeological survey of South Tipperary for the Archaeological Survey of Ireland.

Ms Connie Kelleher is an underwater archaeologist and joint co-ordinator of the Underwater Archaeological Unit of Dúchas The Heritage Service, Department of the Environment and Local Government. She holds a Master's degree in Maritime Archaeology from University College Cork, the focus of which was on the maritime archaeological landscape of Baltimore Harbour. She is presently undertaking a PhD with the University of Ulster at Coleraine on the coastal archaeological landscape of West Carbery, Co. Cork. She has undertaken surveys of several intertidal and subtidal sites, including shipwrecks, and has directed a number of archaeological excavations. She is currently writing a book on *Piracy and privateering in Irish waters.*

Ms Linzi Simpson is a graduate of Trinity College Dublin, and is a Senior Archaeological Consultant with Margaret Gowen and Co. Ltd. She has a special interest in medieval Dublin but has widened her interest to include the built heritage of post-medieval Dublin. She was responsible for directing many of the excavations in the Temple Bar area, the results of which have been published in the Temple Bar Archaeological Series. She is currently working on the publication of a major Viking excavation at Temple Bar West.

Dr Peter Harbison was archaeologist with Bord Fáilte and also editor of its magazine, *Ireland of the Welcomes,* before retiring and taking up the position of Honorary Academic Editor with the Royal Irish Academy. His many books and articles have been devoted to the four 'A's of archaeology, architecture, art and antiquarianism in Ireland, bridging the time-span from the Stone Age to the twentieth century.

Dr Charles E. Orser Jr is Distinguished Professor of Anthropology at Illinois State University and

Adjunct Professor of Archaeology, National University of Ireland, Galway. From 1993 to 2002 he was engaged in a multi-year project in County Roscommon focusing on tenant farm life in the 1780–1850 period. In 2003 his project moved to County Sligo.

Mr Conor Newman is a lecturer in Archaeology at the National University of Ireland, Galway. Probably best known for his work on the Hill of Tara, he has maintained a consistent research interest in the art and archaeology of late antiquity with specific reference to Ireland. A recipient of the NUI Travelling Studentship in archaeology, he studied palaeo-Christian art and archaeology in northern Italy and western France before going on to read Early Medieval Archaeology at Oxford and Edinburgh universities.

Dr Michael Ryan is Director of the Chester Beatty Library and an Honorary Professor in Trinity College Dublin. He has recently been elected President of the Royal Irish Academy. He worked for 22 years in the Irish Antiquities Division of the National Museum, for thirteen of them as Keeper of Irish Antiquities. Co-author of *Reading the Irish landscape*, he has published over 100 papers and edited a number of books.

Professor Etienne Rynne was born in the year of the Eucharistic Congress and educated at Ring College, Co. Waterford, at Terenure College, Dublin, in Normandy, France, and at Clongowes, Dublin. He studied Archaeology and French in University College Dublin, receiving his BA in 1953 and his MA degree in 1955. He was awarded the National University of Ireland's Travelling Studentship Prize in 1956, at which time he travelled around the museums of western Europe. On his return he was employed in the Irish Antiquities Division of the National Museum of Ireland until 1967, when he was appointed Lecturer in Celtic Archaeology at University College Galway (NUI, Galway), and became Professor ten years later. He was made Professor Emeritus on his retirement in 1997.